Babies and Young Children

Book 2   Work and Care

Marian Beaver
Jo Brewster
Pauline Jones
Anne Keene
Sally Neaum
Jill Tallack

Basford Hall College, Nottingham

Stanley Thornes (Publishers) Ltd

First published in 1995 by
Stanley Thornes Publishers Ltd
Ellenborough House
Cheltenham
Glos. GL50 1YD
UK

A catalogue record for this book is available from The British Library.

ISBN 0 7487 1787 0

Typeset by Columns Design and Production Services Ltd, Reading, UK
Printed and bound in Great Britain at The Bath Press, Avon

CONTENTS

KEY FEATURES OF THE BOOK

Both this book and its companion volume *Babies and Young Children: Book 1 – Development 0–7* have been written to support the current modules of the NNEB Diploma and Certificate courses and the standards for NVQs in child care at levels 2 and 3. The books are also suitable for use with other child-care courses at many levels. There are a number of references to Book 1 and students will find it helpful to have access to this.

Each chapter begins with a list of the information you will find in that chapter.

Throughout the book there are exercises to do. They are headed *Check, Think or Do:*

- Check: these sections contain questions to answer. The answers will be found in the chapter you have just read
- Think: these sections contain questions and tasks which ask you to think carefully about what you have read and to apply your knowledge to different situations
- Do: these sections contain practical tasks.

When you do these exercises make sure that you keep a record of the work. It may be useful for evidence of underpinning knowledge for NVQ qualifications.

There is a list of key words at the end of each chapter. You need to know what they mean. Where you are unsure of their meaning you need to go back through the chapter and find out.

ACKNOWLEDGEMENTS

The authors and publishers would like to thank the following people and organisations for permission to reproduce photographs:

Jacky Chapman/Format (page 309); Maggie Murray/Format for the cover photograph.

CHILD CARE AND EDUCATION

This chapter includes:
- **The range of services**
- **The political structure for statutory service provision**
- **Statutory voluntary and private provision:**
  Education
  Social services
  Housing
  Social Security
  Health.

The range of services

There is a wide range of statutory, voluntary, and private services that aim to care for and help children and their families. Britain has a welfare state, introduced by the British Government in the 1940s. The aim is to ensure that all citizens have adequate standards of income, housing, education and health services. The services provided by the state have changed a great deal since then. They continue to be supplemented by voluntary and private provision.

STATUTORY SERVICES

A *statutory service* is one provided by the government after a law (or statute) has been passed in parliament. Such laws say that the service either:
- must be provided (i.e. there is a duty to provide it). Education for 5–16-year-olds is an example
  or
- can be provided (i.e. there is a power to provide it). Nursery education for 3–5-year-olds is an example.

Statutory services are financed by the state, but there may be some fund-raising activities and charging for its services. Most people working in statutory organisations are trained and paid, but volunteers may carry out some tasks.

THINK!

1 Think of some other services that the state either has a duty or a power to provide.
2 What kind of fund raising might take place in these?
3 In what roles do volunteers sometimes work in schools and hospitals?

VOLUNTARY SERVICES

The government also allows and encourages some services to be provided by *voluntary* organisations. Organisations are referred to as 'voluntary' when:

- they are founded by people who see a need and want to meet it (i.e. they are formed voluntarily). No legislation is involved
- they are financed from donations and fund-raising, but may also receive government grants
- some people work without pay (e.g. in self-help groups); others receive a salary (e.g. in the NSPCC). They may or may not be trained and qualified.

There is a long and varied tradition of voluntary work in Britain, and as a result there is a wide variety of voluntary organisations. In many other European countries the church has been the main source of voluntary activity. Voluntary organisations have a number of different functions. Some organisations combine more than one of these functions by:

- acting as information and campaigning bodies (for example Shelter)
- providing money to help people in certain circumstances; these are sometimes called benevolent funds or more commonly charities (for example The Family Welfare Association)
- helping and supporting people who have a range of health conditions and impairments (for example Scope – formerly The Spastics Society)
- supporting families, children and other individuals and groups (for example Barnados).

PRIVATE SERVICES

Private services are provided by individuals or groups of people to meet a demand. They aim both to:

- provide a service
- make a financial profit.

Private nurseries, schools and hospitals are examples of these. The government provides legal guidelines for the operation of most private services, requiring them to be registered and inspected in order to protect the public. People may or may not be trained and qualified when working in the private sector; they work for pay.

DO!

1 Find out what services are provided for families and children in your area on a private basis.

CHECK!

1 What is the difference between a statutory, a voluntary and a private organisation?

The political structure for statutory service provision

The political structure for the provision of statutory services to children and families varies both within Britain and between different European countries. Some services are provided by central government, others by local government. This structure is continuously being changed and modified.

POLITICAL ATTITUDES AND LEVELS OF PROVISION

Differences in levels of provision may reflect the political beliefs of the party that has been in power in a certain area or country. One set of beliefs called 'right-wing' includes the ideas that:
- as little money as possible should be collected in taxes
- people should be free to keep and spend their money to buy the services they want.

Another set of beliefs called 'left-wing' includes the ideas that:
- money should be collected in taxes
- the state should provide services for anyone who needs them, at no further cost to the individual.

THINK!

1 Both the ideas above have positive and negative aspects; can you think what they are?
2 How might these ideas affect the number of day nurseries and nursery schools provided by the state in any area?

DO!

1 Make a study of the area that you live in. Find out how many state-run nursery classes and day nurseries there are. Show where they are located within your area. Find out which political party has been in charge of your council in recent years and whether its views are mainly right- or left-wing. Discuss your findings with someone and then write a conclusion about local provision.

CENTRAL GOVERNMENT SERVICES

Some statutory services are provided by central government. The *political process* involves:
- politicians (who are called members of parliament, and who are elected in a general election), who make policy decisions about the services they want to provide and pass laws to cover this provision
- officers (called civil servants) whom they employ and pay to carry out their

policies. They are based in regional offices throughout the country. The Departments of Health, Employment, Social Security are all organised in this way.

LOCAL GOVERNMENT SERVICES

Some services are provided by local government through a local authority. Most areas of Britain have two tiers (or layers) of local government; both of these have elected councils:

- a district council, which may represent a borough, city or district
- a county council, which will contain several districts.

The political process involves:

- the local councils, made up of councillors elected in district and county council elections. Their powers come from acts of parliament and local by-laws.
- officers (called local government officers) whom the councillors appoint and pay to organise and provide services, including education, personal social services and housing.

The government is at present aiming to bring county and district councils together to provide a single tier of government at a local level. These will be called 'unitary authorities', because the aim is that one (uni-) body will provide all the services for an area.

DO!

1 Carry out some research to find out the structure of local government in your area. Find out what services they provide and who is responsible for each. This information is often enclosed with a council tax bill. It can also be obtained from the headquarters of your council(s), which may be at a county hall, a civic centre or a town hall. There are also many books which give a general description of the structure of local government.

Statutory voluntary and private provision

EDUCATION

Statutory education

The state is required by law to ensure that all children, including those with disabilities, receive education if they are of statutory school age; that is from the beginning of the term after their fifth birthday until the end of the school year in which they have their sixteenth birthday. The structure of provision varies from one area to another. Primary education may be provided for children in:

- one primary school until the age of 11
- an infant then junior school until the age of 11
- a first school followed by a middle school (9–13).

Nursery schools and classes

Local authorities have the power to provide pre-school education. National provision is varied because it is not compulsory and it is expensive. Some councils provide separate nursery schools, others provide nursery units attached to a primary school. Education is usually part-time, either every morning or afternoon. There is a strong emphasis on play and exploration. Where there is no nursery provision some areas take rising fives (children older than 4) into primary schools. Nursery schools are often found in areas of highest social need. Most European countries have more nursery education than in Britain.

There is a strong emphasis on play and exploration in state nursery schools

Grant maintained status

Until The Education Reform Act (1988) was passed, all schools were under the control of their local education authority (LEA). In passing this law the government aimed to encourage all schools to 'opt out' of local authority control and have 'grant maintained status'. This means that they receive their money (grant) directly from the government, not from their local authority. This money is used by the school in the way they wish, to buy any services they need. At present only a small proportion of schools have chosen to do this, but they tend to be grouped in certain areas. Schools have not tended to opt out in areas where the local education authority is supportive and a good provider. It is possible, however, that GMS will be made compulsory in the future.

Local management of schools

Local education authorities now give a large proportion of their education budget directly to schools. The head teacher and the governors of a school decide how to spend this money. They are responsible for the financial and overall management of their school. This system is called the *local management of schools (LMS)*.

The National Curriculum

All state schools are now required by law to follow a national curriculum. The aim is to ensure that all children follow a broad-based and balanced curriculum and study certain subjects. The content of the National Curriculum and arrangements for testing it have been constantly changing.

DO!

1 Investigate how primary education is provided in your area. Information will be available from your LEA.

2 Find out if there is any pre-school provision, what it is and where.

3 If you are able, discuss with a head teacher the advantages and disadvantages of LMS and GMS.

4 Find out about the current requirements of the national curriculum. The arrangements testing it are referred to as 'SATs'. What does this stand for?

Voluntary education

Playgroups

The playgroup movement began in the 1960s with one group and then rapidly spread throughout the country. Groups of local people come together, rent premises and form a committee that organises and appoints workers. Parents usually help at sessions on a rota basis. Playgroups provide play facilities and social contact. There is usually a limited number of part-time sessions available a week and a small charge is made for each child. Playgroups also have to register with and be inspected by the social services department.

Parent and toddler groups sometimes use the same facilities. At these carers bring children from babies upwards, but remain with them while they play.

Private education

Private nursery schools

Private nursery schools exist in some areas where people can afford to pay for them. They provide full- and part-time education for children from 3 to 5 during school hours.

Nannies

Nannies look after children in the child's own home. They may live in or out of the home. They negotiate their contract, which includes hours, pay and duties, with their employer. They do not have to be qualified or registered, unless at the same time they are looking after the children of three or more families.

Workplace crèches
A facility that provides day care at a person's place of work is fairly uncommon, but where it exists it can have many advantages. Crèches are usually subsidised in some way by the employer.

SOCIAL SERVICES

Statutory social services
Local authorities provide statutory social services through their social services departments (SSD). The Children Act (1989) gave them a duty to provide services for children in need in their area to help them to stay with their families and be brought up by them.
A child is defined as 'in need' if:
- the child is unlikely to achieve or maintain, or to have the opportunity of achieving or maintaining, a reasonable standard of health or development without the provision of services
- the child's health or development is likely to be significantly impaired, or further impaired, without the provision of such services
- the child is disabled.

The SSD tries to keep families together by offering them support in the community. It may provide social work support and counselling, practical support in the home, family centres, short periods of relief care, help in providing essential household needs and welfare rights advice.

Day nurseries and family centres
The SSD has the power to provide day care for children in day nurseries and family centres. The emphasis in these centres is shifting away from providing full-time care of children towards therapeutic care and work on a session basis with both children in need and their carers.

Other duties
The SSD has a duty to register and inspect child minders and all day-care facilities provided by voluntary and private organisations. It has a duty to investigate the circumstances of any child believed to be at risk of harm and take action on their behalf (see Chapter 22, *Child protection procedures*).

The SSD provides accommodation for children who, with the agreement of their parents, need a period of care away from their family. It also provides care for children who are made the subject of care orders by the courts. Children will often be looked after by foster carers whom the department approves and pays. It will also provide community homes for some children. All SSDs provide an adoption service.

There are a range of services that may be provided for children with disabilities alongside the Health and Education Authorities.

The National Health Service and Community Care Act (1990) placed on local authorities the responsibility for assessing the needs of individual clients who for a variety of reasons need help to enable them to continue to live in the community.

1 Find out about your local social services department. Where are its offices? (They will be listed in the telephone directory or your local library). The SSD will have some leaflets to inform the public about their services. Try to obtain these.
2 Investigate whether the SSD provides any day nurseries, nursery or family centres in your area, and what these centres provide. (Try also to find out which political party has been in power locally in recent years.)

CHECK!

1 Which Act of Parliament gave the local authority a duty to provide services for children in need in their area?
2 Who is a 'child in need'? Try to put the definition in your own words.
3 Which act gave local authorities the responsibility for assessing the individual needs of clients?

Voluntary social services

There is a wide range of organisations that help to support families and children. These supplement the work of the social services department. Addresses and further information can be obtained from *The Charities Digest*, published by The Family Welfare Association and available in public libraries.

Organisation	Provision
African–Caribbean, Indian, Pakistani community centres	Exist in areas where there are numbers of people of Caribbean and Asian origin. They offer a range of advice and support services for local people. There are also a wide range of local organisations that aim to meet the needs of other minority communities.
Barnados	Works with children and their families to help to relieve the effects of disadvantage and disability. It runs many community projects, including day centres where young children who are at risk can be cared for and their families supported. It also provides residential accommodation for children with special needs.
ChildLine	Provides a national telephone counselling helpline for children in trouble or danger. It listens, comforts and protects.
The Children's Society	Offers child care services to children and families in need. It aims to help children to grow up in their own families and communities.
The National Association of Citizens' Advice Bureaux	Provides free, impartial (not biased), confidential advice and help to anyone. It has over a thousand local offices which provide information, advice and legal guidance on many subjects. These include social security, housing, money, family and personal matters.

(Continued opposite)

Organisation	Provision
Contact a Family	Promotes mutual support between families caring for disabled children. It has community based projects that assist parents' self-help groups, and runs a national helpline.
Family Service Units	Provide a range of social and community work services and support to disadvantaged families and communities with the aim of preventing family breakdown.
Family Welfare Association	Offers services for families, children and people with disabilities. It provides financial help for families in exceptional need, social work support and drop-in centres.
Gingerbread	Provides emotional support, practical help and social activities for lone parents and their children.
Jewish Care	Provides help and support for people of the Jewish faith and their families. Among other facilities it runs day centres and provides social work teams and domiciliary (home) assistance.
Mencap	Aims to increase public awareness of the problems faced by mentally handicapped people and their families. It supports day centres and other facilities.
MIND	Is concerned with improving services for people with mental disorders and promoting mental health and better services.
The National Children's Home (NCH)	Provides for children who are disadvantaged. It runs many schemes including family centres, foster care and aid and support to families.
The National Deaf Children's Society	is a national charity working specially for deaf children and their families. It gives information, advice and support directly to families with deaf children. It helps them to identify local help and support.
National Society for the Prevention for Cruelty to Children (NSPCC)	Has a network of child protection teams throughout Britain. The RSSPCC works similarly in Scotland. It runs a 24-hour referral and counselling telephone line. It investigates referrals and also offers support in family care centres.
PARENTLINE	Offers a telephone support helpline for parents who are having any kind of problem with their children.
PLAYMATTERS: The National Toy Libraries Association	Exists to promote awareness of the importance of play for the developing child. Libraries are organised locally loaning good quality toys to all families with young children.
RELATE: The National Marriage Guidance Council	Trains and provides counsellors to work with people who are experiencing difficulty in their relationships.
The Samaritans	Offer a telephone befriending service to the suicidal and despairing.

National voluntary organisations

Local voluntary organisations

In most areas there are local voluntary organisations that have grown up to meet the needs of the local population. They are often listed and co-ordinated by a local Council for Voluntary Service. They are also listed under Voluntary Organisations in Yellow Pages telephone directories. There are a wide range of these organisations. Some are self-help groups. Others meet the needs of people from a variety of ethnic and national backgrounds. They may provide specific information services, advice and support.

DO!

1 Find out about and list any locally based organisations in your area. You may be able to obtain some leaflets about them.
2 Outline the ways that you could inform the parent and carers of a local school about the local and national voluntary services that are available in their area.

Private social services

Child minders

Child minders are people who in their own home look after other people's children. They have a legal duty to register with the SSD and must conform to standards in The Children Act (1989). They must be of good health and character and have non-discriminatory attitudes. The Act lays down standards for safety, floor space and for children/carer ratios according to the different ages (see Book 1, page 210). Child minders are free to fix their own charges. They are sometimes paid by the SSD to care for children in need.

Childminders are people who, in their own homes, look after other people's children

Private day nurseries

Private day nurseries have to register and conform to standards in the same way as child minders. They provide full- or part-time care for children under school age, as well as providing after-school care in some places. Charges vary, but in general will reflect what people in an area are willing to pay.

Other services

Some support services can be purchased privately, for example personal and family therapy, different forms of counselling, domestic and care assistance. These services tend to be expensive and therefore financially impossible for many people.

HOUSING

Statutory housing

Local authorities have a duty to provide housing for the people in their area and to ensure that families are not homeless. They have provided council housing since the beginning of the twentieth century. There was also a massive slum clearance and rebuilding programme after the Second World War. About 23 per cent of housing is council-owned. However, since the Government introduced the 'right to buy' policy in the early 1980s, this figure is gradually decreasing. People have been encouraged to buy their council houses, but councils have not been allowed to build new houses with the money gained from sales. As a result there are fewer houses available for families. This has, in part, contributed to a rise in the number of homeless families.

Local authorities often have to place homeless families in hostels, of which there are few, or in bed and breakfast accommodation, which is a very expensive and unsuitable provision (see Chapter 18).

Housing benefit is paid by local councils to people who need help to pay their rent.

THINK!

1 What are the advantages and disadvantages both to the individual and to the state of the right for occupiers to buy their council homes?

Voluntary housing

Women's refuges

The local authority helps to finance refuges for women, and their children, who are the victims of violent male partners. These often act as half-way houses until they can re-accommodate the women.

Housing associations

Housing associations provide an alternative to council housing. They exist to provide homes for people in need of housing from different social and cultural backgrounds; they are non-profit making. They provide homes by building new units and improving or converting older property. The government encourages the growth of housing associations and provides money for them through the Housing Corporation, which is based in London.

DO!

1 Find out about the housing associations in your area from your local CVS or from the Housing Corporation.
2 Make a list of those that provide especially for families with dependent children.

Private housing

About 65 per cent of housing in Britain is owner-occupied. There has been an enormous growth in owner occupation during the twentieth century. It is difficult for people on a low income to buy their own home, both because of the deposit required and the high cost of mortgage repayments. In contrast, the number of properties available for private rental has declined enormously. This is especially so at the cheaper end of the market, where for a variety of reasons it is no longer very attractive to owners to let their properties to families.

SOCIAL SECURITY

Statutory social security

The aim of statutory social security is to make sure that all adults have a basic income when they are unable to earn enough to keep themselves and their dependants. There is a range of financial benefits and allowances payable by the Department of Social Security (central government) through its local Benefits Agency to people in a range of different circumstances. The Social Security Act (1986) set out the main recent changes, which were introduced in April 1988.

Logos of Social Security and the Benefits Agency

Contributory benefits

Contributory benefits include sickness, unemployment, disability, old age, maternity and widowhood benefits. These are paid to people in particular categories providing they have previously made a contribution (a National Insurance contribution which is deducted from a person's pay).

Non-contributory benefits

To receive non-contributory benefits a person has to be in a particular category, but does not have to have made a contribution beforehand. Non-contributory allowances fall into two groups:

- universal allowances, which are given to all people in a category who claim them, whatever their income. These include Child Benefit, payable to all mothers, One-Parent Benefit, payable to all one-parent families, and Disability Living Allowance (Some politicians think that these benefits should be means-tested like those below.)
- means-tested allowances, which are only given to people in a certain category providing their income and savings are below a certain level. To claim these people must fill in lengthy forms (tests) about their income (means). This can put people off claiming them.

Income support

Income support is one of the main non-contributory benefits; it is payable to people who are not in paid employment, or who are employed part time, and whose income falls below a certain level. Any income, whether from wages, child or unemployment benefit, will be deducted from income support. The amount of money given in income support includes allowances for members of the family and for different needs. The level at which it is set is a political decision. The government has for many years fixed this at the poverty line. This means that below this level of income people are accepted as living in relative poverty. This benefit is criticised because those who live on income support for a long time are effectively living in poverty.

Family credit

Family credit is paid to families when a parent is in full-time work but their income is below a certain level. The government has advertised this benefit, but many people who are eligible do not claim it and filling in the claim form is difficult for some people.

The Social Fund

The Social Fund is a fund out of which payments are made to meet special needs not covered by income support. Most of this money is given in the form of loans to meet crisis and special household expenses. The criticisms of this benefit are that:

- it is discretionary (officers can chose whether to give it or not)
- it requires repayments by claimants who already have a low income
- there is a limited amount of money in the fund each year.

CHECK!

1 What is a universal benefit?
2 What is a means test?

1 Obtain current information about the whole range of social security benefits, and how much is payable. Leaflets are available at post offices and local Social Security offices (addresses can be found in the telephone directory).
2 What is regarded as full-time and part-time work by the government for benefit purposes?
3 Using this information, make some calculations of your own about the amount of money which would be given in income support to some imaginary families of different sizes and structures.
4 From the leaflets, work out how much some families of different sizes can earn and still be eligible for family credit.

Leaflets are available about a whole range of benefits

Voluntary social security

There are many charities that give financial assistance to people in need in different situations. People need first to be aware of these and then to put in an application stating their case. Gaining awareness and making applications can both be difficult and people may need help with this. A further difficulty is that since the social security changes in 1988, the pressure on charities has been greatly increased and demand far exceeds money available.

1 Go though the Charities Digest and find the names of some charities with funds to help children and families.

Private social security

People are at liberty to borrow money from private sources. Those who are already financially secure, with a job and a house, are more likely to be able to borrow from sources like banks and building societies. Those who are less secure have to go to less reputable sources, private companies and individuals (often referred to as 'loan sharks'). They may be charged higher interest rates and thus put at a further disadvantage.

HEALTH

Statutory health services

The National Health Service (NHS) was created in 1948 to give free health care to the entire population of Britain. Since it was founded:

- the general health of both children and adults has improved
- the demand for services has continued to increase, despite improvements in general health
- more expensive technology and treatments have meant that the cost of the service has increased enormously and is continuing to do so.

This increase in cost has resulted in a series of reforms over the years aimed at cutting costs, and led to what some regard as a decline in standards of care, for example the introduction and gradual increase in prescription charges, and the increase in hospital waiting lists.

The National Health Service and Community Care Act (1990) has led to the most recent series of reforms. This act aimed to bring the 'market place' into the health service. This means that within the service there are some officers who are purchasers (buyers) of services and others who are providers of services.

The Department of Health (central government) is in overall charge of planning the health service. It gives power and money to the 192 district health authorities (DHAs) in Britain. These are now combined with what were the Family Health Service Authorities (FHSAs) who organise general practitioners (GPs) dentists, pharmacists and opticians.

The role of each district health authority is to:

- determine the full range of health needs of the local population, from vaccinations, to mending fractures to treating cancer
- plan the shape of the services required
- purchase the services required to meet local health needs
- review their effectiveness and make any necessary changes.

NHS trusts

The services required by the district health authority are provided by NHS trusts. These are both:

- community trusts, providing community services such as health visitors, mid-wives and clinics at health centres
- hospital trusts providing a range of out- and in-patient services.

DO!

1 Find out more about the changes that are taking place in the Health Service.
2 Find out about the range of services provided by GPs and community health centres for children and their families.

Voluntary health services

There is a long history of voluntary health care provision in Britain. Hospitals with this status became a part of the NHS when it was formed in 1948. There are voluntary organisations and self-help groups for a very wide range of medical conditions and impairments (for example SCOPE, MENCAP, MIND).

DO!

1 Find out about the national and local voluntary health organisations that exist in your area.

Private health services

There has been a large growth in private sector provision since 1979, supported by the government. Increasingly, people who are able and wish to, pay into private insurance schemes and then receive their treatment privately. This usually means that they do not have to wait for treatment. Some people believe that this is contributing to the growth of a two-tier health service, where those who can, pay for a good service, and those who cannot, make do with the NHS.

THINK!

1 It has been found that sometimes the people who most need services are often the least likely to use them. This is especially true, for example, in the use of ante-natal and post-natal care. Why do you think this is? Think of a range of reasons and record them.
2 Think of ways that you could advertise and present services so that all members of the community are aware of them and feel that they could use them.

DO!

1 Draw a chart like the one shown opposite and make a critical evaluation of the day-care facilities available to children and parents in your area. List a range of different types of day care in your area down one side (many of them are mentioned in this chapter). Along the top draw seven columns and write in the headings as shown in the table. Use a star system as your code in each box.

	Relative cost	Flexibility of hours	Physical care provision	Intellectual stimulation	Open access	Child–adult ratios	Ready availability
Day nurseries (private)							
Day nurseries (council)							
Nursery schools (private)							
Nursery units (state)							
Child minders							
Nannies							
Workplace crèche etc.							

Key   ***** Very good   **** Good   ***Acceptable   **Less good   * Poor

2 Discuss your results with another person, preferably as you are completing the chart.

Key terms
You need to know what these words and phrases mean. Go back through the chapter and find out.

A statutory service	GMS
A voluntary service	LMS
A private service	National curriculum
Political process	Children in need
Statutory school age	Means test

2 THE NURSERY NURSE IN EMPLOYMENT

> **This chapter includes:**
> - Structure and roles in the workplace
> - Policies and practice in the workplace
> - Being a professional child care worker
> - Working with colleagues in a team
> - Conditions of employment.

Structure and roles in the workplace

Your workplace may be owned and managed by a statutory, voluntary or private organisation, (see Chapter 1, *Child care and education*). This will influence its aims and objectives and the structure, including staff roles and line management.

In order to function effectively within the organisation you need to be aware of the people who work there, their role, responsibilities and accountability, including their line management. You need to be clear about your own role, responsibilities and who you are accountable to.

DO!

1 Find out who owns and runs your workplace.
2 Draw and label a diagram showing the structure of the establishment, including lines of management, responsibility and accountability.
3 Describe the roles and responsibilities of the staff, including your own.

THINK!

1 Having found out who owns and runs your workplace, think how this influences the aims and objectives, philosophy and practice within it.

Policies and practice in the workplace

Each workplace is likely to have its own specified aims, objectives and policies. These should influence and inform its practice. Good policies and practice will, in turn, be underpinned and influenced by the rights and needs of young children.

THE RIGHTS AND NEEDS OF CHILDREN

The following statements, taken from *Young Children in Group Day Care: Guidelines for Good Practice* by the Early Childhood Unit of the National Children's Bureau, outline a challenging set of beliefs about the needs and rights of young children. They apply equally well to any care or educational setting.

- Children's well being is paramount.
- Children are individuals in their own right, and they have differing needs, abilities and potential. Thus any day-care facility should be flexible and sensitive in responding to these needs.
- Since discrimination of all kinds is an everyday reality in the lives of many children, every effort must be made to ensure that services and practices do not reflect or reinforce it, but actively combat it. Therefore equality of opportunity for children, parents and staff should be explicit in the policies and practice of a day-care facility.
- Working in partnership with parents is recognised as being of major value and importance.
- Good practice in day care for children can enhance their full social, intellectual, emotional, physical and creative development.

Young children learn and develop best through their own exploration and experience

- Young children learn and develop best through their own exploration and experience. Such opportunities for learning and development are based on stable, caring relationships, regular observation and ongoing assessment. This will result in reflective practitioners who use their observations to inform the learning experiences they offer.
- Regular and thorough evaluation of policies, procedures and practices facilitates the provision of high quality day care.

CHECK!

According to the statements listed above:

1 What must always be the most important consideration in the care or education of young children?

2 What are the needs and rights of young children?

3 Why must day-care facilities be flexible?

4 Why is it important to observe and assess young children regularly?

THINK!

1 Why are the following so important in practice:
 a) stable caring relationships?
 b) equality of opportunity and anti-discriminatory practice?
 c) regular evaluation of policies, procedures and practices?

2 For each of the statements of principle think of an example from your workplace that shows how these needs and rights are:
 a) met in practice
 b) denied in practice.

DO!

In your workplace find out:

1 The aims and objectives of the organisation.

2 What is considered to constitute good practice.

3 How staff seek to develop relationships with children and parents or carers.

CODES OF PRACTICE

Within your workplace there are likely to be policies and codes of practice or procedures concerning the following:

- equal opportunities: this means that no adult or child receives less favourable treatment on the grounds of their sex, race, colour, nationality, ethnic or national origins, age, disability, religion, marital status or sexual orientation
- admissions and parental requirements
- financial arrangements
- premises and safety

- emergencies
- child protection
- health, nutrition and food service
- staff rights and responsibilities, qualifications, management, training and development
- ratio of staff to children
- record keeping
- partnerships with parents
- liaison with other agencies.

DO!

In your workplace find out the policy, codes of practice and/or procedures applicable to each of the following:

1 The allocation of places.
2 Equal opportunities.
3 Administration of first aid.
4 Prevention of illness and maintenance of health.
5 Safety of outdoor play.
6 Food hygiene.
7 Provision of a balanced diet.
8 Ratio of staff to children.
9 Staff qualifications, supervision and training.
10 Roles and responsibilities of senior staff and managers.
11 Daily routine within the establishment.
12 Outings for children.
13 Supply of materials and equipment.
14 The authorisation of expenditure.
15 Fire procedures.
16 Methods of keeping records of:
    a) income and expenditure
    b) assessments of children's development in all aspects
    c) accidents
    d) attendance
    e) information concerning family background and emergency contact
    f) stock levels.

STATUTORY REQUIREMENTS

Some policies and procedures result from statutory requirements. These are laid down in legislation. Aspects of the following legislation will have implications for policy and practice within all establishments:

- The Children Act (1989)
- The Education Act (1981)
- The Education Reform Act (1988)

- Race Relations Act (1975)
- Sex Discrimination Act (1975)
- Equal Pay Act (1970)
- Disabled Person's Act (1986)
- Offices Shops and Railway Premises Act (1963)
- Health and Safety at Work Act (1974)
- Food Safety Act (1990)
- Food Hygiene Regulation (1970)
- Food Hygiene Amendment Regulation (1990)

DO!

1 Find out which legislation has implications for the policies and procedures in each of the sixteen areas outlined in the Do! section above.

Policies can increase awareness, but will not, in themselves, change attitudes or practice. Good practice will depend on staff commitment to the needs and rights of children and to their ability and willingness to carry out their duties in a professional way.

Being a professional child care worker

Practising as a professional child-care worker involves several commitments. These are listed and explained under the following headings.

PUTTING THE NEEDS AND RIGHTS OF CHILDREN AND THEIR FAMILIES BEFORE YOUR OWN NEEDS

You will need to meet the needs of children, according to the limits of your work role, irrespective of your personal preferences or prejudices. This will involve recognising the value and dignity of every human being, irrespective of their socio-economic group, ethnic origin, gender, marital status, religion or disability. This is particularly important with young children who may be unable to understand or express their rights and needs fully.

Working with young children may give you a deep sense of satisfaction, but children are not there to provide this for you; you are there to provide for their needs.

RESPECTING THE PRINCIPLES OF CONFIDENTIALITY

Sensitive information concerning children and their families should be given to you only if you need it in order to meet effectively the needs of the child and family concerned. It should not be given, or received, to satisfy your curiosity or to make you feel superior or in control.

Although the principles of confidentiality may be easy to understand, the practice can be complex and will require self-control and commitment to the welfare of the child and their family.

DEMONSTRATING RESPONSIBILITY AND ACCOUNTABILITY

Showing 'responsibility and accountability' involves doing willingly what you are asked to do, if this is in your area of responsibility. You may need to jot down instructions to make sure that you are able to follow them accurately. You must then carry out the tasks to the standard required, and in the time allocated, making sure that you are aware of the policies and procedures of your workplace (see the section *Policies and practice in the workplace*, page 18).

Ask your line manager or someone in a supervisory role if you do not understand what to do, or if you think the task is not your responsibility. You may need to refuse to do some tasks until you have been shown how to do them by someone in a supervisory role, or until you have received appropriate training.

If you have any suggestions for changing things, make them to an appropriate person, rather than grumbling or gossiping behind their back. Open communication of positive and negative issues help staff to develop positive relationships with each other. Assert a point of view, but also be open to the views of other people.

A WILLINGNESS TO PLAN, DO, RECORD AND REVIEW

You will need to spend time thinking and planning in advance for your work with young children. A useful way of doing this is to *plan, do, record* and *review*. Encourage your colleagues to make comments on your work, as this will give valuable feedback and help you to improve your working practice.

Your aim when planning will be to include all children and make sure that they have full access to the curriculum, whatever their cultural background, socio-economic group, religion or disability. A further aim will be to avoid repetitive, adult-centred tasks, but rather to help children to develop their creativity and achieve their full learning potential.

WORKING IN PARTNERSHIP WITH PARENTS OR CARERS

To carry out your duties in a professsional way, you will need to show that you believe in the importance of working with parents or carers. You must respect their views and wishes and recognise that, in many instances, they are the ones who know their own children best. In order to do this it is essential to understand and value individual children's cultural background, and take account of their customs, values and spiritual beliefs.

If there are any religious or cultural issues of your own which may affect your work, you will need to discuss them with your line manager. An example might be if you were unwilling to work on particular days because of your religious practices.

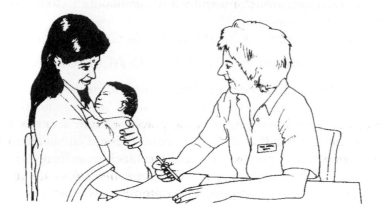

Professionals recognise the importance of partnership with parents or carers

A COMMITMENT TO PERSONAL DEVELOPMENT AND FURTHER TRAINING

As a professional child-care worker, you will want to receive further training, and be open to suggestions for changing your methods of working. You should find that your self-awareness increases through the supervision you receive from experienced workers. In-service staff development and further training will also help to keep you up to date with new developments and improve your working practice.

CHECK!

1 Describe six aspects of professional practice.

THINK!

1 Why is it important to:
   a) put the needs and rights of children and their families before your own needs?
   b) respect the principles of confidentiality?
   c) demonstrate responsibility and accountability?
   d) be willing to plan, do, record and review?
   e) work in partnership with parents?
   f) be committed to personal development and further training?
2 Why may it be necessary to note down the instructions you are given?
3 Why does the practice of confidentiality require self control?
4 Why may professional child-care workers refuse to accept some functions?
5 What enables staff to develop positive relationships with one another?
6 What does partnership with parents involve?
7 What parental actions and choices are not legitimate?

8 Why is it important to understand and value individual children's cultural background?

9 What relevant conscientious objections may child-care workers have?

Working with colleagues in a team

In the workplace, child-care workers usually work with colleagues as part of a team. This may be a multi-disciplinary team, with representatives from a number of other professional groups, for example teachers, social workers. Those who work as nannies or child minders may find it helpful to see themselves as part of a team, with the child's family. The potential advantages of working in a team include:

- individual staff weaknesses are balanced by other people's strengths
- members stimulate, motivate, encourage and support one another
- the skills of all members are used to arrive at the best solutions
- a more consistent approach to the task of caring for children and their families is possible
- individual staff feel a sense of belonging and can share problems, difficulties and successes
- responsibility, as well as insight, is shared
- individuals often become more willing to adopt new ways of thinking or working
- team membership satisfies a need to belong and be respected, and have ideals and aims that are confirmed and shared by others
- the children see the benefits of people working together and co-operating with each other.

In the workplace, child-care workers usually work with colleagues as part of a team

Effective teams will have the following:

1 clearly defined aims and objectives (clarified and redefined regularly) that all members can put into words and agree to put in to practice
2 flexible roles that enable individuals to work to their strengths, rather than in prescribed roles where they must conform to pre-determined or stereotyped expectations (for example, the teacher always does story time, the child-care worker always clears up)
3 effective team leaders who manage the work of the team, encourage and value individual contributions and deal with conflict
4 members who are committed to:
   - developing self-awareness
   - building, maintaining and sustaining good working relationships
   - demonstrating effective communication skills, expressing their views assertively rather than aggressively
   - understanding and recognising their contribution to the way the group works
   - carrying out team decisions, irrespective of their personal feelings
   - accepting responsibility for the outcome of team decisions.

DEALING WITH CONFLICT

Within any team there is likely to be conflict. It is important to deal with this constructively rather than try to ignore it. The following guidelines for behaviour are likely to encourage the resolution of conflict:

- join with the other person so that you can both 'win': people in a conflict often tend to be against rather than with each other. Keep a clear picture of the person and yourself, separate from the issue. The issue causing the conflict may be lost by the strength of bad feeling against the other person. You need to be committed to working towards an outcome that is acceptable to both parties
- make clear 'I' statements: take responsibility for yourself and avoid blaming the other person for how you feel and what you think
- be clear and specific about your view of the conflict and what you want, and listen to the other person's view
- deal with one issue at a time: avoid confusing one issue with another and using examples from the past to illustrate your point. Using the past or only telling part of the story to make your own point can lead to a biased version of what happened. The other person is likely to have forgotten or may remember the incident very differently
- look at and listen to each other: deal directly with each other and the difficulty
- ensure that you understand each other: if you are unclear and confused about the issue, ask open questions and paraphrase back what you think you hear
- brainstorm creative ways of sorting out the conflict: make a list of all the possible solutions and go through them together

- choose a mutually convenient time and place: it is useful to agree on the amount of time you will spend
- acknowledge and appreciate one another: think of the other person's attributes separately from the conflict issue and acknowledge and appreciate them.

CHECK!

1 Describe the potential advantages of team work.
2 What do the following people need to do in order to facilitate effective team work:
   a) the team collectively?
   b) members individually?
   c) the leader?

THINK!

1 Why may team work enable a more consistent approach to caring for children?
2 Why are members more likely to adopt new ways of thinking or working as a result of belonging to a team?
3 Why is it important for a team to have clearly defined aims and objectives?
4 What communication skills do you need to demonstrate to facilitate team work?
5 Why is individual self-awareness important?
6 What is the difference between expressing yourself assertively and expressing yourself aggressively?
7 Why is it important to implement and accept responsibility for the outcome of group decisions?
8 Why is it important to deal with conflict?

DO!

1 Think of any group of which you are a part. Next time you meet, analyse the way the group works by noting the following behaviour or characteristics.
   - initiating: who gets and keeps things going? Is it always the same person? Why don't other people do it?
   - informing: does anyone volunteer information, ideas, facts, feelings, views or opinions?
   - clarifying, summarising or paraphrasing: this should help the group to sort things out, bring things together or round things off. Did it?
   - confronting: this is an important function if groups are to be effective, but it requires some skill and concern for the feelings of others. Did the person upset anyone?
   - harmonising: did anyone work to reconcile disagreements, to relieve tension, and help to explore differences, or did everyone pretend there were none?

- encouraging: did anyone attempt this? Were they successful? What was the outcome?
- compromising: did anyone admit an error or modify a view or position?
- time keeping: who ensured that the group kept to time?
- aggressive behaviour: did anyone attack others or belittle their contribution or put them down?
- blocking: what was done to prevent the group from getting on with the task? Why did this happen?
- dominating: who dominated, interrupted, asserted authority or interfered with the rights of others to participate?
- avoiding: did anyone try to prevent the group from facing issues? Why did they do this?
- withdrawing: did anyone make an obvious display of lack of involvement? How did they show this?

Conditions of employment

The same considerations apply to seeking and obtaining work with young children as for any other profession. Child-care workers need to avoid sentimentality and glamorising the job.

The Employment Protection Acts require that all employees who work for more than sixteen hours a week should have a contract, a document stating their terms and conditions of employment. It may be wise when considering nannying appointments to use a reputable nanny agency.

Once employed you and your employer will have entitlements and responsibilities laid down in employment law. You will need to consider responsibility for paying income tax and national insurance contributions. You may also want to contribute towards a retirement pension. You may wish to consider joining a union and/or a professional association. You will need to be clear about the role of each and what membership entails.

THINK!

1 Consider the advantages and disadvantages of working in the following positions:
   a) A nanny in a private family, living in or coming in daily
   b) A nursery officer in a day nursery or family centre run by the local authority social services department
   c) A classroom assistant in an infant school run by the local authority education department
   d) A play worker in the paediatric department of a general hospital
   e) a residential child-care officer in a residential special school for children with autism, run by a voluntary organisation.
2 What are the advantages of using a reputable nanny agency when you are seeking an appointment as a nanny in a private family?

3 Why is a contract of employment essential? What should be included in it?

4 Who is responsible for the payment of:

    a) income tax

    b) national insurance contributions

    c) retirement pension?

DO!

1 Find out the benefits and costs of belonging to the various trade unions and professional associations for child-care workers.

Key terms

You need to know what these words and phrases mean. Go back through the chapter and find out.

Statutory	Ethnic origin
Voluntary	Gender
Line management	Confidentially
Policy	Record, review, evaluate
Discrimination	Empowered
Reflective practioners	Cultural background
Equality of opportunity	Customs, values, spiritual beliefs
Anti-discriminatory practice	Conscientious objection
Liaison	Religious practice
Code of practice	Multi-disiplinary team
Prejudice	Prescribed roles
Socio-economic group	Stereotyped expectations

3 WORKING WITH PARENTS

> **This chapter includes:**
> - Why work with parents?
> - Making parents welcome
> - Skills for talking and listening
> - Written communications
> - Records
> - Difficult situations
> - Getting parents involved.

Introduction

All those who work with young children will recognise that the relationship between the child-care establishment and the parents (or primary carers) of the child is a very important one. A good relationship will benefit the child, the parent and those who work with the child. The day-to-day nature of this relationship will vary according to the type of child-care establishment and the different needs, at different times, of children, parents and those who work with them. This chapter will look at a number of issues surrounding working with parents and will examine ways of establishing and maintaining an effective partnership between the child-care centre and the parents.

It is recognised that not all children are cared for by their parents. This term has been used for ease of reading and includes other carers who take on the parenting role.

Why work with parents?

Up until quite recently the practice of actively involving parents in the child-care setting was relatively uncommon. You may remember seeing notices that positively discouraged parents from crossing over the threshold into school or nursery. A notice that proclaims NO PARENTS BEYOND THIS POINT is hardly likely to foster good relationships between parents and those who care for their children, and should be harder to find these days. There are a number of reasons why working with parents is considered to be important and necessary.

- Parents have the most knowledge and understanding of their children. If they are encouraged to share this with staff, the child will benefit.
- Children need consistent handling to feel secure. This is most likely to occur

if there are good channels of communication between parents and staff.

- The Children Act (1989) places a legal responsibility on professionals to work in partnership with parents. Services provided for children in both the public and the private sector must take this into account.
- Initiatives such as the Parents' Charter emphasise parents' rights to make choices and be consulted in decisions concerning their children's education.
- Parents have a wealth of skills and experiences that they can contribute to the child-care centre. Participation in this way will broaden and enrich the programme offered to all the children. Many playgroups rely on a parents' rota to complement their staffing.
- An extra person to work at an activity, to help out on a trip or to prepare materials can make a valuable contribution to a busy setting. Parents who are involved in this way will gain first-hand experience of the way that the centre operates and an understanding of the approach.
- Some centres may operate with regulations that require a parent representative on the management committee or governing body. The responsibilities here can be quite significant and will include financial management and accountability, selection and recruitment of staff, as well as day-to-day running of the centre.
- Parents who are experiencing difficulties with their children may be able to share these problems and work towards resolving them alongside sympathetic and supportive professionals.
- Child protection procedures may require that professionals in the day nursery or family centre observe and supervise parents with children as part of an access or rehabilitation programme. (These situations need workers with experience and sensitivity.)
- Parents may experience a loss of role when their child starts nursery or school. Being involved and feeling valued may help them to adjust to this change.
- Provision for young children is often underfunded. Many centres have parent groups that organise social activities and raise funds. This enables parents who are not available during working hours to become involved.

THINK!

1 Read through the preceding section again. Can you think of any other reasons why child-care centres should work with parents? Add them to the list.
2 Choose what you think are the three most important reasons for working with parents from the list above and link these with your own experiences in the workplace. Discuss your choices with another student. Did you agree?
3 Now choose the reason that you think is the least important and compare.

DO!

1 Look at your workplace, ask your colleagues and find out how the centre makes links with parents.

All centres will develop ways of working with parents but naturally there will be differences depending on the emphasis of each particular establishment. For example, a family centre where many of the children are referred by Social Services perhaps as a result of some crisis will work with parents in quite a different way from a workplace day nursery that cares for children during parents' long shifts, or a playgroup where parents operate a daily rota. Nevertheless there are general principles that will always apply:

- be friendly and approachable. Remember that parents might feel uneasy in an unfamiliar setting and it is up to staff to make the right kind of approach
- be courteous and maintain a professional relationship (see Chapter 2, page 23).
- encourage a meaningful exchange of information between the home and centre.

Making parents welcome

First impressions count for a great deal and can make the difference between a parent choosing a particular centre for the child or going elsewhere. Most establishments will recognise this and take particular care to make the way into the building clear with signs directing visitors to an appropriate person. Displays in entrance halls and foyers give an immediate impression of the philosophy of the centre. Well mounted and displayed children's work shows professional standards and says a great deal about what the children do. Named photographs of staff and their roles give parents an indication of how the cen-

Displays in entrance halls and foyers give an immediate impression of the philosophy of the centre

tre operates. The physical condition and upkeep of the building also creates an impression; no parent would choose a gloomy, unsafe or unhygienic environment for their child.

DO!

1 Look carefully at the entrance to your workplace. Does it make parents feel welcome? Could you improve it in any way?

Perhaps even more important than the welcome communicated by the physical environment is the response of the staff. In most establishments there will be a particular person with responsibility for dealing with enquiries and settling in new children and families, but this does not mean that other members of staff should not be involved. Everyone should have time for a greeting and a smile while the required person is found. Remember that parents may feel ill at ease in an unfamiliar setting. Leaving a child for the first time is almost certainly going to be stressful and they will need your support. Remembering the following may help you put parents at their ease.

- Smile or nod when you see a parent, even if they are making their way to another member of staff.
- Make time to talk with parents. If they have a concern that requires time and privacy, agree a mutually convenient appointment.
- Try to call people by name. 'Ellen's mum' may do in an emergency but might not be the most appropriate way to address someone.

NB   Remember that parents may not have the same surname as their children and that not all families will follow the western naming custom of personal names followed by family names. Ask colleagues or consult records to find out parents' preferred forms of address. If you are unsure of the correct pronunciation, ask the parent.

Skills for talking and listening

Pg.1

When talking with or listening to parents, remember the following points.

- Make eye contact, but be careful – a fixed stare can be very off-putting.
- Don't interrupt and make comparisons from your own experiences. Encourage further conversation with phrases such as 'I see . . .', 'Tell me . . .'.
- Make sure that you are at the same level. Do not sit down if the parent is standing, or vice versa. This will make communication less equal.
- If the parent seems upset or wants to discuss something in private, find somewhere suitable to talk.
- Make the limits of confidentiality clear. Assure the parent that you will deal with any information shared professionally but that you may have to pass some things on.
- Summarise the points that have been made during and at the end of a discus-

sion. This recap will be particularly helpful if the parent has come to discuss ways of dealing with a problem.

- Keep your distance. Everyone needs a space around them – if you get too close, the person you are speaking to may feel uncomfortable. (On the other hand, people from some countries might have a different view of personal space and could interpret your distance as hostile.)
- You may feel that a parent is worrying over something quite unimportant. Do not dismiss these concerns as insignificant – the parent will be reluctant to confide in you in future – but try to be reassuring.
- Avoid using jargon (terms that only someone with your professional background would understand). This is off-putting and limits the effectiveness of your communication.
- If you have parents at your centre who do not speak English, try to organise someone to interpret for them. Some local authorities will provide this service or you might find someone locally. All parents, not just those who speak English, will want to share information and be consulted about their children.
- Remember (particularly if you are a student) that you will usually need to discuss with colleagues and your line manager any requests that a parent might make. Don't make agreements that you might not be able to keep!

THINK!

1 When were you last in a stressful situation in an unfamiliar setting? Was it an interview for a job? Your first day in a work placement?
2 What made you feel uncomfortable?
3 What (or who) put you at your ease? How was it done?

DO!

1 When you are next in your workplace, take notice of how your staff interact with parents. What factors encourage communication? Is there anything that hinders communication? (You need to ask permission before you begin this task. It may not be possible to do it unobtrusively.)

Written communications

Most centres will have a brochure that they provide for parents which will give them initial information about the service offered. These will vary, though there will be common factors. These will probably include:
- location, including address, telephone number, person to contact
- the times that the service is available
- the age range of children cared for
- criteria for admission (for example a workplace nursery will require the par-

ent to work in the establishment; some Social Services establishments require children to be referred through a social worker or health visitor)
■ information about meals provided
■ information about the facilities available
■ schedule of fees (if any) to be charged
■ the philosophy of the centre, including any policies they might have (see Chapter 2, page 18)
■ the qualifications of the staff
■ how the children will spend their day
■ what parents are expected to provide, for example nappies, spare clothing
■ details of any commitments the parent must make, for example rota days, notice of leaving, regular attendance
■ information on curriculum methods, for example, learning through play, approaches to early literacy, and so on. The brochure provides the parent with a great deal of information which is also useful for reference once the child has started at the centre.

DO!

1 Collect two or three brochures from different types of establishments.
2 Make a list of the kinds of information each contains. Is anything missing that should be there?
3 Compare the brochures and give each a rating for content, clarity and presentation.
4 Try to comment on the tone of the brochure. Does it patronise parents? Does it confuse with jargon? Does the brochure genuinely welcome the involvement of parents?
5 Design your own brochure for the child-care centre of your choice. Include all the necessary information and show that you value the involvement of parents in your centre.

Parents can expect to receive a whole range of written communications once their child has started at a centre. These could include regular newsletters, invitations to concerts, parents' meetings, requests for assistance and support, information about the activities provided for children, advance notice of holidays and centre closures and so on. These will often be reinforced with notices and verbal reminders. It is important that these notices and letters communicate the information in a clear and friendly manner.

Sometimes there will be a need for a more individual exchange of information, for example if a child has an accident during the session. This might be written in a note to the parent or explained at pick-up time. Parents need to know what has happened and someone needs to have responsibility for passing on this information.

1 Design a letter inviting parents to a nursery open day. Make your invitation attractive, but ensure that all the information is presented in a way that will encourage parents to participate.

Records

Child-care centres will need to keep records of the children and families they work with. The content of these records will vary depending on the type of care that is being provided. Usually parents are asked to complete a form that includes the following:

- personal details about the child: full name, date of birth, etc.
- names, addresses and phone numbers of parents and other emergency contacts
- medical details that will include the address and telephone number of the child's doctor and any information about allergies and regular medications
- details about any particular dietary needs
- details about religion which might affect the care provided for the child
- there may additionally be sensitive information that is necessary for the centre to have; for example, are there any restrictions on who may collect the child from the centre? Are Social Services involved with the family?

Parents will need to be assured that such information will be confidential and stored securely. Centres need to make sure that this essential information is correct and up to date.

Other types of information will also be very helpful to staff. These might include details such as any comfort object the child might have, any likes and dislikes, any particular fears, special words the child might use, for example for the lavatory. The more that the exchange of this type of information is encouraged, the smoother the process of sharing care is likely to be.

Remember that some parents will have difficulty with filling in forms and with written information. They may not be literate, or they may be literate in another language and might need oral support or access to translated information.

Difficult situations

There may be times when there is conflict between the child-care centre and workers and parents. Understanding and resolving this conflict can be a demanding task for staff to manage. Difficulties that arise out of a simple misunderstanding, for example a child coming home with the wrong coat, are usually fairly easy to sort out in a good humoured way. Below are some examples of situations that might not be quite so straightforward.

- The values of the centre, for example methods of disciplining children, may sometimes be quite different from those of the home.

- Parents who are experiencing stresses and strains in their lives may appear to react angrily and aggressively to what seems to be a minor incident, for example a tear in the child's clothes.
- Where there are child-protection procedures in operation and a centre has a role in monitoring and reporting on contact between parents and children, the relationship between child-care workers and parents may be strained.
- There may be agreements over, say, collecting children at the agreed time, paying fees in advance, that are not kept to.
- Parents may disagree with the methods of the centre, for example challenging a learning through play approach.
- Rules such as no smoking on the premises may be broken and challenged.
- Parents may have complaints and concerns directed at particular members of staff. This could result in an official complaint being lodged against the centre.

THINK!

1 Read through the above examples again. Have you had any experience of observing or handling a disagreement with a parent? How was it managed?
2 Can you think of any other situations where there might be misunderstandings or disagreements with parents?

There is no magic formula for resolving difficulties of this, or any, type but a centre that values its partnership with parents will work hard to maintain the confidence of parents by attempting to settle such differences to the satisfaction of all concerned. This is most likely to happen if:

- staff deal seriously and courteously with parents' concerns
- anger and aggression are dealt with calmly and not in a confrontational manner
- parents' skills, feelings and opinions are acknowledged and valued
- the centre has a consistent and well thought out approach to the way that it works with parents, with all staff aware of and supported in it
- any concerns that staff have are communicated promptly and honestly with parents.

To sum up, to work most effectively with parents, child-care workers need to take a non-judgmental approach, that is one that recognises that parents have a great deal to contribute to the shared care of their children, and where professionals value and act on these contributions.

Getting parents involved

All parents will have some involvement with the centre that their child attends. Just what form this involvement takes depends on the type of centre, on the way that the staff interpret their brief to work with parents and on the parents themselves. The following are some examples of ways in which child-care centres can work together with parents to the benefit of their children.

SETTLING IN

Everyone recognises the importance of the settling-in period for both the child and the parents and will encourage parents to play a full part in this transition. Parents will often stay with their child until, with the encouragement of staff, they feel comfortable about leaving. At this stage the exchange of information is vital: staff will want to know all about the child and parents will want to know all about how their child is doing during these early days. Parents who have full-time jobs may find it difficult to stay during these sessions but will be just as concerned and anxious. Day nurseries who cater for working parents will have a programme for introducing parents and children to the setting, sometimes having evening sessions where children and parents can meet staff and visit the building. When the child starts, there is usually someone at the end of a telephone to report back and reassure parents. (Remember, the settling-in period can sometimes be more stressful for the parents than for the child. Parents may take some time to adjust to a new role.)

DO!

1 Find out how children are settled into your workplace.
2 Make a list of practical suggestions to help settle children and parents into your setting.

There are other types of parental involvement which are listed in the following paragraphs.

WORKING WITH THE CHILDREN

Parents are encouraged to stay and become involved in activities with the children, sometimes committing themselves to a regular session, often on an occasional basis. The children benefit from the presence of another adult, parents have a chance to see the setting at work and the child is aware of the link between home and the centre. Cooking, craft and swimming sessions are catered for in this way and many schools rely on parent help for reading activities. Outings with groups of children would neither be possible nor safe without parent volunteers to accompany them. Parents might also be able to contribute in a more specific way, for example by talking about their job, telling a story in another language or playing an instrument.

WORKING BEHIND THE SCENES

Not everyone feels comfortable or is able to work alongside the children. Making, mending and maintaining equipment is a task that can involve parents.

Also in this category of involvement will be the fund-raising and organisation of social events that some parent groups take responsibility for. Parents who are not available during the day can become involved in this way.

SPECIAL OCCASIONS

Most centres have occasions when parents are invited along to parties, concerts, sports or open days. Such events are usually very popular indeed. More parents will be able to take advantage of the invitation if other commitments are taken into account, for example if babies and toddlers are welcome at an afternoon concert, or if there are occasional evening events so that those who are out at work during the day can attend.

SUPPORT FOR PARENTS

In some day nurseries and most family centres the staff have a special brief to work with parents. This is probably because there is some difficulty in the family that affects the child and the parent needs some support. Staff work alongside parents and children in individual programmes. For this kind of work to be successful, it is crucial that the staff have the trust and confidence of the parent. Some centres might also offer 'drop-in' facilities and parents' groups as part of their programme.

TAKING THE CURRICULUM HOME

Most parents will expect to play a part in helping their children to read. Home–school reading diaries, in which parents and staff exchange comments on books and reading, provide a link and show children that everyone is involved. Other schemes such as Impact Maths and Science are available in some areas. These consist of activity packs that children do with parents at home, usually identifying uses for maths (or science) in everyday situations. Such schemes emphasise and recognise the role that the home, and parents, have in children's learning.

OFFICIAL ROLES

Some parents will be involved with the child-care centre in an official capacity. All state schools will have parents, elected by other parents, on their governing bodies and they have an important role defined in law. Playgroups are usually run by a committee of parents for the benefit of the local community. Other types of centre may have parent representatives on their management committees. Sometimes parents may be reluctant to become involved in this way and need to be assured that their contribution is both necessary and valued.

THINK!

1 Read through the above examples again. Can you think of any other ways to involve parents?
2 What might prevent parents from becoming involved?
3 Can you suggest ways to overcome this? Make a list of your suggestions and discuss them with a colleague.

DO!

1 You have been asked to organise an open afternoon in your nursery for new parents. You want parents to find out about the way the nursery operates, meet staff and generally have their questions answered. Plan what you would do.

NB   There are several things you could do before they arrive. Think about display boards, information packs, name badges for staff. What questions do you think the parents might ask?

Key terms
You need to know what these words and phrases mean. Go back through the chapter and find out.

Primary carer	Interact
Family centre	Resolving difficulties
Partnership with parents	Non-judgmental
Eye contact	Transition
Personal space	Parental involvement
Jargon	

PLAY

> **This chapter includes:**
> - **The value of play**
> - **What children learn through playing**
> - **The adult's role in play.**

The value of play

Young children and babies need to acquire many skills and to find out about the world that they live in. They do this through relentless exploration of their environment and constant practising of their developing skills. Adults call this *play*. To enable children to get the most out of their play it is important that people who are involved with children understand the value of play and how to organise play opportunities.

WHY IS PLAY A GOOD WAY OF MEETING YOUNG CHILDREN'S NEEDS?

- Play occurs naturally in young children. It is therefore familiar to the child, a link between home and the establishment. It is a way to harness what the child is already able to do to help their learning.
- Play cannot be wrong. It therefore provides a safe situation for the child to try out new things without the fear of failure. This is important for the child's development of a positive self-esteem.
- Play provides the opportunity for repetition. One of the important ways that learning takes place is through repetition. Play provides the opportunity for the child to practise and consolidate new skills in a enjoyable, familiar and interesting way.
- Play provides the opportunity for extending learning. A carefully structured play environment will provide opportunities for learning across a wide ability range. For example, sand can be a soothing sensory experience and also provide the opportunity for a child to begin to learn about capacity and volume. A child's skills can therefore develop in a familiar situation, one where there is no competition between the physical skills and the intellectual and language skills.
- Play provides the opportunity for a child to practise and perfect their skills in a safe environment. Through play situations children can also try out new skills. This can be done within a safe environment as the child can opt out of the play situation when they want.

- Play is always at the child's own level, so the needs of all children within the group can be met. It is important therefore to make sure that there is a range of play materials and equipment to enable all children to participate at their own level. Adult intervention in a child's play is necessary to move them onto the next developmental level.

What children learn through playing

Young children need to develop a whole range of skills. These need to be practised and developed through the opportunity to repeat them in concrete situations. The skills that a child needs to develop can be categorised into a number of areas to make them easy to understand and learn, but it is important to remember that children's development cannot be divided up in the same way. All the areas of development are dependent upon one another.

Social development
The development of skills needed to interact with other people in both individual and group setting.

Emotional development
Concerned with the development of healthy expression and control of feelings and emotions. This includes feelings about self. This is called self-concept.

THE DEVELOPING CHILD

Physical development
The development of bodily movement and control. It can be divided into two main areas: gross motor and fine motor skills.

Linguistic development
The development of communication through speaking or British sign language; this includes non-verbal communication. It is also the development of early reading and writing skills.

Intellectual development
The development of thinking and learning skills; it includes the development of concepts, problem solving skills, the imagination, creativity, memory and concentration.

Play provides the opportunity for all these skills to be developed. It also has the advantages of being familiar to the child, secure in that mistakes are not permanent and always at an appropriate level. It is also enjoyable and provides the opportunity for the repetition of skills necessary to learning.

PHYSICAL DEVELOPMENT

Physical development is the growth, development and control of bodily movements. Children need to practise these skills by repeating them over and over again. Physical development includes:

- gross motor skills – whole body and limb movements
- fine motor skills – small finger movements and manipulative skills
- balance
- whole body coordination
- hand–eye coordination.

DO!

1 Make a chart of where the skills listed above are practised and/or used in the following activities:
   - building with large bricks
   - playing with wet sand with buckets of various sizes and spades
   - junk and box modelling
   - doing large floor jigsaws.

Outdoor play

Outdoor play is an important aspect of physical development. It provides the opportunity for a range of physical skills to be practised and developed, but there are many other benefits:

- fresh air and exercise that aid growth and development
- space, which allows children to release energy; this provides a contrast to indoor areas within an establishment where physical movement needs to be restricted
- the opportunity to make a noise; indoors low levels of noise need to be maintained. Outdoors children can make far more noise, which may help them to adapt to the usual necessary restrictions
- a different time scale; more space may result in longer play sequences. The space is usually not required for other activities and fewer restrictions are necessary
- adjustment to the school environment; play outside is familiar to most children. It allows a feeling of freedom. Nursery children can get used to playtime.
- discovery of the environment; children can experience different materials (leaves, twigs, pebbles, stones). Outdoor play provides a rich sensory experience where children can develop awareness of many concepts, for example wind, rain, temperature, light and shade, smell, water, heat and cold.

Outdoor play needs to be as carefully planned as all other play activities. Issues that need to be considered include safety, staffing, space, storage, opportunities for all skills to be developed and all children to be involved over a range of abilities and needs.

Children can experience different materials in an outdoor environment

CHECK!

1 Why is outdoor play beneficial to children?
2 What issues need to be considered when planning outdoor play?

THINK!

1 What are the differences in planning indoor and outdoor play?
2 How may these issues be resolved?

DO!

1 List outdoor equipment or activities that promote the development of physical skills.
2 For each piece of equipment or activity that you have listed, identify where each skill can be practised and developed .
3 From your list of equipment and activities draw up a floorplan of a day's outdoor play for a group of young children. Make sure that you consider issues of space, safety, staffing, a balance of skills and a range of abilities.

INTELLECTUAL DEVELOPMENT

Intellectual development is the development of thinking and learning skills. It includes the development of concepts, problem-solving skills, creativity, imagination, memory and concentration. Play provides the opportunity for the early stages of all these skills to be developed.

A painting activity, for example, may develop the following skills:

- concepts of colour, size, shape, properties of water, mixing, thick, thin, wet and dry
- an opportunity to work through problems, for example, how to stop the paint running, how to mix colours, how to stop the paintbrush dripping, what size to draw to fit everything onto the page. These may seen like simple problems, but the child is developing skills that can be applied elsewhere
- an opportunity to use creative and imaginative skills. Children choose what to paint and develop their own ways of representing their ideas. Again, the skills necessary to enable them to do this can be transferred to other situations where the child needs to think through ideas or problems and develop personal responses to them.
- encourages children, by being an absorbing and enjoyable activity, to use their memory and develop their skills of concentration by finishing what they started.

Children choose to paint and develop their own ways of representing ideas

Through play, therefore, children have the opportunity to acquire, practise and consolidate intellectual skills that form the basis of later learning. This can be done in a secure, familiar and enjoyable environment.

LANGUAGE DEVELOPMENT

Language development is the development of communication skills. This includes verbal skills (talking) and non-verbal skills (gesture, eye contact, body movements), reading and writing. Early language development is mainly concerned with expressive language (spoken or signed). Written language and reading are later skills. Again, like all other skills, expressive language skills are acquired, practised and refined through use. As children play they use expressive language for many things:

- describing
- discussing
- reporting
- imagining
- predicting
- asking and answering questions
- practising new words
- forming and maintaining relationships.

To enable children to learn and practise their spoken language they need:

- good role models
- the opportunity to speak and to practise their speech
- adults who are sensitive to both their present level of development and the next stage.

Play provides the opportunity for children to interact with adults and other children to hear and see language, and to practise and develop their own skills. Interaction can occur during any activity or experience.

Non-verbal communication

As well as verbal or expressive language, children acquire non-verbal communication skills through play. These are bodily movements, gestures, eye contact, facial expression, and so on. Non-verbal communication sometimes replaces speech, for example a finger on the lips indicating a command to be quiet. It also forms part of what we are saying when speaking, for example pointing to emphasise a point, facial expression reflecting what is being said. The meanings of these non-verbal signs are understood in the same way as spoken language. They have a powerful impact, and when the non-verbal clues are misunderstood, the meaning of what is being said can be misinterpreted. (It is important to realise that there are cultural differences in the meanings of some non-verbal signs. This can also lead to misinterpretation of what is being said.)

Children's interaction with others in their play provides the opportunity to observe, learn and practise these non-verbal communication signs. For example, a child can become other people in a role play and adopt their use of spoken language, tone of voice and non-verbal signs. They can observe the effect these have on others and adapt and change them as they wish. This is all done in the knowledge that the child can opt out of the play at any time if they begin to feel uncomfortable in the role.

Developing an understanding of reading and writing

Children also need opportunities to develop an understanding of reading and writing. Play provides this opportunity. For example, if notepads, pencils, menus, pricelists and notices are provided in an imaginative play area that is a

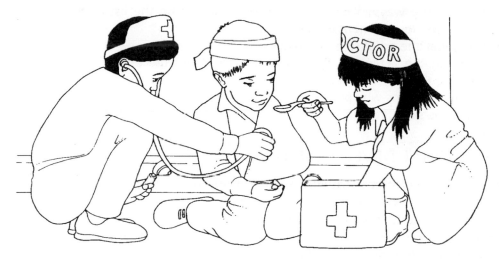

A child can become other people in a role play, but opt out of the play at any time if they begin to feel uncomfortable

cafe or restaurant, children have the opportunity to develop early reading and writing skills. By imitating what they have seen in cafes or restaurants they may pretend to read the menus, make marks on the paper to represent writing when taking orders and refer to pricelists. This puts reading and writing into a realistic context where children can begin to understand the importance of these skills. Older children who have acquired some reading and writing skills can further develop them in similar play situations.

CHECK!

1 What is language development?
2 What are verbal skills?
3 What are non-verbal skills?
4 How can play help language development?
5 List the ways in which children may use language when playing.

THINK!

1 What non-verbal signs can you identify, that either replace speech or form part of what is being said?
2 Are there situations that you can remember where there has been a mismatch between what is being said and the non-verbal messages given?
3 What was the effect of this mismatch?

DO!

1 Observe a group of children involved in an activity.

2 Identify the ways in which they use language. Use the list in the paragraph *Language development* on page 46.

3 What was the adult role in the talking?

4 How did the activity contribute to the children's use and/or development of language?

5 Suggest reasons why play is a good way for children to learn and develop their language skills.

EMOTIONAL DEVELOPMENT

Emotional development includes the development of the healthy control and expression of feelings and emotions. These are learned skills and are often culturally defined. Emotional development is also concerned with the development of feelings about self. This is *self-image* or *self-concept*.

Feelings exist and cannot be changed. It is the behaviour that results from the feelings that can be modified. Through play children have the opportunity to explore feelings that they have. They have the opportunity to experiment with responses to their feelings. Play enables children to express positive feelings openly and begin to develop ways of expressing difficult feelings in acceptable ways.

Play is also a positive self-image builder. The way that we feel about ourselves has a large impact on all aspects of our lives. It is therefore important that children develop a positive self-esteem. Play is familiar and natural to them and so is not a threatening experience – play cannot be wrong. Children play at their own level and so the risk of constant failure is minimised. This familiar positive environment gives them the opportunity to develop a positive sense of their achievements and to begin to feel good about themselves. This in turn affects their later development.

Play is also a positive self-image builder

1 What is emotional development?
2 What is self-image or concept and why is it important?
3 Why is play important in a child's emotional development?
4 List some ways in which play can contribute positively to a child's emotional development.

DO!

1 List the ways in which you can enhance a child's self-concept.
2 Link each of these suggestions to a play activity.
3 Suggest why play is a good way of developing a child's self-image.

SOCIAL DEVELOPMENT

Social development is concerned with the development of skills that enable children to get on successfully with other people. Social skills enable a child to become a reasonable, acceptable and effective member of a community. These skills are learned through interaction with other people. It is a life-long process. Young children need to begin to acquire skills such as:

- sharing
- taking turns
- co-operating
- making and maintaining friendships
- responding to people in an appropriate way.

Play acts as a bridge to social skills and relationships. It provides children with the opportunity to interact with others, both adults and children, at an appropriate level. This in itself helps children acquire the necessary skills for getting on with others and becoming part of a group. Through play children are also given the opportunity to practise and perfect social skills in situations that are not permanent. The activity, game or experience will finish but the social skills used will eventually be remembered. In this way the child is not made to feel inadequate as new skills are acquired.

THE DEVELOPMENT OF SOCIAL PLAY

How children play within the group follows a developmental pattern. Progress through the stages of development depends upon having the opportunity to play with other children. As children learn and develop social skills these are taken into account in their play. The pattern is outlined below and summarised in the table:

STAGES OF PLAY.

- **solitary play:** a child plays alone
- **parallel play:** a child plays side-by-side with another child but without interacting; their play activities remain separate
- **associative play:** play begins with other children; children may make intermit-

tent interactions and/or be involved in the same activity although their play may remain personal

■ **co-operative play**: children are able to play together co-operatively; they are able to adopt a role within the group and to take account of others' needs and actions.

Solitary	Parallel	Associative	Co-operative
Alone	Alongside without interaction	Alongside with some interaction	Together

CHECK!

1 What are social skills?
2 Why are they important?
3 How are social skills acquired?
4 Why is play a good way for children to learn social skills?

DO!

1 List some of the social skills that a child needs to function well within society.
2 Link these skills to activities that give the child the opportunity to develop them.
3 What is your role in promoting social skills during these activities?

The role of the adult

Adults have an important role in children's play to ensure that the maximum benefit is gained from it. The adult needs to plan and prepare the activities carefully. They also need to interact with the children during the activity and monitor what is happening through observation. Study the diagram on page 51 and use it to help you to answer the questions below.

CHECK!

1 Why is the adult important in children's play?
2 What should be taken into account when planning children's play?
3 What is important about the presentation of an activity?
4 List the ways in which adults can interact with children during play.
5 Why is it important to observe and monitor children?
6 What should an adult be looking for when observing and monitoring an activity?

What are the children's developmental levels?
What are the special needs of children within the group?
Which skills do the children need to develop?
How much space is available?
How much time is available?
What are the staffing levels and expertise?
Is there a current theme or topic?
Does the planning reflect cultural diversity?
What activities do the children enjoy?
Are there any safety issues to be considered?

The children:
- Does the play provided meet their needs?
- Who is playing with which activity? Is this significant?
- What interaction with the child/children is appropriate?
- How can the children's play be extended?

The activity:
- Is the activity appropriate for the group of children?
- Is it attractively presented?
- Is all the necessary equipment available so that the children can be as independent as possible?
- Was there enough time and space for the children to play with the activity successfully?
- Was the adult's time and expertise made full use of?

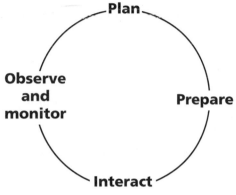

Plan

Observe and monitor

Prepare

Interact

The activity needs to be attractive and easily accessible to the children.
Is all the necessary equipment available?
Is the activity presented in an inviting way? This may include beginning the activity to suggest ways of doing it to the children.
Is there enough space, time and adult help available to enable the child to be successful at the activity?
Is the area safe?

Ways of interacting with the children include:
- joining in the children's play
- playing alongside the children
- providing a commentary on the play
- suggesting new or different ideas for the play
- introducing different equipment to extend the play
- discussing the activity prior to or after the play.

Observe the play without direct intervention allowing the child/children to develop their own ideas.

THINK!

1 Why is it important to plan for children's play?
2 Why should activities be attractively presented?
3 Describe some specific instances where you have seen an adult interacting with a child during play.
4 Suggest some ways that an adult could extend a child's play.
5 Suggest some ways that an adult could observe and monitor children's dvelopment during play.

1 Observe an adult who works with children.
2 Make a note of how they plan for the children's play, how activities are set up and how they interact with the children during play.
3 Ask the adult what they look for when observing children informally during their play.
4 Suggest reasons for their actions.
5 Where possible compare your findings with others. What are the similarities and differences?
6 What conclusions can you draw from the fact that there are similarities and differences?

THE PLAY ENVIRONMENT

There are some important considerations in developing a positive play environment:

- repetition is an important part of learning; children need some consistency in what is provided for them so that they can improve their skills
- there should be a variety of activities provided at any one time to ensure that all necessary skills can be developed
- there should be a balance between play where the children develop their own themes and ideas independently (sometimes called free play) and play where the adult guides the play towards the next stage of development (sometimes called structured play)
- safety should be an important consideration at all times; this includes the maintenance of safe equipment
- the best starting point for a positive play environment is the children's backgrounds, interests and knowledge. These can be extended and built upon and used to develop other necessary skills.

CHECK!

1 Why is it important for children to repeat activities?
2 How can the variety of activities contribute to a child's all-round development?
3 What is the best starting point for a play environment?

THINK!

1 How could you provide free play?
2 How could you provide structured play?
3 How can you ensure that the play environment is safe?
4 Think of some possible starting points for developing a play environment.

Key terms

You need to know what these words and phrases mean. Go back through the chapter and find out.

Physical development

Intellectual development

Linguistic development

Emotional development

Social development

Self esteem

Self-image/concept

Non-verbal communication

Gross motor skills

Fine motor skills

Solitary play

Parallel play

Associative play

Co-operative play

5 THE EARLY YEARS CURRICULUM: PHILOSOPHY AND APPROACHES

> **This chapter includes:**
> - Approaches to the curriculum
> - The National Curriculum
> - Curriculum planning and organisation
> - Equal opportunities and the curriculum.

Approaches to the curriculum

A 'course of study' is the simple dictionary definition of *curriculum*. But in the early years, the curriculum contains more than this simple academic definition. The curriculum also transmits the values of the setting and those who work within it. Through it children learn about themselves and their place in the world. This chapter looks mainly at the content of the early years curriculum but the way that we present this curriculum to young children needs to be guided by what we know about the way that children learn. We must consider **how** children learn as well as **what** children learn.

IN THE PAST

Look in history books and see if you can find drawings or photographs of schools in the early part of this century. You might see very large classes of children, sitting in rows facing a stern-looking teacher, who might be pointing to a list of words on a blackboard with a long stick. There might be a chart or a map on the walls and probably a list of rules, but not much else. The windows would be placed high on the walls so that children could not be distracted by what was going on outside the schoolroom. The only voice heard would be the teacher's or the children chanting their multiplication tables in unison. Children were expected to learn facts by heart, to listen passively and to absorb knowledge from adults. They were not encouraged to take any responsibility for their own learning, to contribute their ideas or to follow up their own interests. Education was not expected to be enjoyable. (*Hard Times* by Charles Dickens or, more recently, *Cider with Rosie* by Laurie Lee both give vivid accounts of bygone schooldays.)

CURRENT PRACTICE

Studies of the way that children learn – Piaget's work in particular – emphasise that concepts are best understood through actual experiences, in effect that children learn by doing. These theories have had a very great influence on the way that we organise early years provision and have led to an approach to learning that takes into account the child's individual capabilities and interests (*child-centred*) and is achieved through experience (*experiential*).

For example, it is impossible for a child of 5 to understand about, say, the absorbency of different kinds of fabrics simply by listening to an adult talk about their relative properties. But if you were to set the child the task of making a raincoat for Teddy, and provided samples of fabric at the water trough, then it is very likely that the child would begin to understand the concept of absorbency and the properties of the fabrics tested.

In most settings the environment is carefully organised so that children have the maximum opportunity for hands-on experience. Equipment will be accessible so that they can make choices and follow up interests, fostering a responsibility for their own learning. A number of activities will be available at any one time and the atmosphere buzzes with busy noise. Children will be involved in planning and working collaboratively and will be encouraged to contribute their own ideas. Staff monitor progress, interact with children and plan and provide for the next learning activity.

This current approach to the curriculum assumes that if children engage with and enjoy what they are doing, then their learning will be both effective and meaningful.

CHECK!

1 Go back through the text. Write down definitions of child-centred and experiential learning. Give examples.

THINK!

1 What can you remember about your early years at nursery or in school?
2 How was your day organised?
3 Can you recall anything that you particularly enjoyed? Anything you hated?
4 Would you describe your experience as child-centred?

DO!

1 Find out about the curriculum in your workplace. What range of subjects are offered to the children ? What methods are used to present them?

The National Curriculum

The National Curriculum was introduced in England and Wales (a similar act relates to Scotland) as part of the of the 1988 Education Reform Act. The main points of relevance to the early years can be summarised as follows:

- the National Curriculum is compulsory for all children between the ages of 5 and 16 in all state schools (this includes special schools)
- the curriculum consists of three *core* subjects – English, maths, science (plus Welsh in Welsh-speaking schools) and seven *foundation* subjects – technology, history, geography, art, music, physical education, with a modern foreign language introduced at 11 (proportionately more time is allocated to core subjects). In addition, teaching in religious education must be provided
- subjects are divided into *attainment targets*, each with a *programme of study*
- schooling is divided into four key stages. Children between 5 and 7 years are at Key Stage 1
- at the end of each key stage children's progress is assessed by Standard Assessment Tasks (SATs) and by teacher assessment. The child's progress is then reported back to parents. Schools' results, but not those of individual children, must be available for consultation.

CHECK!

1 What subjects are studied by children between 5 and 7?
2 Who does the National Curriculum apply to?
3 What key stage applies to 6-year-olds?
4 What are SATs?
5 When are children tested? What happens to their scores?

What does this mean for early years workers? There are several implications, as explained below.

- Though its format and compulsory nature were new, most of the content of the National Curriculum was already being delivered through good early years programmes.
- The importance of science and technology in the early years was highlighted. In-service training and investment in equipment have given staff the opportunity to build on programmes offered in these subjects with increased confidence.
- Planning the programme to meet the requirements of the National Curriculum means that many staff work collaboratively. Nursery nurses and classroom assistants will have much to contribute here.
- Evidence needs to be gathered to support teacher assessment. This may mean observations of the children as well as actual pieces of work. Everyone who works with the children will have a part to play in collecting this.
- Many nursery classes plan their programmes with the breadth of the National Curriculum in mind so there is an effect on under-fives' provision too.
- Children (and parents) may become anxious at the prospect of formal assessment at 7. Care must be taken to reassure and avoid pressure.
- Young children learn most effectively through child-centred and experiential methods. These have been shown to be the most appropriate methods for delivering the National Curriculum too.

- The content and structure of the National Curriculum has been changed a great deal in a relatively short space of time. This has been unsettling for those who have to implement these changes.

DO!

1 Talk with your colleagues in your workplace. How does the National Curriculum influence the way that they work with children?

Curriculum planning and organisation

THEMES AND TOPICS

The curriculum for the early years needs to be both broad and balanced. Planning for under fives will provide activities that meet the needs of children in all areas of their development, intellectual, physical, linguistic, social and emotional. Often these activities will be integrated into a theme or topic that may be developed over a number of sessions.

For example, a nursery class is working on the theme of travel. The following activities have been included:

- the imaginative play area has been presented as a transport cafe. Children are 'reading' menus , 'writing' orders and serving customers
- on the carpet, a road playmat has been set out and small cars are being steered around it
- at the painting easels some children are painting pictures of journeys
- a group of children are making models of vehicles from junk
- a road with traffic signs has been chalked on the outside play area and children are negotiating the 'road' on the wheeled toys
- children are looking at catalogues, selecting and cutting out pictures for a transport collage
- at carpet time the children will sing songs and listen to stories about travelling
- a walk to the nearby station and a trip on a train is planned
- the school's crossing warden is coming in to talk to the children about her job
- children have brought in postcards, tickets and pictures, all linked to travel and these have been displayed on an interest table, providing a focus for conversation.

THINK!

1 Can you add to the list of activities that would develop this theme with nursery-aged children?

This *thematic, topic* or *integrated* approach to curriculum planning is the method

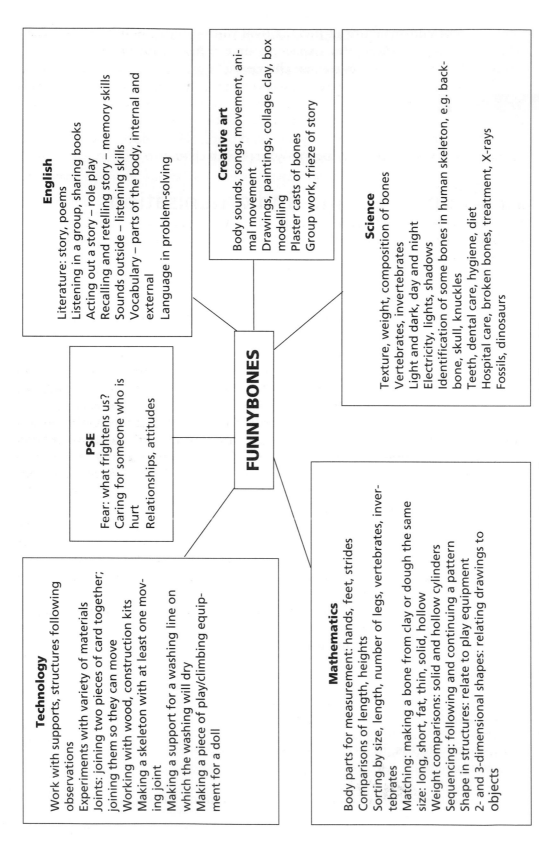

English

Literature: story, poems
Listening in a group, sharing books
Acting out a story – role play
Recalling and retelling story – memory skills
Sounds outside – listening skills
Vocabulary – parts of the body, internal and external
Language in problem-solving

Creative art

Body sounds, songs, movement, animal movement
Drawings, paintings, collage, clay, box modelling
Plaster casts of bones
Group work, frieze of story

Science

Texture, weight, composition of bones
Vertebrates, invertebrates
Light and dark, day and night
Electricity, lights, shadows
Identification of some bones in human skeleton, e.g. backbone, skull, knuckles
Teeth, dental care, hygiene, diet
Hospital care, broken bones, treatment, X-rays
Fossils, dinosaurs

PSE

Fear: what frightens us?
Caring for someone who is hurt
Relationships, attitudes

FUNNYBONES

Technology

Work with supports, structures following observations
Experiments with variety of materials
Joints: joining two pieces of card together; joining them so they can move
Working with wood, construction kits
Making a skeleton with at least one moving joint
Making a support for a washing line on which the washing will dry
Making a piece of play/climbing equipment for a doll

Mathematics

Body parts for measurement: hands, feet, strides
Comparisons of length, heights
Sorting by size, length, number of legs, vertebrates, invertebrates
Matching: making a bone from clay or dough the same size: long, short, fat, thin, solid, hollow
Weight comparisons: solid and hollow cylinders
Sequencing: following and continuing a pattern
Shape in structures: relate to play equipment
2- and 3-dimensional shapes: relating drawings to objects

An example of a topic plan developed from Funnybones by Janet and Allan Ahlberg

usually used at Key Stage 1 as well. In this case the topic might stretch across a longer period, usually a half term, and as many areas of the curriculum as possible will be linked to the theme. Detailed plans, often in the form of diagrams, are developed to include the National Curriculum subject areas and the attainment targets covered in each subject. (NB It may not be possible for all areas of the curriculum to be approached through every theme. In these situations, the subjects will be covered outside the topic.)

An integrated approach is appropriate for the early years curriculum because:

- children do not recognise boundaries between subjects
- a theme is likely to generate interest amongst children
- activities for children at all levels of ability can be provided
- children can make their own suggestions and add to the theme, following up their own interests
- the theme can bring together different types of activities, the less formal as well as the more structured.

THE INTEGRATED DAY

Most early years provision will be organised as an integrated day. A number of activities and tasks are provided and the children either make a choice as to what to do (often the case in nursery) or are directed towards a sequence of tasks that need to be completed. Children can work at their own pace and at a level appropriate to their stage of development. This is especially important given the range of ages and abilities provided for in settings. Most nursery classes will have children between the ages of 3 and 5 and the practice of vertical or family grouping, where classes are comprised of children from more than one year group, is common in primary schools. Space and equipment can be used fully. Adults can spend time with small groups of children at activities that require close supervision or direction, for example reading practice, or introducing a new skill, while other groups of children are given some responsibility for their own learning while they work on activities that they manage themselves. There will naturally be times in the integrated day when the whole group of children come together, for example story time, PE or assembly.

To operate effectively the integrated day takes much careful preparation and organisation. Accurate records need to be kept for each child to ensure that progress is achieved and maintained.

THINK!

1 How is the children's day organised in your workplace?
2 Is there a routine that they follow?
3 How do children move from one activity to another?
4 What kind of records are kept? Do children have any responsibility for recording what they do?
5 Are there any times when children come together as a whole group?

1 Make a 'snapshot' observation of your workplace. Draw a plan of the room and indicate what activities are available in each area. Choose a time and record, at that moment, the position of the children on the diagram. Show where the adults are and what they are doing.

2 What does your diagram tell you about the way that the space is organised?

HIGHSCOPE

Highscope is an approach to the early years curriculum that was developed in the United States in the 1960s as part of the Headstart compensatory education programme. It has been shown to have good results and has now been introduced in a number of centres in this country. Highscope is characterised by the following:

- the Plan–Do–Review routine: children are required to indicate to an adult what they are going to do during a session (plan), to carry out this plan (do) and then together with an adult a small group shows their work and recalls what they have done (review)
- room organisation: the room is arranged for particular activities, usually in a book area, a construction area, a home area and an art area
- equipment organisation: equipment and materials are stored and labelled so that children have independent access to them
- adult involvement that values the children's initiatives and interests.

This approach actively involves children in decisions about their learning and fosters responsibility and independence. (To find out more about Highscope, contact the Highscope Institute 190–2 Maple Road, Penge, London, SE20 8HT.)

Equal opportunities and the curriculum

Treating everyone the same is not going to provide all children with equal opportunities. We need to recognise that some children are disadvantaged in our society and that some positive action might be necessary to enable them to succeed. We need to consider this when we plan the curriculum, and to recognise that we communicate values and attitudes as well as skills and knowledge to the children in our care. The curriculum must be accessible to and reflect all sections of society. It must include and enable all children.

Some practical suggestions for achieving this equality of opportunity are given below.

- Widen your provision of equipment. This includes choosing a variety of cooking utensils and play food for your home corner and clothes for your dressing up rails. Look at the jigsaws, the play figures, the fabrics in your collage box, the tapes and musical instruments. Do they reflect cultural diversity?

- Choose books and tell stories that challenge stereotypes and provide positive role models (see page 71).
- Value the child's home background. This is vital to the child's self-esteem.
- Use cookery sessions to try different recipes and taste a range of foods (you may be able to get parents involved here).
- Celebrate a range of festivals from a variety of cultures. Children who celebrate these festivals at home will feel valued. Those who don't will gain insight and understanding (NB Do your research thoroughly, perhaps enlisting the help of parents or community centres).
- Display positive images in your setting. Include black people, women, people with disabilities, as these groups are often under-represented, even invisible. Visitors can challenge stereotypes too. Invite female firefighters, male nurses.
- Choose stories, rhymes and songs that represent a range of cultural backgrounds.
- Value language diversity. Get children to listen to other languages. Teach greeting words, rhymes.
- Ensure that activities are accessible to all children in your setting, including those with disabilities.
- Monitor activities that are dominated by particular groups of children, for example boys often monopolise large brick play. It might be necessary to exclude one group for a while so that another group can have an opportunity to play.
- Ensure a multicultural approach to arts, crafts and music.

CHECK!

1 Read the section again. Make sure that you understand what the term equal opportunities means.

THINK!

1 Can you make any other practical suggestions for ways to promote equal opportunities?

DO!

Look at your workplace.
1 How does it promote equal opportunities?
2 What positive images can you see?

THE HIDDEN CURRICULUM

The section above deals with the content of the curriculum, but perhaps even more important in ensuring equal opportunities are the attitudes and values of those who deliver it. These are sometimes known as the hidden curriculum and are communicated to children in the way that we talk to them and in the expectations we have of them.

The following are some examples of ways in which the hidden curriculum can hinder equal opportunities:

- an expectation and acceptance that boys' play is rougher than girls'
- adults giving more time to boys (many studies show this to be true)
- having low expectations of the behaviour and achievement of children from minority groups
- regarding particular games and activities as sex-appropriate
- overprotecting children with disabilities
- comments such as;
  'Boys don't cry.'
  'Here's a picture of a wedding. The girls will like this.'
  'Find me two strong boys to move this table.'
  'The girls can wash the cups.'
  'It's not ladylike to fight.'

Children absorb these messages and they can affect their view of themselves. The attitudes and values of the staff as well as the content of the curriculum need to address the issues of equal opportunities.

Key terms

You need to know what these words and phrases mean. Go back through the chapter and find out.

Curriculum	Thematic approach
Learning by doing	Topic
Child-centred	Integrated day
Experiential	Vertical or family grouping
Hands-on experience	Highscope
Working collaboratively	Plan–Do–Review
The national curriculum	Equal opportunities
Core subjects	Language diversity
Foundation subjects	Positive images
Attainment targets	The hidden curriculum
SATs	

6 THE EARLY YEARS CURRICULUM: CURRICULUM COMPONENTS

> **This chapter includes**
> - Early literacy
> - Children's books
> - Developing maths
> - Science and technology
> - Creativity
> - History and geography
> - Physical activities.

This chapter will look at the elements that go together to make up the curriculum for the early years. Children will not be presented with these subjects in isolation but will meet them in an integrated and balanced programme of learning.

Early literacy

We live in a literate world in a society that values reading and writing (*literacy*). Consequently, a great deal of emphasis is placed on becoming competent in these areas. Children begin to notice and respond to this literate world long before they begin the formal process of learning to read and write. Their environment contains many examples of writing, from the signs in the supermarket and on the bus ticket to the postcard from Granny and the bedtime story book.

Through these experiences children become familiar with the *product* of writing. When they see someone take a telephone message or write a cheque, they become aware of the *process* of writing too. This has an impact. Once children realise that writing carries meaning, they have taken their first step towards becoming literate.

CHECK!

1 What does literacy mean? What do you understand by the term a literate world?

THINK!

1 Why is so much emphasis placed on children learning to read and write?

1 List as many examples as you can of the written word in the child's everyday environment.

2 Go through your list again. How many of these involved the process of writing too?

LEARNING TO READ AND WRITE

Learning to read and write is a long and complex process for most children. They will need to learn skills and rules and have plenty of practice to consolidate them. If children have already begun to enjoy books, then it is likely that this will spur them on and give them a reason to persevere. (See *Children's books*, page 69.)

By the age of 5 many children will have a sight vocabulary of a number of words. Most will recognise their own name; some may be able to write it. Formal instruction in reading and writing may not begin until children start at primary school but many pre-school experiences and activities are important in the development of reading and writing skills. These include activities that involve any or all of the following:

- hand-eye co-ordination and fine motor skills – you need to control a pencil to write
- visual discrimination – one letter or word needs to be distinguished from another
- sequencing – the order of the letters or words affects the meaning
- auditory discrimination – hearing the difference between sounds and combinations of sounds helps reading
- use of symbols – reading and writing are representational forms in which one thing, the combination of letters, stands for something else

Also important is using reading and writing as a meaningful part of play, for example, 'reading' the menu in the cafe, 'writing' a telephone message in the home corner.

Remember that reading and writing are essential tools for later learning. They are used and practised in every area of the curriculum.

THINK!

1 Think about the activities that might be available during a typical nursery session.

2 Look at the list of reading and writing skills given above. Link the activities that you thought of with the skills.

READING

There are basically two approaches used in the teaching of reading. They are *Look and Say* and *Phonics*. There is some debate over which is the most effective method. Most teachers use a combination of both methods.

Look and Say gets children to recognise whole words by their shape. Words are often written on flash cards and children will attempt to memorise them, often practising at home. Children can then read simple stories comprised of the words that they have learned. They recognise words from their shapes, from the look of them. The shortcoming of this approach is that they have no way of recognising words that they have not yet learned.

Phonics breaks down words into sounds and encourages the sounding out of words. This disadvantage with this method is that English is not phonically regular: a letter may make one sound in one word and a completely different sound in another. It is not very rewarding for the early reader to be limited to phonically regular words that can be sounded out. On the other hand, a knowledge of phonics will give children a strategy for attempting unfamiliar words.

CHECK!

1 What are the differences between the two methods of reading outlined above?

DO!

1 Talk to your colleagues in your workplace. Find out which methods they use.

READING SCHEMES OR 'REAL' BOOKS?

Reading schemes are carefully structured and graded. A limited number of words is introduced in each book and there is plenty of repetition of these words. The characters usually appear in a number of books so children have the opportunity to become familiar with them. Critics of reading schemes say that the stories are contrived and that the language of the books is stilted. They advocate the use of 'real' books for readers, that is picture books and story books that represent good children's literature. They maintain that these interesting books make children want to read and that this motivation brings success. Critics of this approach say that children miss the step-by-step structure and may choose books that are beyond their capabilities. Many schools use both types of books, using the method that best suits the individual child and the preference of the teacher.

DO!

1 Compare some books from a reading scheme with some picture books. Look at the following:
   - the characters: do they hold your interest?
   - the language: sentence structure and vocabulary

- the story itself: is it interesting, exciting?
- the illustrations.

What are your conclusions?

Early readers need lots of practice. When you listen to individual children you can help them by:

- giving them your attention
- finding a place with minimal distractions
- giving the child thinking time
- helping when necessary: sometimes a bit of encouragement or a clue, for example 'What's that sound?', can help the child move on
- talking about the book and getting them to talk to you; the child may lose the sense of a book reading it word by word
- monitoring and recording their progress; you may notice that a child is not doing very well on a particular book. Suggest something else; different approaches suit different children
- alerting them to patterns in words and sounds
- being positive about their achievements.

You might also be involved in making special individual books for children. These usually consist of photographs of the child with simple text about themselves, their family and so on, mounted on card and bound in some way. These are very popular and are often the first books that children get to read.

Remember that reading is a complex skill that may take years to achieve. As with all skills, some children will grasp it easily and progress quickly while others find it more difficult.

WRITING

Children begin writing by making marks. To adults it may appear to be meaningless scribble, but to the child it is a telephone message, a letter to Santa, their name. During their early years in school we expect children to learn the rules and conventions of writing. It becomes an important tool that they use to communicate with themselves and with the outside world.

Conventions of writing

- Letter formation: children need to know how to form letters correctly and consistently. This means where you start and where you finish and requires a great deal of practice. Children also learn to recognise the feel of a letter when they write it. Tracing in the air and in sand helps to reinforce this.
- Orientation: in English (and many other languages) this means writing (and reading) from left to right and from top to bottom. Bilingual children may have experienced a written language, Urdu or Hebrew for example, that is oriented differently.
- Spacing: groups of letters go together to form words and spaces separate these words. Spacing words correctly needs practice.
- Spelling: children need to learn that there is a standard way of spelling

words, but excessive concentration on this at the early stages will limit and inhibit children's writing.

- Punctuation: this is a skill acquired later, but children notice punctuation early on in their reading and begin to introduce it into their writing. It also includes the appropriate use of upper and lower case letters.

CHECK!

1 Read through the list of writing conventions again. Check that you understand what they mean.

DO!

1 Find some samples of children's writing. Include some early writing as well as a later piece. For each piece, decide which of the conventions are being followed.

Children's writing is not just about the technical skills listed above, it is about content too. Sometimes children become overwhelmed by these technical skills and this affects the content of their writing. A child who is limited to the words that she can spell correctly or who is afraid to make a mistake will not become involved in or enjoy writing. It will become a task to be completed because an adult demands it. A sensitive adult will watch the child's progress and introduce the need for correct spelling at the right stage, ensuring that the child retains confidence in her writing abilities.

Teaching writing

Writing is taught in a variety of different ways. All approaches will ensure that children learn to form letters correctly and develop fluency in their handwriting style. Some schools favour an approach where the child writes completely on their own and then reads the writing back to an adult who may then identify something with the child that can be discussed. This approach is known as *emergent* or *developmental* writing and enables children to get on with what they want to write without waiting for an adult to show them the correct way to write a word. Critics say that technical accuracy takes longer to establish with this method. Other schools place an earlier emphasis on accuracy with children relying on adults for correct spelling at an early stage with independent writing coming later. Critics of this approach say that children become over-dependent on adults and may not have the confidence to make their own attempts. Of course there are merits in both approaches and most schools will strike a balance with the aim of producing children's writing that shows both independence and accuracy.

1 How might the content of children's writing be affected by their lack of technical skills?
2 Evaluate both approaches to writing. Note down strengths and weaknesses.

DO!

1 Investigate the methods used in your workplace to get children writing.

Katy read this back to her teacher:
The snail's teeth is on its tongue and I am going to a party tomorrow and the snail's tongue works like a cheese grater.

Emergent writing

How can you help?

- Sit with children and help them form letters correctly. Left-handed children may need extra help.
- Be a good role model. Let children watch you making notes for your file, filling in a register and so on, so they see that writing is a part of everyday life.
- When you write for children, make sure that your writing is clear, legible and accurate. If children are going to copy your writing, make sure that it is large enough.
- Talk to children about their writing, use it in displays. Let them know that you value it.
- Present children with a variety of writing tasks, not just stories. Get them to make shopping lists, record experiments, write letters and invitations.
- Show children that writing can be found in many different places. Collect examples – involve children in this – and make a display of comics, cereal boxes, bus tickets, labels, and so on.
- Help children to present their writing in different ways, such as making books, using a word processor.

Children's books

Books are an important and integral part of the early years curriculum. They are provided in all nurseries and classrooms. Reading and story time are part of each day. Some children also have books at home and read with parents and carers. This early experience of books is very important in establishing positive attitudes to books and to reading.

WHY ARE BOOKS IMPORTANT?

Books and stories are an important part of children's development. Outlined below are some of the main skills that can be developed and nurtured. Books and stories can be introduced to very young children. Although the child may not fully understand the story, a quiet intimate time reading with a parent or carer forms a positive association for the child. This in turn helps to establish a habit of reading and listening to stories that has many benefits for the child.

Language development
Language is learned: the more exposure a child has to different patterns in language the richer their own language is likely to be. Initially this will be expressive (spoken) language, later read and written language. Listening to stories and talking about books enable young children to listen and respond to the sound and rhythm of spoken language. This is important to speech development at all levels. Initially children need to recognise the sounds and rhythms that occur in their language; once this has been established they need to practise and refine their use of spoken language.

Listening to stories can also extend a child's vocabulary. As long as most of the language in the text is familiar to the child new, imaginative language can be introduced. The child will begin to understand these new words by their context, that is how they are used and linked with the story line and the pictures.

Experience with books and story telling is also an important part of a child's early understanding of symbols. A child who has contact with books begins to understand that the squiggles on the page represent speech. This is a vital skill in the development of reading and writing.

Emotional development
Books and stories are enjoyable. They give children the opportunity to express a whole range of positive emotions. They provide a rich imaginative world that can be a source of great pleasure to the child. Through identification with the characters and the storyline children can develop and practise their own responses to a wide range of events, situations and feelings that are beyond their own life experiences. This can be done in a safe environment where the child has an element of control over events.

Intellectual development

Books, if carefully chosen, can provide a rich source of imagination for a child. They can stimulate interesting and exciting thoughts and ideas. The development of imagination is an important part of being creative. Creative thoughts and ideas are an important part of the quality of life and necessary to the development of society.

Books can also introduce children to a wide range of concepts. Repetition and context enable children to develop their understanding of the world that they live in. Listening to stories, recalling and sequencing the events are also positive ways of extending young children's concentration span and memory.

Social development

Books and stories are more than just the presentation of a sequence of events; they carry in them a whole range of messages about how a society functions. This includes acceptable patterns of behaviour, expectations of groups within the society and moral codes of right and wrong. Children pick up these messages. It is therefore vital that books for young children portray a positive view of society and the people within that society. This positive view of the world contributes towards young children developing a balanced and constructive outlook on life.

Group story time and sharing books contribute to the development of social skills of sharing, turn taking and co-operating with others. Children begin to learn that they have to take other people's needs and wishes into account. Story time can also provide children and adults with the opportunity to build and maintain relationships. If a cosy and comfortable environment is provided it offers a sense of closeness and intimacy for the children and adults involved.

Sharing books contributes to the development of social skills

CHECK!

1 Why is it important to introduce books and stories to young children?
2 Which language skills can be developed through books and story telling?
3 Which emotional skills can be nurtured through books and story telling?
4 Which intellectual skills can be developed through books and story telling?
5 How can books and stories influence children's view of the society that they are growing up in?

THINK!

1 What positive images should be portrayed in children's books of the following groups and themes:
- women?
- men?
- people with a disability?
- black people?
- diverse religious practices?
- diverse cultural practices?
- patterns of family life?

DO!

1 Choose a range of books that present the positive images that you have outlined above.

CHOOSING CHILDREN'S BOOKS

It is important that children's books are chosen carefully. Children have different needs and interests at different stages of their development. The maximum benefit can be gained if the book chosen meets the child's needs. All children are individual and will have different needs, likes and dislikes. This needs to be taken into account. There are, however, are some general points to consider when choosing a book for a young child and these are listed in the table on the following page.

THINK!

1 Why is it important to choose a book or story appropriate to the audience?
2 Why are different books appropriate to children of different ages?

DO!

1 Draw up a checklist for choosing appropriate books within each age range. Make sure that they meet the criteria listed in the table above.
2 Using your checklist, choose a selection of books for each age range.

Books are a powerful way of influencing a childrens's views about the society that they live in. Books for children must therefore reflect positive images of all sections of society in both the text and the illustrations.

0–3
- Picture books are appropriate for this age range, especially for children under 1 year.
- Where there is text it needs to be limited, especially for children aged 0–1.
- The pictures need to have bright colours and bold shapes.
- The pictures need little detail.
- The images need to be simplified so that they are easily identified – the most obvious features stressed.
- Children enjoy familiar themes, for example families, animals.
- The complexity of pictures and text can be increased for children aged 2+.
- The context of the story time is as important as the book itself; the cosy, close and intimate time gives children a positive association with books and reading.

3–5
- Repetition is important – for language development and for the enjoyment of the sound and rhythm of language.
- Books need to be reasonably short, to match children's concentration span.
- Books need minimum language with plenty of pictures that relate to the text.
- Popular themes are still everyday objects and occurrences.

5–7
- A clearly identifiable story and setting are important.
- Children's wider interests, experiences and imagination should be reflected in themes.
- The characters can be developed through the story.
- Language usage can be richer – playing with rhyme and rhythm, the introduction of new vocabulary and the use of repetition for dramatic effect.

3–7
- Illustrations still need to be bold, bright and eye-catching but can be more detailed and have more meaning than pure recognition.
- Sequenced stories become popular – with a beginning, middle and end.
- The storyline needs to be easy to follow with a limited number of characters.
- Repetition is important so that the reader or listener can become involved in the text.
- Animated objects are popular – children can enter into the fantasy.
- Children enjoy humour in stories, but it needs to be obvious humour, not puns or sarcasm.

Guidelines for choosing books for young children

PLANNING STORY TIME

Story time needs to be planned as carefully as any other activity for children. The following points should be considered for all story telling, whether on a one-to-one basis, or in a small or large group:
- the choice of an book should be appropriate to the child/children involved
- allow the child to see the pages as the story is being told
- point to the words as you read them

- tell of the story enthusiastically; show that you are enjoying it
- talk about the book after you have read it through.

When telling a story to a group of children you also need to think about:

- the area: it should be cosy, quiet, warm, comfortable
- the structure of the session: introduction, story, discussion topics and questions, rhymes or songs appropriate, where possible, to the story
- visual aids: story board, puppets, props
- behaviour management: how will you manage the behaviour to minimise interruptions and to make sure that all children can be involved in the session?

THINK!

1 Why is it important to allow the child to see the book as it is being read?
2 Why should the reader be enthusiastic?
3 Why is it important to talk through the story afterwards?
4 Why should an area for telling a story be cosy, quiet, warm and comfortable?
5 What are the benefits of using visual aids?
6 Outline some behaviour management techniques appropriate to a story time session.

DO!

1 Plan three story sessions, one each for children aged 3, 5 and 7 years.
Think about:

- choosing the book
- the area
- the structure of the session
- appropriate visual aids
- behaviour management.

Developing maths

Maths in the early years is approached almost totally through practical activities that children will be able to relate to and understand. During this time they will need the support of concrete experiences to understand mathematical concepts.

Remember that many adults feel nervous about maths, perhaps recalling negative experiences from their own schooldays. It is important that this negative attitude is not passed on to children.

WHAT IS MATHS?

Maths is all around us and children have many mathematical experiences in their everyday lives before they begin to learn maths formally at school.

1. Getting up. Is it still dark? (Time; making logical deductions)

2. Getting dressed; putting clothes on in the right order. Are these socks a pair? (Sorting, sequencing, matching)

3. Having breakfast; pour cornflakes into a bowl and juice into a cup. Oops! Don't spill it! (Estimating quantity, volume)

4. Going shopping. How many oranges? A large packet or a small packet? How much does it cost? (Counting, size, money)

5. Unpacking the bags. Where will these boxes fit? What goes in the fridge? (Sorting, shape, size)

6. Laying the table. How many places? Are there enough plates? How long before we eat? (Matching, counting, time)

7. Out for a walk. How far is it? Have I seen more buses or more lorries? How many ducks on the pond? (Estimating, comparing, counting)

8. Bedtime. Can I have one more story? I'll have the big teddy and the little teddy. How long is it till morning? (Number, size, time)

Mary's mathematical day, showing how maths is a part of children's everyday experiences

1 Using Mary's day as a guide, draw a comic strip of your own mathematical day.

Maths is much more than figures and formulae.

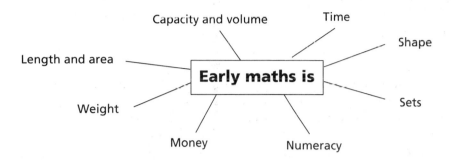

Below are some brief details about each of the areas of maths in the diagram and some examples of activities that are linked to them.

Time
Children need to understand that time can be measured and to be familiar with how we measure time. At about 7 years we expect children to be able to read clock time from both analogue and digital clock faces. They also need to sort events into past, present and future.
- Activities: talking about daily routines, filling in daily calendars, using all kinds of timers. How many jumps in a minute, etc., using movable clock faces. Stories such as *The Sleeping Beauty* deal with the passing of time.

Shape
Children need to be able to recognise shapes, two-dimensional and three-dimensional. They need to learn about the properties of shapes, for example that cylinders roll, cubes have right angles and how they fit together.
- Activities: identifying shapes in the environment, drawing around shapes, sorting junk and modelling with it, making shapes with playdough or clay, building with bricks, making patterns.

Sets
Children need to be able to sort objects into sets and explain why they belong there. This forms part of the development of logic.
- Activities: sorting with special sorting apparatus as well as with collections of shells, beads, etc.; sorting for colour, for shape, for more complex attributes, for example making a set of animals that live on farms. Older children will begin to record their findings on diagrams.

Numeracy
Numeracy includes counting, estimating, recording numbers and the four

rules of number – addition, subtraction, multiplication and division – and also simple fractions.

- Activities: taking every opportunity to count, for example children in the class, coats on the pegs, bottles in the crate; matching one thing to another, children to chairs, saucers to cups; linking number symbols to groups of objects; dividing apples into halves, quarters and sharing them out; using real objects to add to, take away, share. Older children can understand and use symbols to record their work.

Money

Details are the same as for numeracy, but additionally children must become familiar with coins and understand about equivalence, that is that one coin may be worth the same as, say, ten other coins.

- Activities: making shops in the classroom and buying and selling; counting real money, for example milk or trip money; handling play money and sorting coins; making a collection of price tags, receipts, etc.

Weight

Children need to be able to use non-standard (a book weighs as much as three apples) and standard (grams and kilograms, pounds and ounces) measures. They need to be able to apply the concept of equivalence and be able to make comparisons based on weight.

- Activities: practical experience of holding things and talking about heavy and light, then heavier than, lighter than; cooking activities using non-standard (cups, spoons) or standard measures; using balance scales to weigh first with non-standard, then with standard measures (balance scales provide evidence of equivalence – equal weight – that the children can see); investigation of other types of scales.

Length and area

Children need to be able to estimate and measure length and area using non-standard as well as standard measures. They need to be able to select the most appropriate unit of measurement for the task.

- Activities: measuring with hand spans, strides, pencils, etc.; measuring using standard measures, rulers, tapes, trundle wheels; measuring and making charts of height – who is tallest?, who is smallest? – ordering: smallest to tallest, tallest to smallest; drawing around hands, feet, children on squared paper and counting the squares; covering box models with paper and estimating how much is needed.

Capacity and volume

This is a difficult concept for young children to grasp. They need to understand that capacity and volume can be measured using non-standard as well as standard measures. They need to be able to compare containers of different sizes and shapes and to make comparisons about their capacity.

- Activities: filling buckets, beakers, containers with sand or water. Posing problems – how many cups to fill a bucket? Using standard measures to compare the capacity of other containers; 'real life' questions – how many beakers can you fill from a squash bottle?

How can we fit into this box?

CHECK!

1 Go back through this section. List the components of early maths.

THINK!

1 What have you seen in your workplace? Make a list of activities that involved any mathematical learning

DO!

1 Find out what equipment children use for maths in your workplace. List any maths apparatus that you find. How is it used?

HOW CAN YOU HELP?

- Encourage and explain. Many children take a while to grasp new ideas.
- Talk to the children about their work. Introduce mathematical language,

more than, less than, etc. Name shapes accurately.
- Use everyday experiences to reinforce mathematical learning, for example counting stairs, sharing biscuits, laying the table.
- Observe progress on an individual level and use this to plan the next step.

Science and technology

Children are naturally curious, about themselves and about the world that they inhabit. Good early years provision will harness this curiosity and lay the foundations for children's scientific understanding.

WHAT IS SCIENCE?

There are many situations in which the young child can be a scientist. Here are some examples:
- the natural world: caring for plants and animals, looking at the seasons, caring for the environment, life cycles, work on growth, ourselves
- natural materials: discovering the properties of water, wood, clay, sand, air, and so on
- creative materials: identifying the science in painting, collage, junk modelling, music
- the physical world: using magnets and batteries, investigating light and colour with lenses and mirrors, looking at movement and forces
- chemistry: combining substances, watching changes, cooking.

Science is not approached in isolation. In nursery it is an integral part of many of the activities provided routinely such as outdoor play, construction, sand, water, paint. In school scientific themes will be developed through topic work.

How can you help?
The adult's role in promoting the growth of children's scientific understanding is crucial. Their role should be to:
- provide a rich environment for the children
- interact with the children encouraging them to ask questions, to pose problems
- help children decide on ways to try out their ideas, including ways of designing a fair test
- help children to organise their understanding of what has happened (draw conclusions, form concepts)
- encourage children to record their findings using a variety of methods: talking, drawing, making tables, writing
- monitor children's progress and support opportunities to extend learning.

THINK!

1 What activities involving science have you seen in your workplace?

1 Plan an activity for the children that you work with that involves some scientific learning. Think about what you will provide. What questions will you ask? How will children record their work?

TECHNOLOGY

Technology for the early years is closely linked to science. It involves the use of tools and materials in practical projects. Children need opportunities to plan and design as well as to make. As their experience increases their designs will become more complex. In this area the adult's role is to give the children access to a range of materials and to enable them to complete and evaluate their projects. This will include the teaching and practising of techniques such as cutting, joining things and sewing, as well as encouraging the children in their projects.

Information technology, involving the use of computers, is now very much a part of the early years curriculum. Children will become familiar with the operation of the equipment and work on software programs specially designed to meet their learning needs.

Creativity

Creative activities involve the expression of ideas. They provide children with a means of communication with themselves and with the outside world. Creative activities are those which value the *process* as well as the *product*. Opportunities for children to be creative, to develop their own ideas through a variety of media, should be provided throughout the early years.

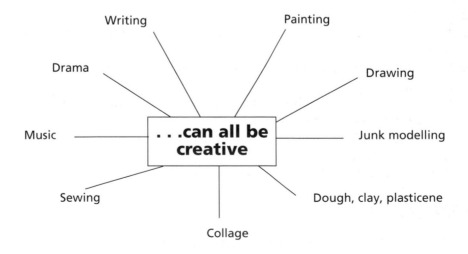

The way an activity is presented will affect how much scope it offers for creativity. Look at the following example.

1 Children have been asked to make a collage using natural materials they collected on an autumn walk. Paper and glue are available and the children are interpreting this brief in a number of ways.

2 Children are busy cutting around circles of paper. They are then sticking them onto an outline drawing of a clown on a piece of paper. They are matching the circles for size to spaces on the paper.

Activity 1 gives the children an opportunity to develop their own ideas, to be creative. Activity 2, which is also a collage activity, is getting the children to practise the skill of cutting and is developing their concepts of size and shape. It is very valuable, but it is not a creative activity.

What we expect from children and what we provide for them in creative activities needs to be linked to their developmental stage. At the early stages they will explore and experiment with the materials, using them in a random manner. They finish quickly and then move on to something else. As they become more experienced they build up a repertoire of skills and techniques that they can then apply creatively. They will work for a longer period at an activity and show more concern for the end product.

CHECK!

1 To be creative, what must an activity allow?

THINK!

1 For each of the kinds of activity shown in the diagram, describe briefly one that you think is creative. Think about the age group of the children you are planning for.

THE ROLE OF THE ADULT

Provision

- Select and present materials and equipment appropriate to the stage of development of the child, for example thick brushes for 3-year olds, finer ones for 7-year olds.
- Organise storage of materials so that they are accessible and easily maintained.
- Introduce new materials. They can act as a stimulus to children's ideas.
- Display children's work.

Planning

- Give time and space to creative activities.
- Organise experiences that will act as a stimulus to creative activities.

Working alongside

- Encourage the child.
- Do not judge by adult standards – value the child's work for its own sake.
- Do not do it for the child. You will make him dissatisfied with his own efforts and dependent on you.
- Children may be affronted if you ask 'What is it?' 'Could you tell me about it?' might be better!
- Teach children techniques. Children's creativity may be hindered if they lack the skills associated with the activity.

DO!

Look at your workplace:
1 How is children's creativity provided for?
2 Is creativity valued? How can you tell?

History and geography

History and geography will be included in any thematic approach to the early years curriculum.

HISTORY

The concept of time is not an easy one for young children to grasp (see the section on maths, above). 'A long time ago' to a small child could equally be last week or when dinosaurs were about. However, there are some ways of making the notion of the past meaningful to children.

- Comparisons with 'then' and 'now' can be very successful, particularly if children have a chance to handle objects from the past and make a direct comparison with now, for example, comparing the dolly tub with an automatic washing machine.
- Many museums run excellent programmes that get children to experience, say, a Victorian schoolroom, complete with costumes and tasks.
- Getting older people to talk to children about the past can be helpful. Children can question their own parents and grandparents for insights about the recent past.
- Old newspapers and photographs can provide useful starting points. Children might search for clues and put them in chronological order.

GEOGRAPHY

The geography curriculum encourages children to investigate the physical and human features of their immediate surroundings, and from this basis to learn about the wider world. The activities listed on the following page would contribute to this understanding.

- making simple maps, perhaps of home-to-school routes
- reading simple maps by following directions and identifying features
- looking at similarities and differences in locations, for example between a city school and a village school. Many schools 'twin' to achieve this
- providing opportunities to look carefully at the local environment, giving children a chance to recognise different land uses and to notice changes. Children could also be asked to suggest how their environment could be improved.

Physical activities

Physical activities are a vital part of the early years curriculum. They are important for the health and development of children and may also provide a starting point for leisure activities. All nurseries will provide regular opportunities for vigorous outside play. This kind of play is important for all areas of development, not just the physical (see Chapter 4, *Play*).

Vigorous outside play is important for all areas of development, not just the physical

Most schools will provide the following as part of the PE curriculum:
- Gymnastics sessions that include floorwork as well as the use of large and small apparatus. Children often work with a theme in mind, for example moving on different parts of the body. They are encouraged to set targets for themselves. (Some smaller children might find the large apparatus daunting

and adults should be sensitive to this and allow the child to stand by and watch until ready to join in. Children also have a part to play in the setting up and putting away of equipment; adequate supervision is vital here.)

- Opportunities for dance to live or recorded music. Dance styles from a variety of cultures may be introduced, sometimes by demonstration.
- Games and games' skills will be introduced during the early school years. These could be indoor or outdoor sessions. Younger children may have difficulty remembering rules but can usually manage simple games. Large team games are not suitable at this stage as the children spend too much time waiting. Remember that there can be quite substantial differences in children's physical co-ordination, balance and manual dexterity at this age and this needs to be catered for in any skills sessions.

    Equipment is important too: a beanbag is easier to catch than a tennis ball; a full-size football is too big for a small child. Make sure that all children take part. They will not enjoy playing the game if they have not had a chance to learn the skills.
- Swimming will be offered in areas where facilities are available. Children who have not experienced swimming before may be frightened at the prospect and need reassurance. If staffing is adequate, an adult in the water will help too. Sessions need to be short but frequent and children should never be forced into situations if they feel unsure.

    (Remember to allow plenty of time for changing both before and after PE sessions, as many children will need help.)
- Playtime will provide another opportunity for physical activities, this time without the direction of an adult. Some children organise themselves in complicated games, others will enjoy just running around. Children new to the situation may find the frenetic activity of the playground frightening and will find a quiet place to watch until they feel more secure.

CHECK!

1 Why is vigorous play important for children's development?
2 What kinds of physical activities are provided in school?

THINK!

1 How does vigorous play in nursery differ from that provided in school?
2 How could you ensure that new children feel secure at playtime?

DO!

1 Make a list of the equipment you would provide for a games session for 5- to 7-year-olds.
2 Plan for a 40-minute session in the playground. What range of activities will you offer?
3 How will you organise the children during this session?

Key terms

You need to know what these words and phrases mean. Go back through the chapter and find out.

Literacy

Product and process

Sight vocabulary

Visual discrimination

Sequencing

Auditory discrimination

Look and say

Phonics

Reading schemes and 'real' books

Conventions of writing

Emergent or developmental writing

Concrete experiences

Non-standard and standard measures

A fair test

Creativity

Chronological

Manual dexterity

7 CHILDREN'S BEHAVIOUR

What is behaviour?

Behaviour is acting or reacting in a specific way. It is what we exhibit to others. It includes all that we do and say, both acceptable and unacceptable.

Patterns of behaviour are learned from the people with whom we have contact, both direct and indirect. This includes such influences as television, books and magazines. However, our earliest and most powerful influences are parents or carers and other influential adults in the immediate community.

Behaviour is therefore socially and culturally defined. We learn our behaviour from the social and cultural groups in which we grow up. There are of course many similarities between societies and cultures. There are also many differences in expectations and what is regarded as acceptable behaviour. This is important: Do not assume that because someone's behaviour is unusual to you it is necessarily unacceptable.

Ideas of what are acceptable patterns of behaviour are acquired from a number of sources.
- historical, cultural and/or national heritage
- immediate and extended family
- local community
- peer group
- national governmental level.

At different times in an individual's life different influences will predominate. For young children the family is the most powerful influence. As children get older peers and the wider community become increasingly important.

CHECK!

1 What is behaviour?
2 Who and what are patterns of behaviour learned from?
3 Who are the most powerful influences in a young child's learning?
4 From what other sources are patterns of acceptable behaviour learned?

How is behaviour learned?

Behaviour is learned through a complex process of imitation of role models, expectation expressed verbally and non-verbally and rewards and sanctions that mould behaviour. Much of this process is subconscious: we are not aware that it is happening. It is a constant life-long process. Both acceptable and unacceptable behaviour is learned in this way.

The patterns of behaviour that are established in childhood influence behaviour throughout our lives. It is essential therefore that young children are given the opportunity to develop acceptable patterns of behaviour from an early age. To enable them to achieve this children need:

- positive role models
- loving adults who have realistic expectations of young children's behaviour
- clear and consistent expectations expressed verbally and non-verbally
- fair and consistent boundaries of acceptable behaviour, rewarded when appropriate.

Where these conditions exist most children will develop acceptable patterns of behaviour with a minimum of conflict.

Behaviours that children learn are more complex merely than what is either acceptable or unacceptable. They also learn different roles. Children pick up the different expectations that society has of different groups of people. For example, how does society expect a female to behave? How is a male expected to behave?

Many people feel that the expectations of society are unfair to some groups of people: the expectation that females should be responsible for all the domestic work in a home, for example, or the expectation that males do not cry when upset. These roles are perceived to be restrictive because they do not reflect what individual people are really like. The learning processes described above, however, are so powerful that many people conform to the expectations.

Children also learn the value placed upon each role by society. They learn that the behaviour of some groups is more highly valued than others. This leads to stigma and discrimination against some groups of people. Stigma and discrimination are not acceptable. People who have contact with young children have a unique opportunity to work towards changing this through the powerful influence they have on children's expectations of what is acceptable and what is unacceptable behaviour.

Young children's behaviour

It is important to have realistic expectations of young children's behaviour. If expectations are unrealistic then the possibility for conflict and labelling arises. Acceptable behaviour causes little concern. Unacceptable behaviour needs more careful consideration and is therefore the focus of this chapter. The following points are important in the discussion:

- The vast majority of children want to be approved by adults and others and therefore wish to behave in an appropriate way. With positive role models, loving adults who are fair and consistent in their expectations and who set clear boundaries, most children will develop acceptable patterns of behaviour.
- Behaviour is not 'naughty' just because it does not conform to adult standards of behaviour. Children need to learn which behaviour is acceptable and which is unacceptable.
- There is often a reason why a behaviour occurs. This reason may be hidden, unconscious or in the past.
- Behaviour can often be attributed to how a child is feeling. The feelings that a child has exist and cannot be changed. It is the behaviour that results from the feeling that is either acceptable or not acceptable. You must never reject a child's feelings, only their behaviour.

- Similar feelings in children can lead to very different behaviours. For example, the feeling of anger may result in a child being physically or verbally aggressive, but a child may well become withdrawn.
- Some behaviours are well established and it is difficult to understand why they occur.

Most young children will exhibit acceptable behaviours as they grow and learn what is expected of them. However, while they are still in the process of learning, it is important that adults have appropriate expectations of what is common behaviour for young children. This will reduce the possibility of conflict and labelling. If the child is in an environment that promotes positive behaviour unacceptable behaviours will diminish with time as the child learns and grows.

SOME COMMON BEHAVIOURS IN YOUNG CHILDREN

Some common behaviours include:
- physical aggression
- aggression in words
- temper tantrums
- defiance
- withdrawing
- jealousy.

WHY DO THESE BEHAVIOURS OCCUR?

There are many reasons for a behaviour occurring. Listed below are some suggestions. However, the reasons are not always straightforward; simple solutions are not easy to find and the feelings and reasons that influence the behaviours are not always obvious.

Curiosity
A child learns by being active and interacting with their environment. There may be a clash between the child's need to be active and the adult's wish for the child to be safe and/or to establish boundaries of what is acceptable.

Imitation
Children will imitate what they see. This may at times be acceptable behaviour for an adult or older child but not for a young child. Who or what are the child's role models?

Egocentricism
Egocentricism means seeing things only from one's own viewpoint. It is not the same as being selfish, when both sides can be seen and the selfish one is chosen. Some psychologists believe that young children are incapable of seeing things from another person's viewpoint. It a skill that children need to acquire over a period of time.

There may be a clash between the child's need to learn through interaction with their environment and the adult's wish to establish boundaries of what is acceptable

Developing independence

Children need to find ways of exhibiting their growing independence and this may result in them trying to influence others in unacceptable ways.

Attention seeking

Human beings need and want attention from other people. Children's behaviour can be a way of attracting this attention. For some children negative attention is better than none at all.

Anger and/or frustration

A lack of experience of the world means that children sometimes have unrealistic expectations of what is and what is not possible.

Anxiety or fear

A lack of experience and understanding of the world may lead to an unrealistic interpretation of events.

Changes in familiar patterns and/or routines in a child's life can also affect their behaviour. Examples might be a new baby in the home, moving house, change in childcare, starting school, changes in friendships, lack of sleep. The feelings associated with these changes and the resulting behaviour is often short-term and behaviour usually settles down once new or different routines are established.

EMOTIONAL NEEDS

Children also have many emotional needs:

- affection: the feeling of being loved by parents, carers, family, friends and the wider social community
- belonging: the feeling of being wanted by a group
- consistency: the feeling that things are predictable
- independence: the feeling of managing and directing your own life
- achievement: the feeling of satisfaction gained from success
- social approval: the feeling that others approve of your conduct and efforts
- self-esteem: the feeling of being worthwhile.

The absence of any of the above *can* lead to unacceptable behaviour as children struggle to get what they need. These can be long-term problems and require long-term strategies to mould behaviour so that it becomes acceptable.

Remember that all children are individuals and that the same feelings or events can result in different behaviours in different children.

CHECK!

1 Why is it important to have realistic expectations of young children's behaviour?
2 List some common behaviours for young children.
3 Suggest some reasons why these behaviours occur.

THINK!

1 Why may unrealistic expectations of children's behaviour lead to conflict and labelling?
2 Why may changes in familiar patterns and/or routines in a child's life affect a child's behaviour?
3 How can an adult who is caring for children meet their emotional needs?
4 Why may the same feeling result in different behaviour in different children?

DO!

1 Draw up a chart similar to the one below, to show feelings linked to possible behaviours.
2 Try to think of different behaviours that may result from each feeling.

Feeling	Possible behaviour
Anger	Physical aggression, verbal aggression, withdrawn

Managing children's behaviour

Behaviour is learned. People who work with children need therefore to be aware of effective ways of managing and moulding children's behaviour. The same techniques can be applied during the child's initial learning and when it is necessary to alter existing unacceptable behaviour.

THE ABC OF BEHAVIOUR

All behaviours that occur, both acceptable and unacceptable, follow a similar pattern, known as the *ABC of behaviour*:

- the *Antecedent*: what happens before the behaviour occurs.
- the *Behaviour*: the resulting behaviour, either acceptable or unacceptable.
- the *Consequence*: the results that occur because of the behaviour, either positive or negative.

The most effective way of managing young children's behaviour is by controlling the antecedent. By being aware of what leads up to a particular behaviour it is possible to have some influence on the behaviour that follows. Careful observation of situations is required for the antecedent to be identified before changes can be made. By anticipating the antecedents to behaviour, carers can encourage children to behave in an acceptable way and the possibility for conflict is minimised. For example:

- reminding children to put their coats on before going outside to play; it is very likely that most children will do as asked
- welcoming children by name to the establishment is likely to produce a feeling of being part of the group; this can exert a powerful influence on behaviour
- being careful about grouping children where there are some within the group who do not work well together
- providing enough space and equipment can reduce the likelihood of problems occurring.
- praising effort is likely to encourage a child to continue trying this and other activities.

Changing the antecedent of unacceptable behaviour is one way of beginning to manage children's behaviour effectively so that it becomes more acceptable. Again, careful observation of situations is necessary to establish the antecedent. For example:

- temper tantrums: when do they occur? What leads up to them? Can this be altered?
- physical aggression: who is involved? When does it occur? What leads up to it? Who or what are the child's role models?
- verbal aggression: who is involved? Who or what are their role models? When does it occur? What leads up to the behaviour?

Children's behaviour can also be managed by altering the consequence of a behaviour. This may mean rewarding acceptable behaviour, or attaching a negative outcome to a behaviour. For this to be effective it is important that the child is aware of the consequence of the behaviour, both positive and negative. It is also important that the resulting outcome is applied consistently. Where possible all the adults who have close contact with the child need to be applying the same consequences to behaviours.

CHECK!

1 What is the ABC of behaviour? Explain each element.
2 What is the most effective way of managing children's behaviour?
3 Give some examples of changing the antecedent.
4 How else can children's behaviour be managed?
5 What are the important features of managing behaviour by altering the consequence?

THINK!

1 Why is altering the antecedent to a behaviour an effective way of managing children's behaviour?
2 List some examples of where this could be effective in an identified establishment.
3 Think of some ways that an antecedent to a behaviour could be established.
4 Why is it important that the children are aware of the consequences of a behaviour?
5 Why is it important for all the adults who have close contact with a child to apply the same consequences to a behaviour?

DO!

1 Observe a child. Make a note of the antecedents, behaviours and their consequences.
2 Can you identify any situations where you could alter either the antecedent or the consequence of behaviour to manage it more effectively? Give reasons for the changes.

BEHAVIOUR MODIFICATION

Behaviour modification is the name given to techniques used to bring about changes in children's behaviour so that it becomes acceptable. It is based on the work of BF Skinner and his theory of *operant conditioning*. It works on the basis that:

- children will repeat behaviour that receives a positive response
- children will not repeat behaviour that receives no response or a negative response.

Behaviour is therefore moulded by manipulating the outcomes of a behaviour.

This may be attaching a positive outcome to a behaviour so that the child is encouraged to repeat it. It may be ignoring a behaviour. It may be attaching a negative outcome to a behaviour so that the child is discouraged from repeating it. (This is the same as altering the consequence of a behaviour in the ABC of behaviour outlined above.)

This way of modifying children's behaviour is a long-term strategy. The rewards and/or sanctions need to be applied over a substantial period of time for them to be effective, especially if the unacceptable behaviour has been evident for some time.

For behaviour modification to be successful an assessment of how a child behaves is essential. This can be done using the ABC of behaviour. Patterns within a child's behaviour can be established through observation. Their needs can then be assessed and decisions made about a suitable behaviour-modification programme.

Attaching positive outcomes to children's behaviour

The following outcomes may be attached to behaviours to encourage repetition:

- adult attention: this can be verbal or non-verbal (nods, smiles, winks)
- adult praise directed solely at the child
- peer group attention: the group's attention is drawn to the child and the behaviour
- attention from other groups within the establishment
- responsibilities within the group
- extended privileges
- choice of activity
- tokens to exchange for privileges/activities/extended time at an activity
- positive reports to the parent or carer.

Attaching negative outcomes to children's behaviour

The following outcomes may be attached to behaviours to discourage children from copying or repeating them:

- ignoring the behaviour
- adult attention directed towards a child who is behaving acceptably
- removal from a positive situation to a neutral or negative situation
- adult disapproval, verbal or non-verbal, directed solely at the child
- peer group disapproval: this must come from the other children, not as a result of humiliating comments from the adult
- loss of responsibility or privileges.

Where a sanction is applied, it needs where possible to follow a pattern of natural justice, which means putting things right; for example picking up litter for dropping it.

For behaviour modification to work effectively it must meet the following criteria:

- rules must be established and the children must be aware of them

- the children must be aware of the outcomes attached to behaviours, whether they are positive or negative
- the outcomes must be appropriate to the children's age and/or stage of development and understanding
- the outcomes must be applied each time the behaviour occurs
- the outcomes must be applied immediately
- outcomes must take individual likes and dislikes into account. What an adult sees as a negative outcome may be positive for a child. For example, removing a child from a group for being disruptive: the child may not want to remain in the group and by removing her the adult has actually rewarded the unacceptable behaviour
- needs to involve all adults who have close contact with the child or children. This means that the rules are consistently reinforced within an establishment and at home.

THINK!

1 Why do you think children will repeat behaviour that has a positive outcome linked with it?
2 Why is it important to establish patterns within a child's behaviour?
3 List the ways that you could do this.
4 Why is it important that the child or children involved in behaviour modification are aware of the rules and the possible rewards or sanctions?
5 Why must the reward be something that is of value to the child?
6 Why must the reward or the sanction be applied immediately following the behaviour?
7 Why is consistency important?

DO!

1 Write a profile of a child who is known to you and who behaves in an unacceptable way.
2 Decide which aspect of this behaviour is most unacceptable.
3 Compile a behaviour-modification programme. Think about:
   - the rule(s), expressed positively where possible
   - the reward for keeping to the rules
   - the sanction that could be applied if using 'Reward and Ignore' does not work.

Making contracts

To encourage a child to behave in an acceptable way over a period of time, a contract may be drawn up between the child and an adult. The child agrees to behave in a particular way over the period of time and the adult agrees to reward the acceptable behaviour.

For young children this can be done by filling in a chart. Each time a child

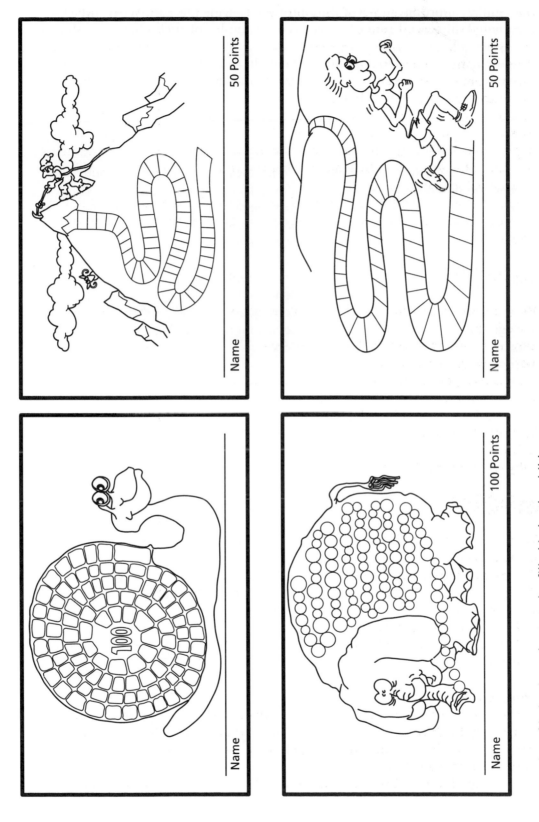

Examples of behaviour charts to be filled in by the child

behaves in an appropriate way a section of the chart is filled in. When the chart is completed an agreed reward is received. Examples of such charts are shown on the previous page.

The benefit of this is to encourage the child to be behave consistently in an acceptable way, as the reward is not received until the child has maintained the behaviour over a period of time.

Key terms
You need to know what these words and phrases mean. Go back through the chapter and find out.

Behaviour	Achievement
Subconscious	Social approval
Curiosity	Self-esteem
Imitation	ABC
Egocentric	Antecedent
Attention seeking	Behaviour
Affection	Consequence
Belonging	Behaviour modification
Consistency	Contracts
Independence	

8 CARE BEFORE BIRTH

> **This chapter includes:**
> - Preconceptual care
> - General health factors
> - Pregnancy: signs and symptoms
> - Antenatal care.

Preconceptual care

Preconceptual care is the phrase used to describe attention to health and lifestyle before pregnancy. It should begin with a decision to have a baby and end when conception occurs.

When a couple decide to have a baby, they should try to make sure that they are both in a good state of health. Although it is impossible to guarantee a healthy outcome, this will help to ensure that their baby is given the best chance to be born in a healthy condition.

During the first three months of pregnancy the baby is developing very quickly and all the systems of the body are formed. All the major congenital abnormalities (disorders that the baby is born with, but which are not necessarily inherited conditions), such as spina bifida, heart disorders, blindness and deafness, will occur during this time of rapid growth and development. The fetus is very vulnerable to substances which can cross the placental barrier (such as drugs and viruses) and harm it.

For the first few weeks of pregnancy a woman may not realise that conception and implantation have occurred, because by the time menstruation stops the embryo is already growing rapidly inside the uterus (see Book 1, page 14). So it is of great importance that the woman and her partner are in the optimum (best) state of health before conception takes place.

Some health clinics run courses for prospective (future) parents offering advice and guidance about important areas of health care (Book 1, page 19). They will also refer couples to the appropriate agencies for advice about financial matters or social factors which may affect pregnancy or future child-rearing.

It is important that both partners attend the clinic. Women are usually the centre of attention and concern during pregnancy and men can feel isolated and not involved in the process. They have an important role to support their partners and take an active part in planning a family. There may be specific areas of health care that the future father needs to consider before pregnancy begins. The preconceptual clinic is able to prepare both partners for a healthy pregnancy.

General health factors

Basic screening checks will be made at the clinic. The following areas of health should also be checked.

WEIGHT

It is advisable for a woman to begin pregnancy as near to her ideal weight as possible. 12–15 kilograms is the average weight gain in pregnancy, and often it is substantially more. The higher the weight at the beginning of pregnancy, the more difficult it is to achieve a healthy weight afterwards.

BLOOD PRESSURE (BP)

High BP (hypertension) is a health risk to everyone and can cause problems to mother and baby in pregnancy. If it is detected before pregnancy begins it may be possible to find the cause and treat it.

DENTAL CARE

Regular dental checks are important for everyone. Tooth decay (dental caries) is a source of infection which can affect the whole body and should be treated before pregnancy begins. Poor dental health before pregnancy will get worse during it, as the fetus takes its calcium requirement from the mother. For this reason dental care is free to all pregnant mothers and for a year after the birth.

CERVICAL SMEAR

This is an ideal time for a woman to have a cervical smear test to detect any changes in the cervix, which could later become cancerous. Pregnancy can increase the growth rate of abnormal cells present before conception.

LONG-TERM ILLNESS

It is essential for women who receive on-going treatment for any illnesses to see their GP to discuss the advisability of pregnancy, any changes in their medicines and the best care for them during pregnancy.

BLOOD TESTS

Rubella (German measles)
Rubella, although not itself a serious disease, has a catastrophic effect on the developing fetus in the first 12 weeks of pregnancy, and perhaps until 24 weeks. The virus crosses the placental barrier and damages the eyes, the brain, the heart and the ears. It may result in fetal death and is certainly responsible for

more than half of the cases of congenital deafness which occur in children.

If a woman is not immune to rubella (if her blood does not contain antibodies), she will be offered immunisation against this condition and advised not to become pregnant for at least 3 months, to allow time for her body to make antibodies to the virus.

Anaemia

Haemoglobin is a protein in red blood cells which contains iron and carries oxygen. Iron-deficiency anaemia is revealed by a low haemoglobin level in the blood. This is usually treated with a diet rich in foods containing iron (green vegetables, egg yolk, raisins, wholemeal bread, baked beans, liver), combined with a course of iron tablets.

The fetus will take its iron and oxygen requirements from the mother, so if she is anaemic, not only will the fetus suffer but the mother may become seriously ill.

Types of haemoglobinopathies (inherited disorders of the haemoglobin) may be screened for preconceptually: sickle cell anaemia may be found in black or mixed race people whose ancestors originated in Central or West Africa or parts of Asia; thalassaemia is most common in people of Mediterranean origin.

Being aware that a mother is affected by one of these conditions will ensure that doctors and midwives give the appropriate care in pregnancy.

The prospective father should also be checked for these conditions because the baby may inherit the affected genes from both parents and be affected itself.

GENETIC COUNSELLING

A couple may be aware that one or both of them have a family history of an inherited condition, such as Duchenne muscular dystrophy, sickle cell disease, cystic fibrosis or Down's syndrome. They may already have a child who is affected by an inherited condition, such as phenylketonuria or haemophilia. A preconceptual care clinic would refer the couple for genetic counselling, which is available to all prospective parents who need it. It is usually a hospital-based service with a team of experts who will be able to give the couple some idea of the risks to a future pregnancy, so that they can make an informed decision (knowing all the risks and weighing them against the benefits).

CONTRACEPTION

Before pregnancy begins a decision must be made to discontinue all forms of contraception. Barrier methods (the condom and the diaphragm) are easy to stop: a couple will simply no longer use them. The intra-uterine contraceptive device (the coil) needs to be removed by a doctor. These methods do not affect the hormonal cycle, unlike the oral contraceptive pill. It is best for women to stop taking the pill three months before pregnancy begins:

- to allow the body's natural hormone cycle to return to normal
- so that accurate dates can be used to assess the length of the pregnancy, which is always measured from the date of the first day of the last menstrual period (LMP).

DRUGS

Any substance taken for its effect on the workings of the body is a drug. Alcohol is a drug; so is nicotine which is present in tobacco; medicines prescribed by a doctor or purchased over the counter without a prescription, or drugs acquired illegally may all cross the placenta and affect the developing fetus.

Smoking

It is much better for both parents to stop smoking before conception takes place. Research has shown that smoking in pregnancy can lead to a higher risk of:
- miscarriage
- premature birth
- low birth weight (on average 200 gm less)
- stillbirth or death in the first week of life (perinatal death).

After birth, babies who are regularly exposed to cigarette smoke are more likely to suffer from respiratory (breathing) problems. Smoking can also affect the male sperm, so the future father should also be encouraged to give up smoking.

Positive help to stop smoking can be given in the form of guidance, counselling, support groups and referral to other agencies. Smoking is an addiction which is not easy to curb, but it may be easier when it is for the sake of a future baby.

Alcohol

Evidence suggests that moderate and high levels of alcohol consumption during pregnancy will affect fetal growth and development. Fetal Alcohol Syndrome is a condition caused by excessive alcohol intake resulting in:
- poor growth, before and after birth
- developmental delay
- congenital abnormalities
- intellectual impairment.

The baby is born addicted to alcohol and has to be weaned off it. Women are advised to cut out alcohol altogether before conception occurs. A session of heavy drinking after conception, but before pregnancy is diagnosed, could seriously damage the fetus.

Excessive alcohol consumption in men can cause infertility and abnormalities in the sperm, so it is better if they too moderate their drinking habits before a pregnancy is commenced.

Medicines

Women are advised not to take any medicines at all during pregnancy. Even such widely used drugs as paracetamol and aspirin are best avoided. Only those medicines prescribed by a doctor should be taken, and only when the doctor has confirmed that they do not damage the fetus.

Those who are on regular medication would be advised to consult their GP regarding the safety of the drug(s) in pregnancy, and whether an alternative would be advisable.

Illegal drugs

All addictions to potentially dangerous substances should be treated before pregnancy begins. Heroin, cocaine, opium, morphine and other illegal drugs in their various forms, and solvents such as glue or lighter fuel, are not only dangerous for a woman to take but could risk the life of a baby. The prospective mother would be given help and guidance about the services available to treat her addiction before she becomes pregnant.

DIET

A well balanced diet is important at all times and especially in pregnancy. Women who are significantly over- or underweight may have difficulty in conceiving, and should be given dietary advice about how to achieve a suitable weight before pregnancy begins. Eating disorders such as anorexia nervosa and bulimia must be treated by experienced doctors.

A diet rich in vitamins, minerals and protein is preferable before conception takes place. The growing fetus will live off its mother, as a parasite, taking all the essential nutrients in preference to her needs. So it is essential that she has good dietary advice and acts upon it before becoming pregnant. This advice should also include a warning to avoid soft cheeses and pate which may contain listeria, and to cook food thoroughly to prevent toxoplasmosis (see Book 1, page 96).

COMMUNICABLE DISEASES

Sexually transmitted diseases, such as gonorrhoea and syphilis, can be detected and treated before pregnancy begins to avoid the possibility of the baby being affected. If they are not treated babies can be born with congenital syphilis, which is eventually fatal. Gonorrhoea can cause blindness as the baby's eyes can be infected during delivery.

Human Immunopathic Virus (HIV) is not yet curable, nor is it routinely tested for before or during pregnancy. Women who think that they may be infected with this virus need professional counselling to help them to decide whether to have a test or not. Women who are HIV positive usually pass on the virus to their babies during pregnancy.

LIFESTYLE

The way women live their lives will affect their general health; this includes the amount of exercise taken and the type of work done. Regular exercise and a stress-free environment will help to improve the general health and well-being of both partners.

Although it may be difficult to achieve in a busy life, this is the time for them to consider their lifestyle and perhaps try to change the parts which can lead to difficulty or stress. This is not always possible, but sometimes an awareness of the causes of difficulties can help.

CHECK!

1 What is preconceptual care?
2 Why is it important to prospective parents?
3 What health checks may be made at the preconceptual care clinic?
4 How long after rubella immunisation should a woman wait before becoming pregnant?
5 Why is the haemoglobin content of the blood important?
6 Which foods are rich in iron?
7 What is genetic counselling?
8 How long before trying to conceive should the contraceptive pill be stopped?
9 Why is this length of time recommended?
10 What is a drug?
11 Why is smoking in pregnancy discouraged?
12 Why is heavy alcohol consumption a health risk for both prospective parents?
13 What condition can alcohol cause to the fetus?
14 Why are soft cheeses and pate best avoided in pregnancy?
15 What problem could maternal gonorrhoea cause to the fetus?
16 Why should men be encouraged to attend for preconceptual care?

THINK!

1 Make a list of all the social factors you can think of which may affect a decision to have a baby. Include positive and negative points and remember to include the influence of family and friends; and local, national and global issues.

DO!

1 Make a chart of your findings from Question 1 above.
2 Design a booklet or a poster about the benefits of preconceptual care.
3 A friend and her partner have been talking about having a baby. Your friend has heard about preconceptual care and is keen to go to the clinic. Her partner refuses to go with her and she asks you to have a word with him. How would you try to convince him of the benefits of the clinic? Why might some men be reluctant to attend?
4 Research the facilities in your area.
   a) How many clinics are there near to your home?
   b) Who are they organised by (for example GP, health visitor, practice nurse or midwife?)
   c) How often are clients invited to attend?
   d) Are men welcome at every session?

e) Are the clinics publicised and if so, where?
Write a report of your findings. Evaluate it in terms of the acceptability of the service offered and, if necessary, how it may be improved.

Pregnancy

Pregnancy begins when fertilisation of the ovum and sperm takes place, usually in the fallopian tubes. It is impossible for a woman to be aware of this happening inside her body. It is only after the conceptus (fertilised ovum) has implanted in the wall of the uterus that the signs and symptoms of pregnancy appear.

These early changes noticed by the mother are caused by the action of the two female hormones, oestrogen and progesterone, produced by the ovary for the first 12 weeks of pregnancy and then by the mature placenta (Book 1, page 14 ff).

Pregnancy is usually confirmed by using a simple urine test to detect Human Chorionic Gonadotrophin (HCG). This a hormone produced by the implanted conceptus which is excreted in the mother's urine.

SIGNS AND SYMPTOMS OF PREGNANCY

Amenorrhoea

Amenorrhoea (stopping of menstruation) is a very reliable symptom of pregnancy in an otherwise healthy woman, who has had a regular menstrual cycle and is sexually active.

Breast changes

Breast changes which take place during pregnancy are outlined in the table below.

Weeks	Changes
3–4	Prickling, enlarging sensation
6	Breasts feel enlarged and tense
8	Surface veins are visible; Montgomery's tubercles appear
12	Darkening of the primary areola; fluid can be expressed
16	Colostrum can be expressed; secondary areola appears

/// Nipple

\\\ Primary areola

Montgomery's tubercules

Secondary areola

Frequent passing of urine

Due to hormonal action and the enlarging uterus women need to empty their bladders more often in early pregnancy.

Nausea and sickness

Often referred to as 'morning sickness', nausea (feeling sick) can occur at any time of the day or night, or be present all the time. Sometimes nausea can be due to particular smells, or foods. This usually passes by the end of the third month.

Tiredness

Lethargy (lack of energy) is common in early pregnancy but usually improves as the pregnancy progresses.

Vaginal discharge

A white, mucousy vaginal discharge, which is not offensive, is normal and is caused by increased hormonal activity.

LATER SIGNS OF PREGNANCY

At 12 weeks the uterus is above the pelvic bone and can be felt by a midwife or doctor. At 16–20 weeks the mother may begin to feel the baby move (quickening), and it is possible to feel parts of the baby when she is examined at antenatal clinic. The fetal heart can be heard using a stethoscope.

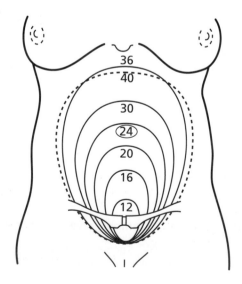

The growth of the uterus during the weeks of pregnancy

Antenatal care

The concept of antenatal care was introduced as recently as 1915, but was not available to all women free of charge until the National Health Service was created in 1948. Antenatal care has been greatly responsible for:

- the reduction in the maternal mortality rate: this is the number of women whose death is caused by pregnancy or childbirth. Until about 1935, 40–50 women died per 10 000 total births. The current rate is 1 death per 10 000 births.
- the reduction in the infant mortality rate: this is the number of children who die in the first year of life. In 1900, out of 100 children born alive, 14 would die before their first birthday. Today the statistics show that 1 out of 100 will die in the first year.

Antenatal care alone cannot take all the credit for these large reductions. Improvements in living conditions since the turn of the century are also responsible for the improved health of the population; but people who live in poverty and deprivation today still suffer from higher than average maternal and infant mortality rates.

THE AIMS OF ANTENATAL CARE

Antenatal care is care offered free of charge by professionals to a woman and her partner during pregnancy. The professionals might be a midwife, general practitioner, health visitor or obstetrician, who specialises in care of the mother and unborn child. The care includes all aspects of health and social conditions to promote well-being, and its aims can be listed as follows:

- to maintain and improve health in pregnancy
- to find any abnormality as early as possible and treat it
- to prepare both parents for labour and a safe, normal delivery which is a pleasurable experience
- to encourage breast-feeding
- a live, healthy mature baby who is happily accepted into the family
- health education of the parents.

EARLY PREGNANCY

Women are encouraged to see their own doctor (GP) as soon as think that they may be pregnant. The doctor may confirm their condition by doing a simple urine test for HCG (see page 103). It is important to see a doctor as early as possible in pregnancy so that:

- a baseline of recordings and observations can be made. It is much easier then to see if any abnormalities occur later
- advice can be given about health and lifestyle to promote a healthy pregnancy.

The doctor should explain to the mother about the choices available to her regarding antenatal care and where she wants her baby to be born. A general health check may be performed (weight, blood pressure and urine test) and advice given about diet, smoking and lifestyle. Blood tests may be performed for rubella antibodies, haemoglobin estimation and grouping.

If the woman chooses to have a hospital delivery the doctor will refer her to the local maternity unit, and she will be sent an appointment to attend the booking clinic.

BOOKING CLINIC

This is the first visit to the hospital antenatal clinic (ANC). A bed is booked for the time the baby is due. Several observations, tests and recordings are made at this clinic and the information is put into the woman's hospital notes.

HISTORY TAKING

General particulars
Accurate records of the woman's name, age, address, GP and midwife are taken.

Present pregnancy
- Calculation of the expected date of delivery (EDD).
  The woman is asked the date of the first day of her last menstrual period (LMP). 9 calendar months are counted forwards and 7 days added, for example:

  LMP: 1.1.97 → add 9 months and 7 days → EDD: 8.10.97.
- Health during this pregnancy is assessed, for example the mother may report excessive sickness, vaginal bleeding or any other abnormality.

Previous pregnancies
Details of previous pregnancies are recorded, because this may affect the care given during this pregnancy, for example:
- date of birth of previous children
- type of delivery
- weight and sex
- method of feeding
- miscarriages, terminations, stillbirths, abnormal babies.

Medical history
Any illnesses affecting the mother are recorded, especially if they may affect the baby, for example diabetes, heart disease.

Family history
Twins, multiple births, genetic conditions or medical problems are recorded.

THE MIDWIFE'S EXAMINATION

Weight
Weight is recorded as a base measure for future weight gain. (The average gain in pregnancy is 12–15 kg.)

Height
Height may indicate the size of the pelvis.

Urine test
The urine is tested for protein, ketones and sugar. These substances are not usually found in the urine; if they are present further investigation will be required:
- protein: this may be an early sign of toxaemia (Book 1, page 96), or it may be caused by an infection or contamination of the specimen
- ketones: these are produced by the breakdown of body cells to provide energy. Dieting or constant vomiting may be the cause.
- sugar: this is not uncommon in pregnancy because the kidneys are less efficient than usual; it could, however, be an early sign of diabetes.

Blood pressure (BP)
This again provides a baseline for future recordings. High BP in pregnancy can indicate toxaemia.

MEDICAL EXAMINATION

A full medical examination will be performed by an obstetrician. This will include examination of:
- teeth
- breasts
- heart and lungs
- abdominal examination (see illustration on page 104)
- lower limbs, for varicose veins or swelling (oedema)
- internal vaginal examination to check the size of the uterus; an ultrasound scan will give an even more accurate assessment. A cervical smear will be done if necessary.

BLOOD TESTS

At this first visit to the ANC a sample of blood is taken for a variety of tests:
- ABO group and Rhesus factor: with information from this test, blood can be cross-matched without delay in the case of anaemia or bleeding during pregnancy, when a transfusion may be needed; see Book 1, page 99 for the importance of the Rhesus factor
- serology: to detect syphilis (a venereal disease), which can be treated to prevent damage to the baby

- haemoglobin: the iron content of the blood is recorded and is taken at monthly intervals thereafter. All mothers of African, Asian or Mediterranean descent have their blood tested for sickle cell disease and thalassaemia
- rubella: blood is tested for rubella antibodies (see previous section)
- serum alpha-fetoprotein (SAFP): this test is taken at 16 weeks of pregnancy when a raised level of SAFP indicates that the baby may have spina bifida; this high level could mean, however, that it is a multiple pregnancy or that the date of the LMP is incorrect. An amniocentesis is offered to mothers with a raised SAFP, and a detailed ultrasound scan will usually be performed to check for twins, or more, and to examine the spine
- Bart's (Triple) test: this new test may be offered to women over 35 years of age, or it may be requested. The test calculates the risk of the baby having Down's syndrome.

THE CO-OPERATION (CO-OP) CARD

Every pregnant woman is given a co-operation card to record every antenatal assessment made by the hospital, GP or midwife. As its name implies, the card is to enable co-operation between all the providers of ANC as well as the mother. She should carry it with her at all times because pregnancy is not predictable – a problem could occur at any time, even when out for the day or on holiday. Whoever cares for her will need to know the progress of the pregnancy so far, so that the best treatment can be offered.

As the pregnancy progresses it will be possible to record the fetal heart and feel the fetal parts when the mother is examined. The mother will begin to feel the baby move, at about 20 weeks for a first baby, and earlier for subsequent pregnancies because an experienced mother will recognise the sensation of fetal movement. These observations will be recorded at each antenatal visit together with records showing:
- weight
- urinalysis
- blood pressure
- height of the fundus (see the illustration on page 104)
- fetal heart
- oedema (swelling of tissues).

This is shown on the sample card opposite.

The position of the baby
The following abbreviations are used to describe the way the baby is positioned in the uterus. O = occiput, the crown of the baby's head; a = anterior, i.e. in front and p = posterior, at the back.
ROA: right occiput anterior
ROP: right occiput posterior
LOP: left occiput posterior
LOA: left occiput anterior

ANTE - NATAL RECORD

INVESTIGATIONS	DATE	RESULTS
A.B.O.Blood Group		A Rh +
Rhesus Blood Group	24/8/93	3/12 10668
Antibodies		
WR/KAHN		
X-Ray Chest		
Other		

IMPORTANT NOTE - In the event of a transfusion this record of the blood grouping should always be checked and cross-matching should always be carried out

FIRST EXAMINATION		Date	Sig. Wishes to breast feed
Height 5. 6"			
Teeth			
Breasts			
Heart		NAD	
Lungs			
Varicose veins			
Pelvis			
Cervical smear Aug. 91			

Special observations:
URINE CULTURE
CERVICAL CYTOLOGY
K.P. INDEX
SERUM: ALPHA FOETO - PROTEINS — 28/9/93 by GP
RUBELLA

EXAMINATION 33/37 week	
Date	
Head/Brim relationship	
Pelvic capacity	
Sig.	

This patient is fit for inhalation analgesia

Date

Signature of Doctor

DATE	WEEKS	WEIGHT	URINE ALB SUGAR	B.P.	HEIGHT FUNDUS	PRESENTA-TION AND POSITION	RELATION OF P.P. TO BRIM	F.H.	OEDEMA	Hb	NEXT VISIT	SIG	NOTES e.g. antibodies, other tests, infections, drugs
26.7.93	7	57 kg	n.a.d.	95/60					nil			SB	Well.
24.8.93	11	59g	No-d	100/65	Just palp				Nil	12.6	2wk	Jo Harris	SAFP here
20.9.93	15	59kgs	NAD.	94/60	16				nil		4wk	SB	BKD MISS BAKER CHN
18.10.93.	19	59kgs	N.A.D.	100/60	19			FHH	nil		4wk	SB	Well.
5.11.93.		Home visit Community midwife.			Home conditions suitable for 24hr discharge.							Cudby	Breasts examined : satisf. Br care advice
15.11.93	22+	62½kg	NAD	95/60	23			FHH	nil		4wk.	SB	Well.
13-12-93	27	65kg	N.A.D.	100/60	27	Ceph.	Free	"	nil		4wk.	SB	Well.
10.1.94	31	69kg	NAD	90/50	31	Ceph.	Free	H	nil		31stJan	SB	well -
19/1/94	32	67kg	NAD	100/60	32	Vx mobile	LOT	FHH	nil	11.4	4wk.	A5	Asilone tabs
31.1.94	34	67kg	NAD	90/50	34	Vx mobile		H	nil		2 wk.	SB	Well,
6/2/94	36	69.35	NAD	100/60	36	Vx at brim	LOT	FHH	nil		2 wk.	A5	Well,
21.2.94.	37	69 kgs	N.D.	90/54	37	"	LOT,	FHH	nil	11.7	1wk.	SB,	Well.
28.2.94.	38	69.5kgs	N.D.	88/54	38	Vx.	LOT,	FHH	nil.		1wk.	SB,	Well.
5-3-94	39	70.0 kgs	NAD	95/55	39	Vx.		"	nil.		1wk.	SB,	
13-3-94	39+	70.0	NAD	95/55	40	Vx.		✓	nil.		1wk-	SB,	Well.

A co-operation card

FREQUENCY OF ANTENATAL VISITS

Visits should be made as shown in the following table:

Until the 28th week of pregnancy	Every four weeks
Until 36 weeks	Every two weeks
Until delivery	Weekly

COMMON TESTS AND INVESTIGATIONS DURING PREGNANCY

Ultrasound scan

The ultrasound machine is an echo sounding device which uses high-frequency sound waves. It can be used to:

- check the position of the fetus in the uterus
- measure the size of the fetus
- find the position of the placenta
- detect and confirm multiple pregnancies
- diagnose some fetal abnormalities.

At 18 weeks of pregnancy women are offered a detailed scan for doctors to look at the structure of fetal organs in detail.

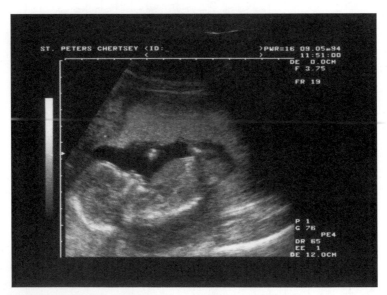

An ultrasound scan taken in the 18th week of pregnancy

Placental function tests

A healthy placenta is essential for a fetus to grow and develop normally. It is possible to test the health and strength of the placenta by checking the amount of pregnancy hormones it produces.

Hormones are carried in the blood and then excreted in the urine. Blood or urine tests, to test the presence and amount of hormone, will indicate how well the placenta is working.

Amniocentesis

Amniocentesis involves the removal of a small sample of amniotic fluid from the uterus, via the abdominal wall. It may be performed after the 16th week of pregnancy, when it is possible to check that the chromosomes, including the sex chromosomes, are normal.

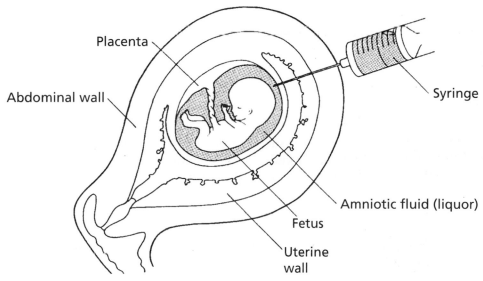

Amniocentesis

Amniocentesis may be offered to women who have:
- a history of chromosomal abnormalities, such as Down's syndrome
- raised SAFP
- a history of sex-linked disorders, such as Duchenne muscular dystrophy.
- passed the age of 35 years (the risk of chromosomal abnormalities, especially Down's syndrome, increases with age).

Chorionic villus sampling (CVS)

CVS is carried out between 8 and 11 weeks of pregnancy. With the help of an ultrasound scan to find the position of the placenta and the fetus, a small sample of placental tissue is removed via the cervix. CVS is used to detect inherited disorders such as:
- Down's syndrome
- haemophilia
- thalassaemia
- sickle cell disease
- cystic fibrosis.

It can also be used to detect the sex of the fetus if there is a family history of sex-linked conditions.

A couple may decide to terminate a pregnancy because of the results of amniocentesis or CVS. Whatever their decision, they will need a great deal of support and empathy from all the professionals involved in their care. Some concern has been expressed about the safety of this test, and professionals should ensure that prospective parents are fully informed about this.

NEEDS OF EXPECTANT PARENTS

Physical needs

Physical needs include:

- housing
- equipment
- finance
- information.

Emotional needs

Emotional needs include:

- security: feeling secure reduces stress and promotes well-being
- communication, with professionals, to understand the process of care
- family support, to minimise worries and concerns
- reassurance, from family and professionals
- self-confidence, to ask questions and be assertive
- a stable relationship
- maturity, to cope with the inevitable changes that pregnancy produces
- a compassionate midwife.

Professional guidance

The midwife, doctor and health visitor will provide a great deal of emotional support, as well as physical care. As the pregnancy progresses they will be available to discuss, advise and give reassurance on any issues which may be causing the parents concern.

Parents will be invited to preparation for parenthood classes towards the end of the pregnancy, when a mother who has been in employment will by that time be on maternity leave. These classes are organised by the local health authority and are run by the local midwife and/or health visitor in the health centre or hospital. They usually last for 2 hours and take place once a week for 6 to 8 weeks, and include evening sessions which the mother's partner can attend. They aim to:

- educate the parents about pregnancy and childbirth
- reduce any anxieties
- educate parents about child development and child-rearing practices.

Areas covered include:

- relaxation, to help towards an easier labour
- signs of labour
- what happens in labour and what to do
- methods of feeding
- details of layette

- home safety
- child development
- the immunisation programme
- the role of the health visitor
- future family planning.

The course usually includes a visit to the local maternity unit, to look at the labour suite and postnatal wards and the neonatal ICU (intensive care unit). This visit helps to reduce anxiety about going into hospital.

CHECK!

1 What are the aims of antenatal care?
2 How often are visits made to the antenatal clinic?
3 What is the importance of the co-operation card?
4 Assuming that the following dates are the first day of the last menstrual period (LMP), work out the expected date of delivery (EDD):
   a) 28-4-95
   b) 25-9-96
   c) 15-11-96
   d) 25-12-97
   e) 6-5-98
   f) 29-1-99.
5 What is the fundus?
6 Which two dates on the co-operation card should roughly correspond?
7 What is the midwife looking for when she records the BP at each visit?
8 What tests are made on the urine sample and how often is the urine tested?
9 Why is the position of the head in the uterus so important?
10 Describe anaemia.
11 What is oedema?
12 What observations are made at each antenatal visit and why?
13 Describe the blood tests taken during pregnancy.
14 When are these blood tests performed?
15 What are the signs of toxaemia of pregnancy?
16 Explain the value of:
   a) ultrasound scan
   b) blood test for serum alpha fetoprotein (SAFP)
   c) amniocentesis
   d) chorionic villus sampling (CVS).
17 What are the needs of the expectant parents?
18 How can these needs best be met?

DO!

1 Study the co-operation card on page 109 and find out the meaning of the following abbreviations: NAD, PP, BP, FHH, Vx, Hb.
2 Write a detailed report describing the importance of antenatal care for mother

and baby. Describe the reasons why some women may need investigations during pregnancy.

3 Try to find out what antenatal services are like in another country.

4 Research the antenatal care offered to women from different generations; for example ask a friend or relative aged:

a) 70 or over

b) about 50

c) about 30.

Make a list of questions to ask them about their experiences of antenatal care:

- who gave the care?
- where was it given?
- was it the same midwife or doctor all the time?
- how often was she examined?
- where was the delivery?
- was the father present?
- types of investigations, and so on.

Report on your findings of the differences in ANC. Has antenatal care improved, and if so how and why?

Key terms

You need to know what these words and phrases mean. Go back through the chapter and find out.

Preconceptual care	Antenatal care
Dental caries	Maternal mortality rate
Hypertension	Infant mortality rate
Rubella	Booking clinic
Anaemia	Ketones
Haemoglobin	Oedema
Genetic counselling	Ultrasound scan
Perinatal	Serum alpha fetoprotein
Fetal alcohol syndrome	Amniocentesis
HIV	Bart's test
Colostrum	Co-operation card
HCG	Chorionic villus sampling

9 CARE AT BIRTH AND STIMULATION OF EARLY DEVELOPMENT

The birth process

Labour is the process by which the fetus, placenta and membranes are expelled through the birth canal.

SIGNS THAT LABOUR HAS STARTED

the onset of strong and regular contractions.
- a 'show': the discharge of blood-stained mucus from the vagina
- 'waters breaking': rupture of the membranes resulting in some amniotic fluid escaping via the vagina.

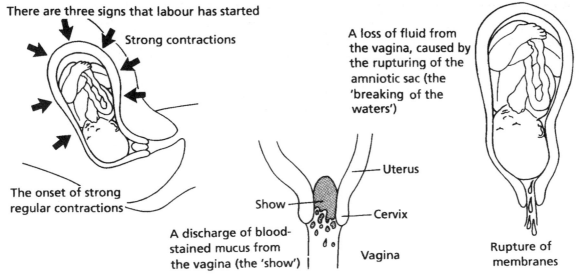

There are three signs that labour has started

Strong contractions

A loss of fluid from the vagina, caused by the rupturing of the amniotic sac (the 'breaking of the waters')

The onset of strong regular contractions

Show

A discharge of blood-stained mucus from the vagina (the 'show')

Uterus

Cervix

Vagina

Rupture of membranes

The onset of labour

One, or any combination of these, may indicate that labour has begun. A mother should contact her midwife for advice as soon as she thinks that she may be in labour. The rupture of the membranes may allow infection to enter the uterus, so the mother should contact the hospital immediately if the baby is to be born there.

NORMAL LABOUR

A normal labour will have the following characteristics:
- it starts spontaneously, in other words naturally, without any help from the doctor or the use of drugs
- it starts at term, that is between 38 and 42 weeks of pregnancy
- there is a *cephalic* (head-first) presentation
- it is completed in 24 hours
- the baby is born alive and healthy
- there are no complications.

Stages of labour

Labour is divided into three stages.

Stage one
The first stage of labour begins with the onset of regular uterine contractions, during which the cervix dilates (widens or gets larger) to allow the baby to be delivered. It ends with full dilatation of the cervix, when it is about 10 cm dilated and cannot get any bigger.

Stage two
The second stage of labour begins with full dilatation and ends with the birth of the baby.

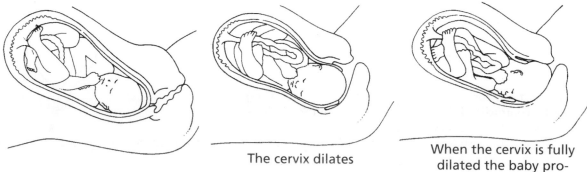

The first stage of labour

The cervix dilates

When the cervix is fully dilated the baby progresses down the birth canal

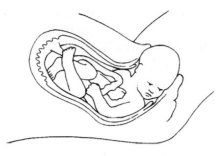

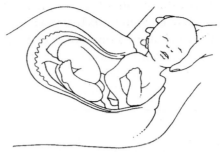

The head 'crowns'   Delivery of the baby

The second stage of labour

Stage three

The third stage begins with the birth of the baby and ends with the complete delivery of the placenta and membranes.

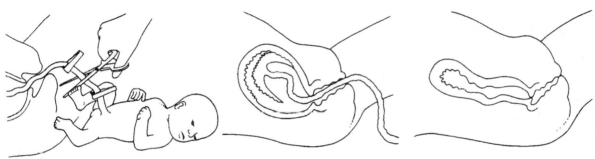

The cord is clamped and cut   The placenta is delivered   The uterus contracts

The third stage of labour

TYPES OF DELIVERY

Some babies and mothers need help with the birth process, and some type of medical intervention may be necessary to make sure that both mother and baby are healthy at the end of labour.

Induction

Labour may need to be induced (started) if:

- the baby is very overdue
- the mother is ill, for example with toxaemia
- the placenta is failing.

Labour may be induced by rupturing the membranes and/or giving artificial hormones to stimulate contractions.

Episiotomy

An episiotomy is a cut made in the perineum (the area between the vagina and the rectum) during the second stage of labour. It is a fairly common procedure performed for two main reasons:

- to allow the baby to be delivered more quickly
- to prevent a large tear which may involve the rectum.

Forceps delivery

Delivery may be with forceps if the baby is becoming distressed. Forceps are spoon-shaped and fit around the baby's head so that the doctor can help with the delivery of the head.

Ventouse extraction

A ventouse extraction involves the use of a cup-shaped instrument which fits onto the baby's head and is also attached to suction equipment. The baby is gently helped down the birth canal with the help of suction.

Caesarian section

A Caesarian section is a surgical operation to remove the baby, placenta and membranes, via the abdominal wall. It may be performed when the mother is awake, but under an epidural anaesthetic or spinal block, which prevents any feelings of pain. Some women may prefer to have a general anaesthetic. Caesarians are performed for many reasons. Some are 'elective' which means that they are done before labour starts, and some are done as an emergency procedure because of an abnormality occurring during labour.

PAIN RELIEF IN LABOUR

The best form of pain relief in labour is having a positive attitude and knowing what is happening. Women who have been to parentcraft/relaxation classes usually cope well, and their partners are aware of how best to help. Having a familiar hand to hold, a sympathetic midwife and remembering breathing techniques may help to prevent the use of analgesics (painkillers) and anaesthetics. The following are, however, used by many women:

- Pethidine: a strong drug which can be injected every four hours, to take the edge off contractions
- Nitrous oxide and oxygen: NO_2 and O_2 is a gas which the mother can breathe in to help with contractions; she controls the amount she takes by holding the mask; when her muscles relax she cannot hold the mask, so she cannot be given too much gas.
- Epidural: an epidural anaesthetic is the injection of a painkilling drug into the space around the spinal cord; it numbs the pain of contractions by anaesthetising the nerves that carry sensations to the brain. This type of anaesthetic does not harm the baby and leaves the mother fully conscious

- TENS (Transcutaneous Nerve Stimulation) consists of equipment that produces electrical impulses which block any sensations of pain before they reach the brain; the equipment is loaned to the mother before labour begins so that she can begin to use it as soon as she thinks that labour has begun.

CHECK!

1 What are the three signs that labour has begun?
2 What do you understand by 'normal labour'?
3 What are the three stages of labour?
4 Why may labour be induced?
5 What is an episiotomy?
6 What types of pain relief may be offered in labour?

THINK!

1 Think about how women may be encouraged to feel relaxed during labour.
2 Why do women remember the events of childbirth so clearly, years after the event?

THE NEWBORN BABY

The arrival of a new baby is a time for celebration

The arrival of a new baby is a time for celebration. Parents are usually overjoyed with the new addition to their family. The first question they ask, however, is usually 'Is she alright?', closely followed by 'How much does she weigh?'

To make sure that the baby is in the best of health and that her progress continues, the midwife and doctor will be making sure that the baby is alright and will eventually get the baby weighed!

Immediate care at birth

ESTABLISHING RESPIRATION

As soon as the head is delivered, the midwife will wipe the baby's nose and mouth so that when the first breath is taken it is not contaminated with mucus or blood. She may use a mucus extractor to gently suck away the debris of delivery. Most babies breathe spontaneously, but specialised equipment is available in the delivery room for resuscitation if necessary.

MAINTAINING BODY TEMPERATURE

Babies are wet at birth and lose heat very quickly. That is why hospital delivery suites are so hot! It is important to dry the baby as quickly as possible, usually by wrapping her in warm towels to be cuddled by her mother. Radiant heaters over the cot will warm it in preparation for the baby.

The temperature of the baby is taken within an hour of birth.

BONDING

It is extremely important that the parents have close contact with their new baby, so that their relationship can begin positively. Bonding can be encouraged by:

- the mother helping with the delivery, by holding the baby's shoulders and lifting him out
- the baby being delivered into the mother's arms, or onto her tummy if possible
- the mother or her partner cutting the umbilical cord if they wish; this is a symbolic gesture of the start of a new life
- the mother being encouraged to breast feed as soon as possible after delivery, if that is her chosen method of feeding.

IDENTIFICATION

The baby will be labelled immediately after she is born by attaching small bracelets to one wrist and one ankle. These labels contain the name and hospital number of the mother and the date and time of birth. The baby's cot will also be labelled.

OBSERVATIONS

The Apgar score

While all this is happening the midwife will be closely observing the baby. She will be looking at his vital signs:

- heart rate
- respiration
- muscle tone
- response to stimulus.
- colour.

From observing these specific areas she will be able to assess the Apgar score. This is an internationally used system for assessing the condition of babies at birth. Each of the five areas above is observed and the baby is given 0, 1 or 2 points for according to their condition. These points are added to give a maximum score of ten.

Sign	0	1	2
Heart rate	Absent	Slow (below 100)	Fast (above 100)
Respiration	Absent	Slow, irregular	Good, crying
Muscle tone	Limp	Some flexion of extremities	Active
Response to stimulus (stimulation of foot or nose/mouth)	No response	Grimace	Cry, cough
Colour	Blue, pale	Body pink/dusky; extremities blue	Completely pink/ healthy colour

The heart and respiratory rate are the most important.
Babies of black, Asian or mixed parentage will be assessed by monitoring the blood flow to the skin.

The Apgar score

The test is first performed when the baby is 1 minute old, then 5 minutes later, and every 5 minutes afterwards until the maximum of 10 is achieved. A score of 8–10 indicates that the baby is in good condition at birth. Most babies score 9 at 1 minute, losing a point for colour, as the fingers and toes often remain blue until the circulation becomes fully established.

The Apgar score may be referred to later in childhood if the child shows any signs of developmental delay which may have been caused by their poor condition at birth. A record of the score is kept in the child's health records held by the parents, the health visitor and later by the school nurse.

Measurements

The baby will be weighed soon after birth and the weight recorded in kilograms.

The circumference of the head is also recorded to give a baseline reading against which to measure future growth.

Some centres may continue to measure the length of the baby, but this is now generally thought to be of little value.

Temperature

The temperature is taken to ensure that the baby is warm enough.

Stools and urinary output

It is very important that the midwife observes and records whether the baby has passed urine, and passed *meconium* (a greenish-black soft stool). Failure to do either indicates an abnormality which will need investigation.

EXAMINATION

The midwife will perform a detailed examination of the baby in the presence of the parents, starting at the head and working downwards, checking for any abnormalities in the baby, and making sure that everything is normal.

General observations

The midwife will check for regular, effortless breathing and skin colour – a healthy bloom will indicate that blood is circulating oxygen around the body.

All babies are varying shades of pink at birth, regardless of their racial origin. There may be lanugo (soft, downy hair mainly found in pre-term babies, but some may still be present in babies born at term). Vernix caseosa is a white, greasy substance that protects the skin in its watery environment in the uterus. In mature babies it may be found in the skin creases, but may also be present on the trunk if the baby is premature.

The midwife will note the baby's activity, whether the limbs are moving .

Detailed observations

The head

Fontanelles and suture lines are felt; the eyes are examined to confirm their presence and that formation is normal. The ears are checked for skin tags and the mouth for cleft lip and palate, tongue tie (if the frenulum – see Chapter 20 – is attached near the tip of the tongue) and for the presence of teeth.

The arms and hands

The arms and hands are checked for full movement; fingers are counted (an extra digit is not unusual) and webbing (rare, but it may be missed in a check) noted.

The body

An umbilical cord clamp is applied; external genitalia is noted and checked. The anus is checked by taking the temperature. With the baby in prone (face down) the back is examined to look for any evidence of spina bifida. There may be an open lesion (wound) or a small dimple to signify the presence of a hidden lesion.

An umbilical cord clamp

The baby may have mongolian blue spots, areas of blue tingeing to the skin which look like bruising. They are commonly found at the base of the spine (the sacrum), although they can be anywhere on the body. They are usually found in babies of Asian, Afro-Caribbean or Mediterranean descent or in babies of mixed race. They disappear before the age of 5 years, but should be recorded to prevent any later allegations of child abuse (see Chapter 20).

The legs
The baby's hips are tested for congenital dislocation. Leg movements are noted, to exclude paralysis, and talipes (club foot, an abnormality of the foot) is noted. The toes are counted.

Within 24 hours of birth the baby should be examined by a paediatrician (a doctor who specialises in the care of children). This check will include listening to the heart and lungs and *palpating* (feeling) the abdominal organs.

Postnatal care

Registered midwives have a legal right and responsibility to examine all mothers and babies for a minimum of 10 days after birth. They may continue to visit for 28 days if necessary.

DAILY OBSERVATION AND CARE

During the first 24 hours most abnormalities and illnesses will be identified. It may be considerably longer before some disabilities, such as deafness or developmental delay, are confirmed. Daily observations, as well as noting temperature, respiration and feeding patterns, should include the following areas.

The skin

Many babies have milia (tiny, white, milk spots) over the nose. These disappear in time, but occasionally they become infected and need treatment.

Birthmarks may appear in the first few days after birth; not all are present at birth.

Stools

Meconium is the first stool passed by the baby. It is dark green and sticky, composed of the contents of the digestive tract accumulated during fetal life. After milk feeds it becomes greenish-brown, then yellowish-brown. These are called *changing stools* as the last of the meconium is excreted together with the waste products of the milk feeds. This normally takes place around the 4th day.

The stools of a breast-fed baby are typically watery, bright yellow and passed 3 to 4 times a day (although the frequency will vary). There is little or no odour. Those of a bottle-fed baby are firm, paler, putty-like, with odour. Green stools occur naturally in some babies, depending on the mother's diet if she is breast-feeding, or the type of artificial milk. Yellow or green, watery frequent stools may indicate gastroenteritis. Small dark green stools are usually due to under-feeding.

The eyes

Sticky eyes (ophthalmia neonatorum) are common, because a new baby cannot yet produce tears. They are easily treated with antibiotic drops if discovered early. The eyes are examined daily and cleaned, using separate swabs for each eye.

The mouth

The mouth is checked for oral thrush, a common fungal infection. It looks like milk residue on the tongue and cheeks.

The umbilical cord

The cord should be checked daily and kept clean and dry to avoid infection. The cord stump usually drops off by the 6th day.

Feeding

Whether breast- or bottle-fed, babies will establish their own routine. Demand feeding (feeding when the baby is hungry rather than on a strict four-hourly schedule – but see Chapter 10) is recommended.

Bathing

Babies can be bathed daily and the midwife will teach the new mother the correct procedure. However, topping and tailing (washing the face, hands and bottom), is quite adequate with a full bath every 2 to 3 days, if this fits in more easily with the home routine.

Crying

All babies cry during the early weeks. The cause can usually be detected by process of elimination: the carer checks whether the baby is hungry, thirsty, in pain (wind) or uncomfortable (too hot, too cold, soiled nappy, uncomfortable position).

Screening tests

Various screening tests are performed in the early neonatal period to check for specific abnormalities that can be successfully treated if detected early enough.

THE GUTHRIE TEST

The Guthrie test is performed on the 6th day of milk feeding, to detect phenylketonuria (PKU). A sample of blood is obtained by pricking the baby's heel. This sample is also checked for levels of thyroxine so that hypothyroidism (cretinism) can be treated.

BARLOW'S TEST

This hip test is performed by the midwife and later by the doctor, to check for congenital dislocation of the hip. The health visitor will repeat the test, and so will the GP when the baby has a 6-week medical and development check.

Low birth-weight babies

Not all babies are born at term; some are born early and an increasing number of these are surviving because of improved neonatal care. Low birth-weight babies can be divided into two main categories:

- pre-term (premature): these babies are born before 37 completed weeks of pregnancy, i.e. at 36 weeks' gestation or less
- light-for-dates (small-for-dates): these babies are below the expected weight for their gestational age – the length of the pregnancy, according to percentile charts.

Some babies are both premature and light-for-dates.

7 to 8 per cent of all babies are low birth-weight but almost half of all deaths in the first month occur in this group. This shows how important the birth-weight of a baby is. There is a greater chance of a baby surviving if it weighs more than 2.5 kg.

Women who have undergone fertility treatment are more likely to have a multiple pregnancy; their babies are more likely to be born early, with the problems described in this section.

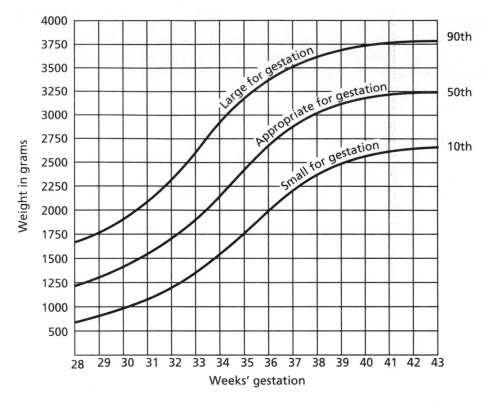

A centile chart, showing weight and gestation

PRE-TERM BABIES

Pre-term babies are immature and are not yet ready to survive alone outside the womb. They have a better chance of survival if their weight falls between the 90th and 10th percentile.

Characteristics
There are several characteristics common to pre-term babies:
- the head is even larger in proportion to the body than normal
- the face is small and triangular with a pointed chin
- the baby looks 'worried'
- they may be reluctant to open their eyes
- the sutures and fontanelles are large
- the skin may be red
- the veins are prominent
- the baby may be covered in lanugo
- the limbs are thin
- nails are soft
- the chest is narrow
- the abdomen is large

- the umbilicus is low-set
- there are small genitalia, poorly developed
- muscle tone is floppy
- arms and legs are extended
- they are feeble and drowsy
- reflexes are poor, the baby may be unable to suck.

Causes

Causes of premature delivery are often unknown, but are commoner in mothers who smoke and in those with pre-eclampsia or with a multiple pregnancy. Prematurity is also associated with poverty and deprivation which may indicate the importance of a good diet and healthy lifestyle in pregnancy.

Complications

Complications which might arise for a pre-term baby are:
- birth asphyxia: pre-term babies may be slow to breathe at birth due to an immature respiratory centre in the brain.
- respiratory problems: immaturity of the lungs may make breathing difficult.
- intracranial haemorrhage (bleeding in the brain): fragile blood vessels in the brain may bleed easily. This may cause long-term damage.

The care of premature babies is a highly specialised field; they are prone to many difficulties. For example, like all babies they cannot control their temperature but the smaller the baby the greater the risk of hypothermia; they are more likely to become jaundiced or anaemic and are vulnerable to infections. Some pre-term babies do survive and develop well, but some suffer long-term damage as a direct result of their prematurity.

Possible effects on development are:
- generalised developmental delay: this 'global' delay may affect all areas of development, with milestones being achieved at a much later age, if at all
- specific developmental difficulties: there may be a particular problem with one area of development, such as motor or communication skills
- sensory loss: blindness and deafness are much more common in children who have been born very early.

CHECK!

1 What immediate care is given to the baby at birth?
2 Why are delivery rooms kept very warm?
3 Why is the Apgar score such an important observation?
4 What measurements of the baby are recorded after birth?
5 What is the first stool called?
6 What is lanugo?
7 What is vernix caseosa?
8 What is a mongolian blue spot?
9 For how long after a birth does a midwife have the responsibility to visit a mother and baby?

10 What are milia?
11 Describe the typical stool of a breast-fed baby.
12 Describe the typical stool of a bottle-fed baby.
13 Why are a baby's eyes vulnerable to infection?
14 What is demand feeding?
15 Why do babies cry?
16 When is the Guthrie test performed? Why is it done?
17 What are the two categories of low birth-weight babies?
18 What are the characteristics of pre-term babies?
19 Why is the birth-weight of a baby important?
20 What may be the cause(s) of prematurity?
21 What effects may prematurity have on future development?

DO!

1 Describe the Apgar score.
2 Briefly describe the midwife's first examination of the new baby.

Early development

There are wide variations in the ages at which babies will develop particular skills. Parents and carers will inevitably compare their child to others of the same age to assess progress. It is common to hear conversations concerning the ages at which particular goals are reached, for example 'John smiled at 3 weeks', 'Shazia sat up at 4 months'. If another child has not made similar progress it can arouse parental anxiety. It is important to remember that all children develop in a very individual way (See Book 1, Chapter 3), and that their progress should be measured against:
■ what is typical for their age range
■ cultural/biological origin
■ parental/genetic background
■ social group
■ gestational age
■ level of stimulation
■ medical background.
■ their own achievements, that is whether or not any new skills have been learnt by them within a period of time.
It is important to remember that all areas of development are linked and dependent on each other, and should not be viewed in isolation.

STIMULATING DEVELOPMENT

All babies need to be stimulated in order to progress through the developmental stages. Stimulation can be as simple as talking to a young baby and achieving or maintaining eye-contact. Babies need a lot of physical contact with adults who will spend time with them, caring for them and meeting their needs. This will enable babies to communicate and feel secure.

Stimulation does not mean a hot-house of toys and activities which are often beyond the capabilities of the child, although some toys do make learning through play exciting and challenging. It is possible to over-stimulate a baby which can cause stress, anxiety and unhappiness in the child, and so defeat the purpose.

Above all babies need close and secure contact with adults. It is through this trusted relationship that development will proceed and skills will be learnt. A feeling of security and of being well cared for is essential for a child to reach full potential.

All methods of stimulating development can be achieved without great financial cost. Not all families can afford frequent shopping trips to purchase the latest toy or aid to development. Manufacturers can make parents or carers believe that development cannot be maintained unless a certain article or gadget is purchased, often at great cost. But this is a fairly recent phenomenon. For thousands of years babies have developed with little more than parental care and home-made equipment, so however attractive and necessary the latest toys appear, parents should be reassured that their children are not deprived if they cannot afford to purchase them all. A little ingenuity and imagination, combined with an awareness of safety, can provide a multitude of learning experiences with everyday household articles.

There are facilities for loaning, renting or giving children the opportunity to play with different toys at a specific venue. It may be possible to purchase toys second hand. The following should be investigated as possible sources for varied play experiences:

- toy libraries
- toy loan facilities
- playgroups
- mother and toddler groups
- jumble sales and car boot sales
- newspaper and shop advertisements.

It costs a great deal to buy new clothes and equipment for a new baby, but looking through the small advertisements section of any local newspaper will show that all the necessary items can be purchased at a fraction of the retail price. Nor do all toys and equipment need to be purchased: some organisations will loan the necessary items or make a small weekly charge for rental. The health visitor, Social Services Department or Citizens' Advice Bureau should be able to give details of such charitable organisations in any area.

The following pages show, in table form, activities and toys that are appropriate to the different ages and stages of development.

Methods of stimulating development

Age	Area of development	Stage of development	Stimulating activities/toys
0–3 months	Gross motor	Head control developing; kicking legs with movements becoming smoother and more symmetrical in supine; enjoys being held sitting; begins to support head and chest on forearms in prone	Time for lying on the floor to kick and experiment with movement; opportunity to be without nappy or clothing to encourage co-ordination; change positions from prone to supine so that the baby feels comfortable in either; sitting supported on carer's knee and in bouncing cradle
	Fine motor	Fascinated by human faces; grasp reflex diminishing; outwards direction of development progressing: trying to co-ordinate hands and eyes to control environment; fingerplay: beginning to discover the hands; may begin to hold objects for a few moments when placed in the hand	Bright colourful objects to encourage focusing within the visual field of 20–25 cm, e.g. mobiles, watching the washing line, pictures of faces around the cot, toys with facial characteristics; opportunity to watch what is happening around her; use of noise to attract attention, e.g. rattle placed in her hand or objects strung over the cot, which make a noise when touched; baby-gym, or other objects within reach of waving arms
	Hearing and speech	Recognises main carer's voice; vocalising in conversational pattern; beginning to look for the origin of the sound; cries to indicate need	Opportunity to bond with main carer and recognise their voice; lots of physical contact and cuddles with loving conversations which maintain eye contact and give the baby the opportunity to respond; carers need to show lots of pleasure when they do; enjoys being sung to
	Social and play	Smiles from about 5 to 6 weeks; enjoys all caring routines and responds to loving handling; imitates some facial expressions; beginning to recognise situations, e.g. smiles, vocalises and uses total body movement to express pleasure at bathtime or feeding time	Lots of contact with adults and children to widen the social network, but mainly with primary carer, to strengthen the bond; routines for meeting needs to ensure security and comfort; stimulating areas of development, as above; opportunity for eye contact and to watch faces and mimic them, e.g. sticking tongue out
3–6 months	Gross motor	Head control established; beginning to sit with support; rolling over; playing with feet in supine, and raising head to look around; supporting head and chest on extended forearms in prone; weight bearing and bouncing when held standing	Opportunity to practise sitting, on carer's knee, then protected by cushions for a soft landing when she topples! Physical play: bouncing on the knee with suitable songs, rough and tumble on the bed, rolling and bouncing (NB Never leave a baby alone on the bed or other high surface); carer's knee is ideal gymnasium at

(Continued on facing page)

		this age: some babies love to stand and bounce up and down for long periods of time; baby bouncer may be useful purchase; time to practise and experiment skills on the floor
Fine motor	Beginning to use palmar grasp and transfer objects from hand to hand; watches all activity with interest; moves head around to follow people and objects	As baby is finding her hands, toys which rattle are essential; as she holds an object, the noise it makes will attract her attention and she will see the clever thing she is doing; colourful, small, safe toys which can be grasped by tiny fingers are invaluable, e.g. soft animals, box of bricks, chiming ball, home-made toys, e.g. transparent plastic bottles with coloured water inside or half-filled with sugar or dried beans which rattle (lid must be tightly on and baby supervised); old plastic cotton reels strung together provide useful tactile experience; baby needs things to reach out for and things to hit
Hearing and speech	Turns immediately to familiar sounds; screening hearing test may be performed from 6 months onwards; tuneful vocalisations, sing-song sounds, laughs and squeals with pleasure; responds to different emotional voices in carer	Lots of physical contact and play using songs and voice; conversations with carers and others, who give baby time to respond, reinforce responses by showing pleasure and repeating sounds; enjoys listening to nursery rhymes and finger games with tune and rhythm; *This little piggy* and *This is the way the farmer rides* encourage listening and fun
Social and play	Beginning to put all toys in mouth to explore them and investigate the world object by object; recognising objects which make a noise, trying to utilise them; finding the feet as a source of investigation and pleasure; enjoys strangers if they are friendly and gentle	Safe, non-toxic toys to put in the mouth; some babies may enjoy finger feeding too; make bean bags with various fillings, e.g. dried peas, crunchy cereals, to give oral experience; make books suitable for chewing, using photographs and/or pictures in plastic covers; waterproof bath books useful purchase; opportunity to play and investigate both alone and in the company of other children

(Continued overleaf)

Methods of stimulating development (*continued*)

Age	Area of development	Stage of development	Stimulating activities/toys
6–9 months	Gross motor	Can sit unsupported for lengthening periods of time; may begin to crawl; may stand and cruise holding on to furniture or other stable objects; some may begin to walk with hands held or even alone	Needs to be given time to play on the floor, placed in sitting position, with support until stability is established; fun toys big enough to see and attract attention, just out of reach to stimulate mobility, but not enough to increase frustration; surround baby with toys in sitting position to encourage balance skills as he reaches to grasp to sides and the front; time spent bouncing on feet and encouraging strength in legs; stable furniture for baby to pull to stand
	Fine motor	visually very alert to people and objects; developing pincer grasp with thumb and index finger; uses index finger to poke and point; looks for fallen objects	Needs lots of exciting visual activity, e.g. going to the park, shopping; toddler group good opportunity for observing other children play; smaller objects can be introduced with supervision, (remember that everything will go into the mouth), e.g. small pieces of biscuit or bread, hundreds and thousands to encourage a pincer grasp and yet be safe to eat; build towers of bricks to be knocked down with glee; look at picture books, encouraging baby to point at familiar objects with you; encourage baby to look for and find items 'lost' over side of highchair, to help make sense of the world and cause and effect, e.g. something dropped does not disappear forever
	Hearing and speech	Babbles loudly and tunefully, repeating sounds again and again e.g. *da da*; beginning to understand commonly used words and phrases e.g. *No, Bye bye*; varies volume and pitch depending on mood, whether happy or cross; still cries for needs	Talk to baby about what is happening all the time; repeat their interpretations of words; sing repetitive songs, encouraging them to vocalise with you; finger rhymes encourage language; read books together, naming objects; encourage imitations of verbal and non-verbal language; name objects and people baby points at
	Social and play	Now wary of strangers; plays games like *Pat-a-cake, Peep-bo*; claps and waves; offers toys to others; finger-feeds; attempts to use	Games and activities to encourage language development also stimulate play and social skills; as baby now discovers values of objects, she will need things that respond

(Continued on facing page)

		cup and/or bottle; looks for partly hidden toys	differently when same thing is done to them, e.g. ball will roll when pushed, brick will not; biscuit will crumble when squeezed, bread will not, toys that squeak, bricks that do not; safety mirror in plastic frame to allow the baby to recognise herself; post table-tennis balls down kitchen-roll tube; toys or safe household items that can be banged to make a noise, wooden spoon, saucepan or xylophone; babies are beginning to make music and be delighted by achievements
9–12 months	Gross motor	Will now be mobile, crawling, bottom-shuffling, bear-walking or walking; may be able to crawl upstairs; mobility has frustrations as well as pleasures: baby can reach areas previously out-of-bounds, so needs attention in providing suitable playthings within reach	Large-wheeled toys fun to push around, brick-trolley or similar push-along toy to help develop skills of getting around corners, reversing, etc.; small climbing frames used with supervision to increase balance and co-ordination; swimming; walking outside with reins
	Fine motor	Mature pincer grasp; throws toys deliberately; points to desired objects; bangs toys together	Pull-string musical box or similar to encourage dexterity and also teach cause and effect; nesting toys, building bricks, etc. will encourage balance and concepts of shape, size and colour; roll balls for baby to fetch, she will soon roll them for you; tin or basket filled with interesting objects to take out and put back in; plastic jars and bottles with removable lids to encourage investigation of what is inside, or simple delight at removing lid
	Hearing and speech	Understands several words and phrases; obeys simple commands, lots of vocalisations with sounds for certain objects, e.g. dud may mean cup	Talk to baby constantly, repeat names of people and objects, sing songs, games and rhymes, read stories with familiar situations and few characters; baby must be surrounded by language to develop communication skills effectively

(Continued overleaf)

Methods of stimulating development *(continued)*

Age	Area of development	Stage of development	Stimulating activities/toys
9–12 months	Social and play	Usually loving and affectionate, likes to be near someone familiar; can drink from cup with a little help; tries to use spoon; likes to put objects in and out of containers; participates in routines	Make sure that care is consistent and familiar; give opportunity to learn to feed, e.g. allow practice with cup and spoon, regardless of inevitable mess; valuable for sensory experience; offer lots of opportunity for play with interaction from adults, e.g. taking turns, stop and go; baby sometimes acquires a new skill by making something happen by mistake – if it is fun he will want to do it again; adult must observe this and reinforce positive actions; opportunity to watch and imitate others, perhaps in routine domestic chores; small dustpan and brush or similar to encourage this and make help valued; needs own equipment, e.g. flannel, toothbrush, cup, spoon to foster feeling of personal identity, and encouragement to take part in caring routines

Some stimulating toys for a baby's pram or cot

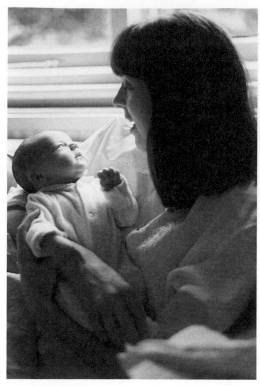

0–3 months: babies are fascinated by human faces

0–3 months: the baby cries to indicate a need

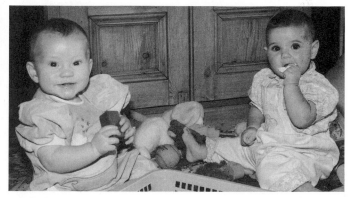

At 6–9 months babies will sit unsupported for longer periods

The hearing test may be performed from 6 months when the baby turns to sounds

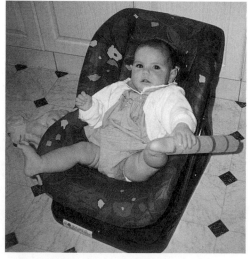

6–9 months: everyday household articles can easily provide learning experiences

CHECK!

1 What factors should be taken into account when assessing development?
2 Why is personal contact especially important to a young baby?
3 How could you stimulate:
   a) gross motor development from birth to 3 months?
   b) fine motor development from 3 to 6 months?
   c) social and play from 6 to 9 months?
   d) hearing and speech from 9 to 12 months?
4 Where are toys and equipment available for families who do not wish to purchase them?

THINK!

1 Think of 3 activities to encourage all-round development in a baby from 6 to 12 months.
2 Think of all the household items you could use to provide stimulation during the first year.

DO!

1 Make an article for a baby to provide sensory experience. Observe the baby using your toy and encourage them to use all aspects of it.
2 Collect together several safe items for a baby from 6 to 12 months to explore to stimulate all areas of development. Observe babies playing with these items and evaluate how effective they are.
3 Make a playbox full of interesting and safe items for a baby to examine.
4 Select toys from a shop or catalogue that are suitable for a baby during the first year. Give reasons for your choices and include methods of adapting these toys for the baby as she goes into the second and third year.

Key terms	
You need to know what these words and phrases mean. Go back through the chapter and find out.	
Labour	Mongolian blue spot
Term	Talipes
Contraction	Milia
Forceps	Meconium
Induction	Sticky eyes
Ventouse	Thrush
Episiotomy	Screening
Caesarian	Guthrie test
Epidural	Low birth-weight
TENS	Pre-term
Apgar score	Light for dates
Lanugo	Birth asphyxia
Vernix caseosa	

10 MEETING NEEDS

Equipment

Having a baby will necessarily incur some financial cost unless the family has a baby already and has kept all the required items. Even so, they will need to ensure that the equipment is still suitable and safe to use. There are many factors to consider, the well-being of the infant being of prime importance. Some of these factors are outlined below.

SAFETY

All equipment bought, loaned or rented, new or second-hand, must comply with safety legislation and carry the BSI safety kitemark.

LIFESTYLE

If, for example, the family uses a car for most journeys, a pram may not be an essential item, but a car seat will be.

ACCOMMODATION

The family may have plenty of space for large equipment, or may be living in a small flat, bedsit, or perhaps with extended family. Carers may need to consider how to cope with transporting the baby up several flights or narrow stairs.

Marks of safety

ADAPTABILITY AND DURABILITY

Equipment that is to be purchased must be justified in terms of long-term use-fulness and be strong enough to withstand normal wear and tear. A cot, for example, will be in use for two years and perhaps more. It should be strong enough to continue to be safe for this and subsequent babies. Prams and push-chairs must be suitable for continued use as the baby becomes a toddler to avoid having to replace it unnecessarily early.

PRACTICALITY

It is easy to fall for the pretty items that look so appealing but are of little practical value. The frilly pram may prove difficult to clean when the baby has vomited on it! Highchairs with fabric seats may look lovely in the shop, but are not practical when the baby begins to feed himself.

ESSENTIAL ITEMS

All babies need a place to sleep, provision for feeding and hygiene routines, such as bathing, changing nappies, and to be safely transported. The tables on pages 140–3 summarise the advantages and disadvantages of different types of essential items.

Layette

The layette is the first set of clothes provided for a baby. Some guidelines for purchasing baby clothes are given below.

- Avoid ribbons, ties and bows which can trap tiny fingers and toes and be very difficult to take on and off. Garments of a loose weave (for example hand-knitted) can also be similarly hazardous.
- Buttons are a dangerous choking hazard and fiddly for large fingers.

Sleeping and transport

Item	Features	Advantages	Disadvantages
To try to prevent avoidable cot deaths, current research recommends that all babies should sleep:			
• on their backs			
• without a pillow			
• without a duvet for the first year; sheets and blankets prevent overheating by removing a layer when necessary.			
Moses basket	Wicker basket with decorative lining and covers, with or without a canopy; usually with two handles for transport; may have a stand or be placed on the floor	Baby feels secure in small, enclosed space; easy to carry from room to room; looks pretty and appealing	Cannot be used to transport baby outside; unsafe for use in the car; unsuitable for older/ heavier babies due to lack of internal space; may topple as baby moves around
Cradle	Wooden crib with rocking mechanism, either on rockers or suspended between two upright supports	As for Moses basket, except for ease of use between rooms; baby may respond well to being rocked to sleep	As for Moses basket
Carrycot	Rigid structure with mattress, waterproof cover and hood and carrying handles; covered in washable fabric or plastic	Enclosed space so baby feels comfortable and secure, used for night and daytime sleeping; easy to transport from room to room using handles; suitable for use outdoors, may be available with transporter (wheels) to convert to pram; restraining straps for transport by car	Babies will grow out of a carrycot sooner than a full size pram; may be heavy and cumbersome to lift when the baby is older

(Continued on facing page)

(Continued overleaf)

	Features	Advantages	Disadvantages
Pram	Rigid, frame-built structure with hood and waterproof cover on wheels, with brakes, washable fabric, plastic or metal exterior and fabric interior with mattress; harness fixing points	Baby feels comfortable, safe and secure; can be used for sleeping downstairs at home; ideal for use outside, for journeys on foot or for letting the baby sleep in the fresh air; suitable for use in all weathers; large enough to carry the baby for the first year and longer; shopping tray makes transporting groceries easier; possible to transport a toddler as well on a specially designed pram seat	Unsuitable for getting up and down stairs, so alternative night-time sleeping arrangements required; may be a problem in a block of flats if lifts not working; unsuitable for transportation by car; may create storage problem in a small house/flat or bedsit
Cot	A purpose built sleeping area for a baby and toddler; should be strong and stable; bars should be no more than 7 cm apart to prevent hands, feet and head getting stuck; waterproof, safety mattress that fits tightly within the frame; dropside cots should have childproof safety catches; option of high or low mattress position, depending on age/stage of the baby	Safe secure sleeping environment individual to each baby, whether room is shared or not	No disadvantages provided that all specifications under Features are met

Sleeping and transport (continued)

Item	Features	Advantages	Disadvantages
Rearward facing baby car seat	Designed for safe car travel using standard inertia seat belts; contains harness to restrain the baby within it; carrying handle to move the seat to and from the car	Safe transportation in a car; easy to carry with a sleeping baby in it; back support for a very young baby; can be used from birth until about 9 months; useful for babies who need motion to get to sleep; can be used in the house as a first seat	Can be expensive; will need replacing with a fixed car seat at about 9 months; some models can be difficult to carry and attach car seat belts to
Bouncing cradle	Soft fabric seat for a baby from birth to about 6 months; may include a row of toys	Used from birth; baby can be transported from room to room and can see what is happening everywhere; babies can rock themselves to sleep; easy to wash fabric cover	Dangerous if left on a bed or worktop when the baby can bounce themselves off; not suitable when babies can sit unsupported
Carrying slings	Fabric baby slings, attached to the carer's body to enable the baby to be carried in an upright position on the chest	Baby feels comfortable and secure, can hear carer's heartbeat and feel body warmth; comfortable sleeping position; babies can be carried indoors and out, invaluable for fractious ones who find sleep difficult or crave constant contact; leaves two hands free to cope with a toddler or other children needing supervision and attention; allows carer to continue with routine tasks	May be difficult to put on and take off depending on the mechanism; may strain the back as baby gets heavier; flat shoes and careful posture essential to prevent injury to the back by falling

(Continued on facing page)

Bathing

Item	Features	Advantages	Disadvantages
Warmth is essential when bathing a new baby. A wall thermometer will ensure that the room is at least 70° C before you start.			
Baby bath	Plastic, purpose-built baby bath, usually bought with a stand	Large enough to use until the baby is about 6 months; can be used in any room where there is sufficient heat; comfortable for baby and carer, who can sit in a chair to bath when the bathstand is in use	Limited life, and of little use when the baby is bathed in the big bath; difficult and heavy to carry when full of water; storage may be difficult in small accommodation
New washing-up bowl or storage box	Large plastic container	Can be used for its original purpose when no longer needed for bathing; easy to transport to a warm environment when full of water; large enough to bath a baby in the early weeks; avoids expense of purpose-built models	Baby will need to transfer to the big bath by 2 to 3 months

Feeding

It is largely personal preference which will decide whether a mother will begin to breast- or bottle-feed her baby. The advantages and disadvantages of breast-and bottle-feeding will be discussed later in the chapter. It is advisable to have some artificial feeding equipment to provide extra water or fruit juices, even if the baby is being breast fed; 2 to 3 bottles and teats should be sufficient. If the baby is being bottle fed, then 8–10 bottles and teats will be required to make up enough feeds for a 24-hour period. Sterilising equipment will be essential, and a good supply of formula milk; there are many brands available

- Choose clothes that are easy to launder; babies need changing often.
- Natural fibres are the most comfortable; cotton, for example is more absorbent than synthetic fabrics.
- Clothing should be comfortable, to allow for ease of movement, and not too tight, especially around the vulnerable feet. Clothes made of stretch fabric and with raglan sleeves make dressing and undressing much easier. Avoid suits with feet as it is tempting to continue using them after they have been outgrown. A footless suit with a pair of correctly sized socks is a better alternative.
- Garments should have a flame-retardant finish.

CLOTHING FOR A NEWBORN

- 6 vests: bodysuits prevent cold spots and help to keep the nappy in place.
- 6 all-in-ones: Babygros, preferably footless.
- 3 pairs of socks or bootees.
- 3 cardigans (matinee jackets).
- Hat: sunhat in the summer or bonnet in colder weather.
- Outdoor clothing: type will depend on method of transporting the baby. A knitted pramsuit may suffice or a quilted all-in-one may be required.
- Warm mittens and scratch mittens.
- Nappies: whether disposable nappies or terry nappies are to be used a good supply is required. Do not buy more than one pack of first size nappies until the baby is born and its size is known. Dial-a-nappy services are available in some areas.
- 24 terry nappies are sufficient, and will perhaps last for a subsequent baby. Nappy pins, nappy liners and plastic pants will also be required.

Clothing for the first year

- Babies grow very quickly, so it is sensible not to buy too many clothes of the same size. There will be little chance to wear them all before they are outgrown.
- Shoes are unnecessary until a child needs to walk outside. Bare feet are preferable, even to socks, if it is warm enough and the flooring is safe.
- Choose clothes that will help development and not hinder it; baby girls trying to crawl in a dress, for example, will become increasingly frustrated as they crawl into their skirts.
- Clothing needs will vary according to the season.
- Sort out clothes regularly and remove all that has been outgrown from the baby's drawers. This will prevent anyone who does not dress the baby often trying to squeeze them into garments that are too small.

A baby's layette

CHECK!

1 Which factors need consideration when buying equipment for a new baby ?
2 How should babies be put to sleep to try to prevent cot death?
3 What are the features of a Moses basket?
4 List the advantages of a carry cot.
5 Why should a bouncing cradle always be placed on the floor?
6 What is a layette?
7 What guidelines should be followed when buying baby clothes?
8 When are shoes necessary?

DO!

1 Prepare a booklet for parents to show the range of equipment available for a new baby. Include diagrams or photographs to illustrate each item. Draw attention to the advantages and disadvantages of each item.
2 Visit shops in your area to price all the essential items. Look through the small advertisements section of the local paper and cost similar second-hand equipment. Work out the savings to be made by buying in this way. What factors must be taken into account when buying second-hand articles for a baby? Why do some parents reject the idea of buying previously used equipment?

Clothing for the first year: garments should allow for ease of movement – and be easily washable

1 Think of all the essential clothing items for a baby during the first year. Include the various items for a winter as well as a summer birth.

Feeding

All babies should be fed on milk only for at least the first three months of life, so parents must decide how the baby will be fed. The decision to breast- or bottle-feed is a very personal one. Most women have an idea of how they will feed their babies before they become pregnant. This may be influenced by how their mother fed them, how their friends feed their babies, health education at school, the influence of the media and how they feel about their body.

There are advantages and disadvantages to both methods, but it is agreed that breast milk:

- is the natural milk for babies as it is the ideal source of nutrients for the first months of life
- should be encouraged as the first choice for infant feeding.

However, breast feeding may not be possible for a number of reasons and women should not feel inadequate if they bottle-feed their babies.

BREAST-FEEDING

The primary function of the breasts is to supply food and nourishment to an infant. During pregnancy the breasts enlarge by about 5 cm and prepare for feeding. Successful breast-feeding does not depend on the size of the breasts; women with very small breasts can breast-feed just as successfully as those with large breasts.

Each breast is divided into 15–20 lobes containing alveoli which produce milk. Each lobe drains milk into a lactiferous duct which widens into an

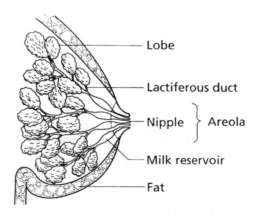

The lactating breast

ampulla (small reservoir) just behind the nipple. It narrows before opening on the surface of the nipple.

From the 16th week of pregnancy the breasts produce colostrum. This will feed the baby for the first 2–3 days after birth. It is a thick, yellowish fluid which has a high protein content but is lower in sugar and fat than mature human milk. Only a few ml are produced at each feed but it satisfies the baby, it helps to clear the meconium from the intestine and is very easy for the new baby to digest.

On the 3rd or 4th day the milk comes in and a mother may notice that her breasts become fuller. Breast milk is not fully mature until about 3 weeks after birth.

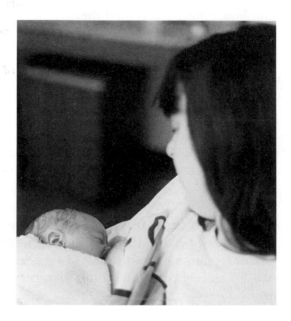

Breast-feeding

Advantages of breast-feeding
- Breast milk from a well nourished mother is the ideal food: it is made especially for babies. It contains all the right nutrients in exactly the right proportions to meet the changing needs of the baby. It is easily digested.
- Colostrum has a high concentration of maternal antibodies so protects the baby from some infections.
- It is sterile (contains no germs) and reduces risk of infection.
- There are fewer incidences of allergies, for example asthma or eczema, in babies who are breast-fed.
- It is always available at the correct temperature.
- It is more convenient: there are no bottles to prepare or heat.
- It is less expensive than purchasing modified milks.

Management of breast-feeding

- Demand feeding (the baby is fed when hungry) is preferable to a strict regime of feeding by the clock, every 4 hours. Babies have differing requirements and although they may feed often in the first few days, they will often have established their own 3–5 hourly feeding routine by 3–4 weeks. Some days they will require feeding more often – the only way they can stimulate the breast to produce more milk is by sucking for longer.
- Avoid giving complementary (extra) feeds in a bottle.
- The mother must be taking a well balanced diet, especially high in fluids. Her diet will affect the composition of the breast milk and some foods may cause colic. The baby will not need extra vitamins if the mother is taking a healthy diet.
- Breast-feeding is tiring in the early weeks, so mothers should be encouraged to relax. Extra help at home until breast-feeding is established will benefit mother and baby.
- Allow the baby to finish sucking at one breast before offering the other. Avoid timing the feeds on each side because the more filling milk, with higher fat content, is the last to be expelled from each breast. This will help the baby to settle for longer between feeds.
- Breast milk can be expressed using the hands or a breast pump for use when the mother is unavailable. The expressed breast milk (EBM) can be stored for up to 3 months in a domestic freezer and offered in a bottle.

Breast feeding can continue for as long as the mother desires (feeding for even a few days is better than none at all). Weaning onto solid foods should begin between 4–6 months and milk consumption will gradually reduce, but some mothers may feed for 2–3 years, mainly as a comfort rather than a source of nutrients.

BOTTLE-FEEDING

Most modern infant formulas (modified baby milks) are based on cow's milk, although some are derived from soya beans, for babies who cannot tolerate cow's milk. Manufacturers try to make the constituents as close to human breast milk as possible. All modified milks must meet the standards issued by the Department of Health. There are, however, basic differences between breast and modified milks:

- cow's milk is difficult to digest; it has more protein than breast milk, especially casein, which the baby may be unable to digest. The fat content is also more difficult to digest and this may cause wind or colic
- cow's milk has a higher salt content; salt is dangerous for babies as their kidneys are not mature enough to excrete it. Making feeds that are too strong, or giving unmodified cow's milk, can be very dangerous.
- cow's milk contains less sugar (lactose, needed by human infants) than breast milk.

Advantages of bottle-feeding

The advantages of bottle-feeding are:

- it is possible to see exactly how much milk the baby is taking
- fathers and other carers can help with the feeding regime, which may give the mother a chance for a good rest, especially at night; she may have more opportunity to go to work or pursue her own interests
- the baby can be fed anywhere without embarrassment
- it is less tiring for the mother in the early weeks.

Equipment for bottle feeding

All equipment for bottle-feeding must be thoroughly sterilised following the manufacturer's instructions on the sterilising solution bottle or packet. Equipment must be washed and rinsed before it is sterilised. Do not use salt to clean teats, as this is thought to increase the salt intake of the baby. Feeds should then be made up according to the guidelines on the modified milk container. The following equipment will be needed:

- bottles (some have disposable plastic liners)
- teats
- bottle covers
- bottle brush
- plastic knife
- plastic jug
- sterilising tank, sterilising fluid or tablets, or steam steriliser.

There are some important points to remember:

- always wash your hands before and after making up feeds
- wipe down the work surface before preparing feeds
- rinse the feeding equipment with boiled water after it comes out of the sterilising fluid
- always put the water into the bottle or jug before the milk powder
- never add an extra scoop of powder for any reason, pack the powder too tightly into the scoop nor give heaped scoops; the baby will be thirsty because too much salt has been given, the baby will cry, more food will be given, only increasing the salt intake. The baby can quickly become seriously ill
- use cooled boiled water to make up feeds
- demand feed, rather than time-feed, bottle-fed babies
- the primary carer should give the baby most of its feeds to encourage a close bond to develop
- never leave a baby propped with a bottle
- wind the baby once or twice during a feed; check the size of the hole in the teat: if it is too small the baby will take in air as she sucks hard to get the milk, which will cause wind; if the teat is too large the feed will be taken too quickly and the baby may choke
- always use the same brand of baby milk; do not change without the advice or recommendation of the health visitor or doctor
- never add baby cereals or other food to the bottle; when the baby is ready for solid feeding, it should be offered on a spoon.

Weaning

Weaning is a gradual process when the baby begins to take solid foods. This process should not be started before 3 months, and not later than 6 months.

WHY IS WEANING NECESSARY?

Milk alone is not nutritionally adequate for a baby over the age of 6 months. The baby has used the iron stored during pregnancy and must begin to take iron in their diet. Starch and fibre are also necessary for healthy growth and development. Weaning will also introduce the baby to new tastes and textures of food.

Babies at around 6 months are ready to learn how to chew food. The muscular movement helps the development of the mouth and jaw, and also the development of speech.

Mealtimes are sociable occasions and babies need to feel part of a wider social group. As weaning progresses they will learn how to use a spoon, fork, feeding beaker and cup. They will also begin to learn the social rules associated in their cultural background with eating, if they have good role models; rules such as using a knife and fork, chopsticks, chewing with the mouth closed or sitting at the table until everyone has finished eating.

WHEN TO START WEANING

Between 3 and 6 months babies will begin to show signs that milk feeds alone are not satisfying their hunger. There are no strict rules regarding the weight of the baby before weaning. The following are signs that the baby might be ready for weaning:
- still being hungry after a good milk feed
- waking early for feeds
- being miserable and sucking fists soon after feeding (this may also be a sign that the baby is teething)
- not settling to sleep after feeding, crying.

HOW TO WEAN

As young babies cannot chew, first weaning foods are runny so that the baby can easily suck it from a spoon. Start weaning at the feed at which the baby seems hungriest: this is often the lunchtime feed. Give the baby half their milk feed to take the edge off their immediate hunger, then offer a small amount of baby rice, pureed fruit or vegetables (first foods must be gluten-free) mixed with breast or formula milk to a semi-liquid consistency from a spoon.

The baby should be in a bouncing cradle or similar, but not in the usual feeding position in the carer's arms. There should be a relaxed atmosphere without any stress or distractions which may upset the baby. The carer should sit with the baby throughout the feed and offer their undivided attention. It may take a few days of trying for the baby to take food from the spoon successfully.

GUIDELINES FOR WEANING

Never add salt to food, and never sweeten food by adding sugar. Do not give very spicy food; avoid chilli, ginger and cloves.

Try different tastes and textures gradually – one at a time. This gives the baby the chance to become accustomed to one new food before another is offered. If a baby dislikes a food, do not force them to eat it. Simply try it again in a few days' time. Babies have a natural tendency to prefer sweet foods. This preference will be lessened if they are offered a full range of tastes.

Gradually increase the amount of solids to a little at breakfast, lunch and tea. Try to use family foods so that the baby experiences their own culture and becomes familiar with the flavour of family dishes.

As the amount of food increases, the milk feeds will reduce. Baby juice or water may be offered in a feeding cup at some feeds. The baby still needs some milk for its nutritional value, and also for the comfort and security of feeding from the breast or bottle.

COW'S MILK

After 6 months babies may be given cow's milk in family dishes. They should not be offered it as a drink until they are over 1 year old. Milk drinks should continue to be modified milk or breast milk.

IRON

By 6 months the baby's iron stores are low, so foods containing iron must be given. These include:
- liver
- beef
- lamb
- beans
- dahl
- green vegetables
- wholemeal bread
- cereals containing iron, for example Weetabix, Ready brek
- eggs, but these should not be offered until 6 months; because of the risk of salmonella they must be hard boiled and mashed.

WEANING STAGES

Stage 1
Early weaning foods are pureed fruit, pureed vegetables, plain rice cereal, dahl. Milk continues to be the most important food.

Stage 2

The baby will progress from pureed to minced to finely chopped food. Using a hand or electric blender or food processor is helpful to enable babies to enjoy family foods. Milk feeds decrease as more solids are taken. Well diluted, unsweetened fresh fruit juice or herbal drinks may be offered.

Stage 3

Offer lumpy foods to encourage chewing. The baby may be offered food to hold and chew, such as a piece of toast or apple. A cup may be introduced.

Three regular meals should be taken as well as drinks.

FEEDING DIFFICULTIES

Most feeding problems are caused by adults who are unfamiliar with the feeding or weaning process or who have unrealistic expectations of babies and children. Problems may be prevented by following these guidelines:

- be aware that weaning is a messy business; disapproval will prevent the baby from exploring and experimenting with food
- encourage independence by allowing the baby to use their fingers and offering a spoon as soon as the baby can hold one – it will eventually reach the mouth! Offer suitable finger foods too
- allow the baby to find eating a pleasurable experience – mixing yogurt and potato may seem revolting to an adult but if the baby eats this and enjoys it, so be it!
- babies have not learnt that courses conventionally follow a pattern and may prefer to eat them in a different order; never start a battle by insisting that one course is finished before the next is offered. When the baby has had enough of one dish, calmly remove it and offer the next.
- Remember that babies will not wilfully starve themselves; they know when they are or are not hungry, so never force a baby to eat anything that they do not eagerly want.

FOOD ALLERGIES

Food allergies can be detected most easily if a baby is offered new foods separately. Symptoms may include :
- vomiting
- diarrhoea
- skin rashes
- wheezing after eating the offending food.

The advice of a doctor should be obtained, and the particular food avoided.

Some babies may have cow's milk intolerance. If the baby is bottle-fed it may fail to thrive as expected, and should be referred to a paediatrician to confirm the condition. A dietician will give feeding advice and should be consulted before weaning begins.

The allergy may be apparent in a breast-fed baby and the mother may be advised to restrict the cow's milk in her diet. In all cases of cow's milk allergy, re-introduction should be carried out with medical supervision. There are substitute milks available, usually derived from soya beans.

CHECK!

1 What may influence a mother's decision to breast- or bottle-feed her baby?
2 Why is it generally agreed that 'breast is best'?
3 What is colostrum?
4 List the advantages of breast-feeding.
5 List the advantages of bottle-feeding.
6 Describe the process of sterilising equipment and making up feeds.
7 What is weaning?
8 Why is weaning necessary?
9 How may a baby show that it is ready for weaning?
10 Describe the management of introducing the first solids.
11 Which foods are rich in iron?
12 Describe the weaning stages.
13 How can feeding problems be avoided?
14 What are the symptoms of food allergies?

DO!

1 Make a booklet for parents describing the weaning process.
2 Produce a weekly weaning timetable from 4 to 6 months, and a monthly weaning time table from 7 to 12 months. Include the timing of meals from first foods to 3 family meals. Include suggestions for meals and drinks, emphasising home produced foods.
3 Look at the picture opposite and make a list of reasons for this baby's unhappiness about mealtimes.

Routines for care

Babies are completely dependent on an adult to meet all their needs. Although the babies' needs are generally the same, the manner in which they are met will differ in the first year: all babies are different, some will sleep well, others will not, some are happy and contented, others not. Caring adults need to be flexible, patient, to accept change and be aware of how and when these changes may occur. The needs of babies and young children can be summarised under the following headings of emotional and physical needs.

Emotional needs are:
■ continuity and consistency of care
■ physical contact
■ security

Distractions at feeding time

- socialisation
- stimulation.

Physical needs are:
- food
- warmth, shelter, clothing
- cleanliness
- rest, sleep, exercise
- fresh air, sunlight
- safety and protection from injury and infection
- medical intervention if necessary.

Babies will eventually settle into a routine that meets their need for food. The regularity of feeding and the urgency with which a baby signals its hunger is the basis of any routine in the early weeks. Feeding the baby on demand, as described earlier, is the most satisfactory method. The baby will develop a pattern of 2–4-hourly feeding and sleeping for periods between feeds.

As the baby gets older, he will sleep for longer at night, although some babies require a night feed or drink well into the second or third year. There are no rules which control how babies behave: they are all individuals with very individual needs.

As the baby begins to sleep for longer at night, he will probably stay awake for longer periods in the day, until by the end of the first year he may only have one long, or two shorter, sleeps during the day. This increasing wakefulness provides the opportunity to develop in all areas, with good care and stimulation (see the table in Chapter 9, pages 130–4). It also gives the carer the opportunity to perform the caring routines which the baby will enjoy if he is treated with affection, patience and understanding.

CARE OF THE SKIN AND HAIR

Students should refer to *Care of the hair*, skin and teeth in Chapter 13 for information on the structure and functions of the skin and hair.

It is important to give careful attention to caring for a baby's skin and hair, because:

- the baby is very vulnerable to infection
- the skin must be able to perform its functions (again, see Chapter 13).

As well as giving attention to keeping adequately clean, this routine care includes frequent observation of the condition of the skin for any rashes or areas of soreness.

DAILY CARE

Babies do not need to be bathed every day. They are not active enough in the early months to require their hair and whole body to be washed more than 2–3 times a week. Some carers prefer to bath the baby every day so that it becomes part of the routine, whether in the morning or evening.

As babies gets older and begin to explore the world and investigate their food as they try to put it into their mouths, a daily bath will become an essential way of removing the grime of the day.

Bathtime gives an ideal opportunity to talk and play with the baby. Topping and tailing can, however, be equally pleasurable, and is more reassuring for young babies who can feel insecure when their clothes are removed and they are submerged in water.

Topping and tailing

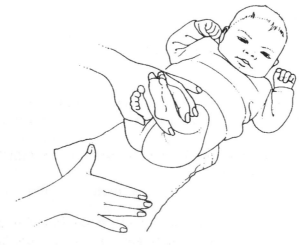

Topping and tailing

Topping and tailing involves cleaning the baby's face, hands and bottom.

Preparation
Collect all the necessary equipment:
- a bowl of warm water
- a separate bowl of cooled, boiled water for the eyes in the first month or so
- cotton wool balls
- baby sponge or flannel
- towel
- change of clothes
- nappies
- creams if used
- blunt ended nail scissors.

Method
- Lie the baby on a towel or changing mat.
- Remove outer clothing, if it is to be changed.
- Gently wipe each eye with a separate cotton wool ball, moistened with water, from the inner corner to the outer (nose to ear).
- Wipe the face, neck and ears with cotton wool balls.
- Make sure that the baby is dry, especially where the skin rubs together, such as in the neck creases.
- Clean the hands, using a sponge or flannel. Check that nails are short and that there are no jagged edges that the baby may scratch herself with. Cut them straight across.
- Remove the nappy and clean the bottom area, using cotton wool or a separate flannel. If the baby has soiled the nappy, soap is advisable to clean the area. Wet wipes may be used, but these may sometimes cause soreness.
- Put on a clean nappy, after the bottom is completely dry.
- Replace clothing.

Bathing
Bathing should eventually become a 'fun' time for the baby and carer, but there are nevertheless some conditions which are essential:
- the room should be warm: at least 20°C
- the water should be warm: at body temperature, 37°C
- always put the cold water in the bath first
- collect all the equipment together before starting the bath
- never leave a young child alone in the bath; babies can drown in only 1 cm of water.
- after the bath ensure that the baby is completely dry, especially in the skin creases, to prevent soreness.

Safety in the bath
As the baby gets older it may feel more comfortable in a sitting position in the bath. Constant physical support must be given to prevent the baby from sliding

under the water, or feeling insecure. Such an experience could put a baby off bathing for a considerable time. A non-slip bath mat is a wise investment for safety. As the baby gets older, standing may seem fun. This should be discouraged, as serious injuries could result from a fall.

Bath time is fun
If the baby is safe in the bath, she will feel secure and begin to enjoy the experience. There are many toys available for the bath, and many can be improvised from objects around the house. Empty washing up bottles will squirt water, squeezed sponges make a shower. But in the first year a baby is more interested in physical contact and play. Blowing bubbles, tickling, singing songs with actions will all amuse and give pleasure. Hair washing can be fun too. If the baby is accustomed to getting her face wet from an early age, hair washing should be easy. If it proves difficult, leave it for a couple of days. Wipe over the head with a damp flannel and gradually re-introduce the hair-washing gently, using a face shield if necessary. Above all, never let this area become a battle. It is not that important and may create a real fear of water that could hinder future swimming ability.

Bath time is fun

Non-infectious skin problems

Cradle cap

Cradle cap is a fairly common condition affecting the scalp, especially the area around the anterior fontanelle (soft spot). It is a scaly, greasy or dry crust appearing by about 4 weeks and disappearing by 6 months. It is probably caused by unnecessary fear of rubbing that area of the scalp. Prevention is by washing the hair once or twice a week, and rinsing it very thoroughly. If it becomes unsightly or sore, the crust can be removed by special shampoo or by rubbing olive oil into the scalp, leaving it for 1–2 hours and washing off thoroughly.

Heat rash

Heat rash is caused by over-heating and appears as a red, pin-point rash. The treatment is to bath the baby to remove sweat and to apply calamine lotion to reduce the itching and make the baby feel comfortable.

Eczema

Eczema is fairly common in babies, especially if there is a family history of allergies. It begins with areas of dry skin which may itch and become red, scaly patches. Scratching will cause the skin to weep and bleed. The treatment is to avoid perfumed toiletries, use oil such as Oilatum in the bath and an aqueous cream instead of soap. Biological washing powders and some fabric conditioners can irritate the condition, so use a gentle alternative. Cotton clothing is best, and try to prevent the baby scratching if possible. The GP should be consulted if the condition is severe or causing distress.

Nappy rash

Nappy rash usually begins gradually with a reddening of the skin in the nappy area; if this is not treated it will proceed to blistering, spots and raw areas which may bleed. It is extremely uncomfortable for the baby, who will cry in pain when the nappy is changed. Causes of nappy rash are:

- a soiled or wet nappy left on too long; this allows ammonia present in urine to irritate the skin
- concentrated urine (a result of the baby not drinking well)
- an allergy to, for example, washing powder, wet-wipes, baby cream
- infection, for example thrush
- inadequate rinsing of terry nappies
- use of plastic pants, which do not allow the skin to breathe.

Treatment is as follows:

- remove the nappy
- wash the bottom with unperfumed baby soap
- let the baby lie on a nappy with the bottom exposed to the air
- leave the area free of nappies as often as possible, as contact with fresh air will help the healing process
- change the nappy as soon as the baby has wet or soiled it, at least every 2 hours

- do not apply any creams unless the bottom is completely dry; creams can cause nappy rash by sealing dampness in
- do not use plastic pants or rubbers.

If there is no improvement, the carer should consult the health visitor or GP.

Nappy care

There are two main types of nappy:
- terry nappies
- disposable nappies.

Muslin nappies may be bought, but are rarely used on the baby's bottom. They are ideal first bibs, or to throw over the shoulder as the baby is winded! The choice of nappy is based on personal preference. The factors to consider are as follows:

- cost: terry nappies involve a larger initial cost (24 will be needed), but are thought to be cheaper in the long term, especially if they are used for a subsequent baby as well. Research shows that this may be misleading, however, as the cost of electricity for washing (and sometimes drying), sterilising solution, washing powder, nappy liners, nappy pins, plastic pants and nappy buckets must also be considered. The cost of disposable nappies may prevent them from being changed as often as they should be
- time: disposable nappies certainly take less time generally, but they are bulky and inconvenient to carry. This may be insignificant if the lifestyle is very busy and the carer does not want the inconvenience of washing and drying nappies
- hygiene: a row of freshly laundered, white nappies drying in the wind is a satisfying sight to a carer. However, biological washing powders and other detergents do cause nappy rashes if they are not rinsed out properly.

Both types of nappy are quite adequate if they are used with care. Whichever type is used babies should be changed 3–4 hourly, at each feeding time, and between if they are awake and uncomfortable. Avoid using nappy creams unless necessary. Clean the baby's bottom with water, baby soap, baby lotion, wet-wipes or baby oil. Make the experience fun, never show disapproval. Talk to the baby and let them enjoy some freedom without the restriction of a nappy.

Care of black skin

All babies may have dry skin, but it is especially common in black children and should be given special care. The following are general guidelines:

- always add oil to the bath water and do not use detergent-based products, as these are drying
- massage the baby after the bath, using baby oil, massage gel or almond oil. This is a wonderful experience for both parties!

- observe the baby frequently for signs of dryness and irritation – scaly patches need treating with a moisturising cream
- beware of sunshine: black skin is just as likely to burn as white skin; always use a sun block on a baby's skin in the sun, and a sun hat
- wash the hair once a week, but massage oil into the scalp daily, as the hair is prone to being brittle and dry
- comb the hair with a large-toothed comb
- avoid doing tight plaits in the hair as this can pull the hair root out and cause bald patches.

Signs and symptoms of illness

Because a young baby cannot say when he feels unwell, or where there is pain, it is very important to be able to recognise the signs of illness. Babies can become seriously ill very quickly, and the advice of a doctor should be obtained whenever there is any concern about a baby's state of health.

Babies usually recover very quickly too, and with the correct treatment can be transformed from misery to smiles in the space of 24–48 hours or less.

The signs to look out for are as follows:
- the baby looks pale and lacks energy (babies with black skin look paler than usual) or looks flushed and feels hot, due to a high temperature
- loss of appetite: a baby on milk alone may refuse feeds or take very little; an older baby may refuse solid foods and only want to suck from the breast or bottle
- vomiting persistently after feeds and in between: this should not be confused with normal *possetting* (regurgitation of milk) after feeds. Projectile vomiting in a baby of 4–8 weeks may be a sign of pyloric stenosis and the doctor should be consulted urgently
- diarrhoea: persistent runny, offensive stools which may be green, yellow or watery should be treated immediately; babies can dehydrate very quickly.
- sunken anterior fontanelle: this is a serious sign of dehydration, perhaps after a period of vomiting and/or diarrhoea or insufficient fluid intake due to loss of appetite.
- bulging anterior fontanelle: the 'soft spot' is visible as a pulsating bump on the top of the baby's head, and is caused by increased pressure inside the skull; this requires urgent medical treatment
- crying constantly and cannot be comforted: this may be together with any other sign(s) of illness; the cry may be different from any of the usual cries
- lethargy: the baby lacks energy and may seem to regress (go backwards) in development
- rash: if the baby develops a rash and has any other signs of illness, consult the doctor; a rash alone may be due to heat or allergy. It may be possible to treat this without medical intervention
- persistent cough: coughing is very distressing to a baby and carer; if it does not clear up in a few days, is associated with any other signs of illness or is worse at night, the doctor should be consulted

- discharge from the ears, or if the baby pulls at the ears and cries (especially if there are any other signs of illness): a doctor should be consulted. Ear infections are common in young children and should be treated promptly to avoid damage to the hearing. Further information on this topic is given in Chapter 16, *Caring for sick children*
- changes in the stools or urine: apart from changes due to diarrhoea (loose, frequent stools) and dehydration (scanty urine output) other changes may be observed. The stools may contain blood or pus or become bulky and offensive. Stools should be observed for colour, consistency and frequency, and any abnormality recorded and investigated – it may be due to a change in diet. Any concerns should be reported to the doctor, preferably with a sample.

Positive health for babies

Babies should be checked regularly by a professional carer to ensure that they are thriving and developing within the average range. This monitoring begins as soon as the baby is born, with the first examination by the midwife. A paediatrician will also examine the baby before she is discharged to go home. If the baby is born at home the community midwife and GP will be responsible for these checks. The baby will be seen daily for the first 10 days by the midwife, who is responsible for her care. The GP should also visit the home to see the baby. When the midwife discharges the mother and baby (usually on the tenth day if there are no problems) the health visitor will arrange to examine the baby. This 'birth visit' is usually at home. The health visitor will use her professional skills to decide how often the baby needs to be seen.

6-WEEK CHECK

All babies should have a full medical examination at about 6 weeks of age. This may be performed by the GP, community paediatrician or hospital paediatrician.

HEARING TEST

All babies are offered a hearing test between 6 and 9 months. This is usually performed by the health visitor in the child health clinic. A developmental assessment may be done at this time.

CHILD HEALTH CLINICS

Throughout the first year of life carers are encouraged to attend child health clinics with their baby. Here they can have the baby weighed, discuss progress with the health visitor and see the doctor if necessary. It is also an opportunity to meet other babies of a similar age and stage.

The immunisation programme (see page 174) is also commenced in the first year, at 2, 3 and 4 months. This is another opportunity for the baby to be observed and for a carer to report progress and any difficulties.

SUPPORT GROUPS AND SERVICES

There are often local support groups for parents and carers with young babies. Groups of mothers who have met at relaxation classes may keep in touch and have regular meetings as a form of mutual support. The National Childbirth Trust, the La Leche League and hospital-based post-natal support groups are other alternatives. Gingerbread is a national organisation to help to support single-parent families. There are probably others in your area.

There should be no need for anyone to sit at home worrying about a baby; there are lots of services and people who are very willing to help. However, there may be barriers, such as language, for example, which prevent people from using the services they are entitled to.

In areas where there is a high proportion of people who do not speak English as their first language there should be specialist help available, for example interpreters in clinics, leaflets printed in the relevant mother-tongue and additional supportive home visiting by specially trained health visitors.

Key terms	
You need to know what these words and phrases mean. Go back through the chapter and find out.	
Pram	Complementary feeds
Carrycot	Weaning
Moses basket	Food allergies
Sudden infant death syndrome	Cradle cap
Bouncing cradle	Eczema
Layette	Heat rash
Breast feeding	Nappy rash,
Alveoli	Pyloric stenosis
Colostrum	Sunken anterior fontanelle
Demand feeding	Lethargy

11 CHILD HEALTH SURVEILLANCE

> **This chapter includes:**
> - Principles of child health surveillance
> - The child health surveillance programme
> - Screening for hearing impairment
> - Screening for visual defects
> - The Guthrie test
> - Immunisation.

Introduction

Child health surveillance is a system of reviewing a child's progress. These reviews are carried out at certain ages in the child's life. Programmes with regular reviews at fixed ages safeguard children from slipping through the net, especially when families move home frequently and change doctors and health visitors. In many areas of the country the child health record is held by the main carer of the child in the form of a book. This book, the child health record, has spaces which can be filled in by the parent or main carer and any other people who care for the child. These may be:

- health visitors
- family doctors
- child health clinic staff
- hospital emergency department staff
- hospital outpatient staff
- school health team
- dentists.

In this way information can be shared and is easily available to all those caring for the child. Parents or carers have an ongoing record to which they can refer.

Principles of child health surveillance

There are certain principles which underpin the effective use of a child health surveillance programme. Child health surveillance should be:

- carried out in partnership with the parents or carers. They are the experts and the best people to identify health, developmental and behavioural problems in their own children

- a positive experience for parents or carers
- a learning experience for the parents or carers, the child and the health professional; it should involve exchanging information
- an opportunity to provide guidance on child health topics and health promotion
- a continuous and flexible process; as well as fixed assessments there should be opportunities for other reviews as required by each child
- carried out by observation and talking with the parents or carers; tests and examinations should complement the process
- based on good communication and teamwork.

THE PROFESSIONALS INVOLVED

Most child health surveillance is carried out in the child's own home or at the child health clinic. Clinics are held in health centres, GPs' premises or in other convenient places, like church halls. The professionals most concerned with child health surveillance are health visitors and doctors. Health visitors are trained nurses who have undertaken further training in midwifery and health visiting. The doctors have a special interest in child health and could be the child's GP. Each of these professionals is responsible for part of the child health surveillance programme; they work as a team with the parents or carers. The general practitioner and the health visitor are part of the primary health care team.

The primary health care team

The child health surveillance programme

Assessment of the developmental progress of the child is part of each review. A detailed account of development can be found in Book 1, Chapter 3.

BIRTH REVIEW

The birth review is normally carried out before discharge from hospital, or by the family doctor if the birth is at home. The birth review includes:

- measurements: weight and head circumference are recorded on a percentile chart (see Book 1, pages 6 and 87)
- Guthrie test, to exclude phenylketonuria. There is more information about the Guthrie test later in this chapter
- hip examination to detect any congenital dislocation or instability of the hip (see Book 1, page 247)
- general examination to exclude congenital conditions or acquired disease
- health promotion topics include: advice on feeding, safety, car transport.

10–14 DAYS REVIEW

The 10–14 days review is usually carried out by the health visitor at the child's home and includes:

- review, with the parent or carer, of progress and development since the birth
- general examination
- hip examination repeat
- measurements: head circumference and weight are recorded on the percentile chart
- health promotion topics include: feeding, immunisations, further health reviews, safety.

6-WEEK REVIEW

The 6-week review is usually carried out by the doctor at the child health clinic and includes:

- review, with carer, of progress and development from 2 weeks
- physical examination
- measurements: weight and head circumference are recorded on the percentile chart
- hip examination repeat
- health promotion topics include: feeding and safety.

3–4 MONTHS REVIEW

There is a another hip examination for any signs of disability or instability.

6–9 MONTHS REVIEW

The review at 6–9 months is usually carried out by the health visitor at home or at the clinic and includes:
- review, with parent or carer, of progress and development from 6 weeks
- measurements: weight and head circumference are recorded on the percentile chart
- hip examination
- hearing test, using a distraction test (described later in this chapter)
- observation of visual behaviour
- check for undescended testicles: in males the testes, which are in the body before birth, should come down into the scrotum (see the diagram in Book 1, page 12)
- health promotion topics include: safety, use of fireguards, stairgates, car seats, dangers of glass doors.

18–24 MONTHS REVIEW

The review at 18–24 months includes:
- review, with parent or carer, of development and progress from 9 months
- measurements: weight is recorded on the percentile chart
- language development is checked (language development is treated in Book 1, Chapter 8)
- vision test
- health promotion topics include: accident prevention, water safety, for example ponds, safe storage of medicines and other dangerous fluids, kitchen safety.

HEART CHECK

Between 1 and 3 years, all children should have a heart check by the doctor.

TESTICULAR EXAMINATION

Between 1 and 3 years all males should have their testes checked again to make sure both of them have come down into the scrotum.

3–3 YEARS 6 MONTHS REVIEW

The review at 3 years includes:
- review of progress and development with parent or carer, especially of language development
- measurements: height is recorded on the percentile chart
- health promotion topics include: road and car safety.

At this stage the doctor and health visitor will review the records with the parents or carers and discuss the need for further regular reviews.

SCHOOL ENTRY REVIEW

The school entry review is undertaken by the school nurse and doctor. The review involves:

- review, with parent or carer, of progress and development
- measurement of height and weight
- vision test
- hearing test
- health promotion topics: road safety, stranger danger
- immunisation booster (see *The immunisation programme*, page 174).

8 YEARS APPRAISAL

This appraisal is carried out by the school nurse and involves:

- review of progress and development
- measurement of height and weight
- vision test
- health promotion topics include: road safety, stranger danger, dental health, diet, exercise.

CHECK!

1 Who writes in the child health record?
2 Who are the best people to identify health and developmental problems?
3 How are reviews carried out?
4 Which professionals are most involved in child health surveillance?
5 What measurements are recorded in the first year?
6 Where are the measurements recorded?
7 What is the starting point of each review?
8 What does the hip examination detect?
9 What is the testicular examination for?
10 When should all children have a heart check?

THINK!

1 Think of all the benefits of child health surveillance.
2 Think of the benefits of a parent-held child health record.
3 What do you think 'slipping through the net' means in terms of child health surveillance? How might this happen? How might it be prevented?

DO!

1 Find out if parent-held child health records are in use in your area. Try to see one.
2 Look for a diagram of the hip joint (for example Book 1, page 247) and copy it into your notes. Find out more about congenital dislocation of the hip.
3 Find a diagram of the male reproductive organs (for example Book 1, page 12) and make sure you know where the testes are normally located.

4 Find out about the members of the primary health care team. Who are they and what are their roles?

5 Look back at the health promotion topics suggested at each review. Can you add to these? Make sure that your additions are appropriate to the age and stage of development.

6 If you can, try to arrange to go with a parent or carer and their child to a child health surveillance review.

Screening for hearing impairment

Parents or carers will often recognise that their child has a hearing loss. Child care workers should listen carefully to these concerns and refer the child for further investigation. There are special tests which are done as part of the child health surveillance programme, but tests can, and should, be done at any time if a hearing problem is suspected. There is more information about deafness in Book 1, page 251.

NEONATAL (NEWBORN) SCREENING

Parents or carers will know whether their child is responding to sounds. Responses to loud sounds at this age include:

- stiffening
- blinking
- the Moro reflex
- crying.

The baby may respond to quieter, prolonged sounds by becoming still and quiet. There are methods of testing the hearing of neonates, but these are not tests which are done routinely on every newborn baby. Tests include:

- auditory response cradle (ARC)
- otoacoustic emissions (OAE)
- brainstem evoked response audiometry (BSERA).

These are complex tests and are not routine. They are usually used if there is some reason to suspect a hearing problem.

DISTRACTION TEST: 6–9 MONTHS

The best age for screening hearing in the first year of life is at about 7 months old. All babies should have their hearing tested at this age. Developmentally the baby must be able to sit and have good head control. The distraction test needs two people as well as the carer: one to observe and one to test.

The baby sits on the carer's lap facing the observer. The observer holds the baby's attention with a soundless toy. When the observer has engaged the baby's attention, the toy is withdrawn and the tester makes the stimulus sound at ear level. The baby should turn, search for and find the source of the sound. This is called *localising*. Both ears must be tested with a range of quiet sounds, both high- and low-pitched.

The sounds are made very quietly   The baby locates the sound

A distraction hearing test

Stimulus sounds include:
- rattles: there are specialised rattles such as Manchester and Nuffield rattles
- voice: low-pitched sound such as *oo*, high-pitched sound such as *ss*, quiet conversation using the baby's name.

There are many reasons, for example illness or tiredness, why a baby might not respond to a hearing test. If the baby does not respond to all of the test it is repeated after 2 to 4 weeks. Further failure to respond needs referral for a full audiological assessment.

TESTS FOR OLDER CHILDREN: 2–5 YEARS

As children develop it becomes possible to use tests which need the child's co-operation. Examples of these are the Go game and the Speech Discrimination test

Go game
In the Go game test the child is asked to post a brick into a box when she hears the word 'Go'. An experienced tester can vary the pitch and sound level of the voice and each ear can be tested separately.

Speech discrimination test
This test is more difficult than the Go game and the child's co-operation and understanding are needed. The child is presented with a selection of toys, specially selected to test the child's ability to hear different consonants, for example p, g, d, hard c, s, m, f, b. After naming the toys in a normal voice with

the tester, the child is asked in a quiet voice to identify each of the toys, for example 'Show me the duck'; 'Give the brick to Mummy'. Again, each ear is tested though the range.

The speech discrimination test

Pure tone audiometry (from 5 years)
For pure tone audiometry the child puts on earphones and listens for the tone produced by the audiometer. The tones are given at different pitch and intensity. Each ear is tested separately. This is a lengthy and complicated test.

Audiometry: using an audiometer to measure hearing

Sweep audiometry

Sweep audiometry is a less complicated method of pure tone audiometry, where a range of selected frequencies is tested. This test is usually performed at school entry.

Screening for visual defects

In many instances visual defects are first detected by parents or carers. The child-care worker should be sure to listen carefully to any concerns expressed and refer the child for further investigation to the GP or health clinic. Some of the general signs that will indicate that a baby's vision is developing normally are given in the following check list:

- at birth the baby will look briefly at the mother's face
- at 1 month the baby will watch the carer's face intently while being fed and follow the carer's face as it moves from side to side
- at 3 months the baby will follow a dangling toy held in front of his face; he starts to look at his own fingers
- at 6 months the baby can see across a room and can see small objects like a smartie
- at 9 months the baby can recognise toys across a room and see small crumbs on the floor and try to pick them up.

If a child does not seem to be doing these things, it is important that further tests on vision are carried out.

ROUTINE CHECKS ON VISION

In addition to general observation of the child's progress there are routine checks on children's vision which are part of the child health surveillance programme:

- at birth and 6 weeks: the doctor will examine the eyes for any signs of abnormality, in particular any evidence of *cataract*, a condition where the lens of the eye is not transparent
- 6 weeks to 6 months: the doctor and health visitor will look for any sign of a *squint*, a condition where the eyes do not work together properly and the baby seems not to look straight at you. There are special tests used to identify a squint: the corneal reflection test and the cover test
- 2 to 5 years: by this age children are able to co-operate with vision testing. Distance vision can be assessed using single letters with a letter matching chart. The child looks at the letter being held up by the tester, then points to the matching letter on her chart. Older children will be able to name the letters. Each eye must be tested separately from a distance of 3 metres
- pre-school: routine screening of vision is usually carried out at school entry and at 3-yearly intervals
- colour vision defects: screening for colour vision impairment is usually recommended at the beginning of secondary school.

Vision testing for near and distance vision

The Guthrie test

The Guthrie test is a screening test to detect phenylketonuria (PKU), an inherited condition which affects the baby's ability to metabolise part of protein foods (see Book 1, page 253). Other conditions such as hypothyroidism (a condition in which the thyroid gland is not working properly) may also be detected. The test is carried out when the baby is about 6 days old and has been taking milk feeds for several days. Blood is collected from a heel prick to cover four circles on a specially prepared card which is then sent to the laboratory. Early treatment of PKU gives the child a good chance of developing normally.

Immunisation

Immunisation is the use of vaccine to protect people from disease. You will need to read Chapter 15, *Childhood illnesses and ailments* to find out more about how the body remembers and recognises infections so that people become immune to diseases.

Vaccines used in immunisations contain either small parts of the viruses or bacteria which cause the disease, or very small amounts of the chemicals (toxins) they produce. These have been treated to make sure that they do not cause the disease, but are still capable of stimulating the body to make antibodies. In this way the body will be able to defend itself against future infections. Vaccines provide most children with effective and long-lasting protection. Some immunisations need topping up and boosters may be needed as the child gets older.

Immunisation protects children from serious diseases. It also protects other children by preventing diseases being passed on.

THE IMMUNISATION PROGRAMME

Advice and guidance on immunisation is part of the programme of child health surveillance. Doctors and health visitors will advise parents or carers about immunisations and discuss any worries they may have about their child. More information about each of the diseases and their treatment is given in Chapter 15.

Age	Vaccine	Method
2 months	Hib	1 injection
	Diphtheria, whooping cough, tetanus	1 injection
	Polio	By mouth
3 months	Hib	1 injection
	Diphtheria, whooping cough, tetanus	1 injection
	Polio	By mouth
4 months	Hib	1 injection
	Diphtheria, whooping cough, tetanus	1 injection
	Polio	By mouth
12–15 months	Measles/mumps/rubella (MMR)	1 injection
3–5 years (school entry)	Diphtheria, tetanus	Booster injection
	Polio	Booster by mouth
Girls 10–14 years	Rubella	1 injection
Girls/boys 10–14 years	Tuberculosis	1 injection (BCG)
School leavers 15–19 years	Tetanus	1 injection
	Polio	Booster by mouth

The immunisation programme

SIDE EFFECTS AFTER IMMUNISATION

After immunisation some children may be unwell, have a fever or be irritable for a while. Sometimes the skin becomes red and swollen around the place where the injection was given, or a small lump appears. If the child does develop a fever after being immunised, keep them cool and give plenty to drink. The doctor or health visitor may advise a dose of paracetamol syrup but always check first to make sure the right dose is given. Any red or swollen area around the injection site should gradually disappear. If there are any other worrying symptoms such as a high temperature or a convulsion, consult the doctor immediately.

Side effects of the DTP triple immunisation
Side effects after having the DTP (diphtheria, tetanus, pertussis – whooping cough) immunisation are mild. The baby may become miserable, fretful and slightly feverish in the 24 hours after the injection. Some children may have a convulsion (fit) after the DTP immunisation. It is the whooping cough part of

the triple vaccine that often worries parents and carers. There have been questions about the safety of the vaccine and the possibility of brain damage. New research has not found a link between the vaccine and permanent brain damage.

Side effects of the Hib (haemophilus influenzae type B) immunisation
About one baby in ten will have some redness or swelling at the site of the injection. The swelling goes down very quickly and has usually disappeared after a day or so.

Side effects of the measles mumps and rubella (MMR) immunisation
Some children develop a mild fever and a rash about seven to ten days after the immunisation. This usually lasts for a day or two. A few children get a mild form of mumps about three weeks after their immunisation. These are all mild symptoms and are not infectious to other children or pregnant women. A few children may have more serious reactions such as a convulsion or encephalitis (inflammation of the brain) but this is very rare.

Side effects of the polio immunisation
The polio vaccine is a live virus given by mouth. The virus is passed through the digestive tract and into the stools. It is very important for care workers to wash their hands carefully after changing nappies to avoid becoming infected. Childcare workers need to check that their own polio immunisation is up to date.

Immunisation protects children from serious diseases. It also protects other children by preventing diseases being passed on.

CHECK!

1 What is the best age to test a child's hearing using the distraction test?
2 Name two other tests used to assess hearing.
3 What might lead you to suspect that a baby of 6 weeks was not able to see?
4 What is the test for PKU called?
5 Give two reasons why it is important for children to be immunised.
6 Describe the most common mild reactions to an immunisation.
7 Describe the more serious side effects.
8 Which vaccine is given by mouth?
9 If a baby has had the polio vaccine, what special precautions should the carer take?
10 What is contained in the triple vaccine?

DO!

1 Devise a check list showing some of the signs to look for, in the first year, that will indicate that a baby's hearing is normal.
2 Write a page outlining what you would say to a parent or carer who was unsure about the value of immunisations.

Key terms

You need to know what these words and phrases mean. Go back through the chapter and find out.

Child health surveillance

Health visitor

Primary health care team

Undescended testicles

Distraction test

Localising sound

Audiometry

Guthrie test

12 FOOD AND NUTRITION

Introduction

Good nutrition is essential for general good health and well being. We need food for four main reasons:
- to provide energy and warmth
- to enable growth, repair and replacement of tissues
- to help fight disease
- to maintain the proper functioning of body systems.

The food we eat each day makes up our diet and contains the nutrients we need. Before these nutrients can be used the food must be digested by the body. Digestion is the process which breaks down food into smaller components which the body can absorb and use.

Inadequate dietary intake is still the most common cause of failure to thrive. Good eating habits begin at an early age and child-care workers need to ensure that children establish healthy eating patterns which will promote normal growth and development.

The nutrients in food and drink

To be healthy the body needs a combination of different nutrients. These nutrients are:
- protein
- fat
- carbohydrate
- vitamins
- minerals
- water.

Protein, fat, carbohydrates and water are present in the foods we eat and drink in large quantities. Vitamins and minerals are only present in small quantities, so it is much more common for those to be lacking in a child's diet.

PROTEIN

Protein foods are essential for:
- growth of the body
- repair of the body.

Protein foods are divided into *first-class* and *second-class* proteins. Sources of first-class protein include:
- meat
- fish
- chicken
- cheese
- milk and milk products.

Sources of second-class proteins include:
- nuts and seeds
- pulses (for example black beans, chick peas, lentils, soya beans, kidney beans)
- cereals (rice, cornmeal, oats) and cereal based foods such as bread, pasta, chapattis, noodles).

Protein foods are made up of *amino* acids. There are ten essential amino acids. First-class protein foods contain all of them, second-class protein foods contain some.

Some sources of protein

CARBOHYDRATES

Carbohydrate foods are divided into *starches* and *sugars*, which provide energy for the body. Sources of starch include:
- cereals
- beans
- lentils
- potatoes
- plantain
- pasta
- yams.

Sources of sugar include:

- sugar from cane or beet
- fruit
- honey
- milk.

Carbohydrates are broken down into glucose before the body can use them. Sugars are quickly converted and give a quick source of energy, starches take longer to convert to glucose so they provide a steadier longer lasting supply of energy. That is why marathon runners eat large quantities of pasta the night before they race.

Some sources of carbohydrate

FATS

Fats provide energy for the body and contain essential vitamins. They also make food more pleasant to eat and aid its passage through the digestive tract. Fats are divided into *saturated* fats and *unsaturated* fats. Sources of saturated fat include:

- butter
- cheese
- milk
- lard
- meat
- palm oil.

Sources of unsaturated fat include:

- fish oil
- olive oil
- sunflower oil
- corn oil
- peanut oil.

Saturated fats are solid at room temperature and come mainly from animal fats. Unsaturated fats are liquid at room temperature and come mainly from vegetable and fish oils.

Some sources of fat

VITAMINS AND MINERALS

Vitamins and minerals are only present in small quantities in the foods we eat, but they are essential for growth, development and normal functioning of the body.

The following chart shows the main vitamins and minerals, which foods contain them and their main function in the body.

Vitamin/mineral	Food source	Function	Notes
A	Butter, cheese, eggs, carrots, tomatoes	Promotes healthy skin, good vision	Fat soluble, can be stored in the liver; deficiency causes skin infections, problems with vision
B group	Liver, meat, fish, green vegetables, beans, eggs	Healthy working of muscles and nerves; forming haemoglobin	Water soluble, not stored in the body, so regular supply needed; deficiency results in muscle wasting, anaemia
C	Fruits and fruit juices, especially orange, blackcurrant, pineapple; green vegetables	For healthy tissue, promotes healing	Water soluble, daily supply needed; deficiency means less resistance to infection; extreme deficiency results in scurvy
D	Oily fish, cod liver oil, egg yolk; added to margarine, milk	Growth and maintenance of bones and teeth	Fat soluble, can be stored by the body; can be produced by the body as a result of sunlight on the skin; deficiency results in bones failing to harden and dental decay

(continued on facing page)

Vitamin/mineral	Food source	Function	Notes
E	Vegetable oils, cereals, egg yolk	Protects cells from damage	Fat soluble, can be stored by the body
K	Green vegetables, liver	Needed for normal blood clotting	Fat soluble, can be stored in the body
Calcium	Cheese, eggs, fish, milk yoghurt	Essential for growth of bones and teeth	Works with vitamin D and phosphorus; deficiency means risk of bones failing to harden (rickets) and dental caries
Fluoride	Occurs naturally in water, or may be added artificially to water supply	Combines with calcium to make tooth enamel more resistant to decay	There are different points of view about adding fluoride to the water supply
Iodine	Water, sea foods, added to salt, vegetables	Needed for proper working of the thyroid gland	Deficiency results in enlarged thyroid gland in adults, cretinism in babies.
Iron	Meat, green vegetables, eggs, liver, red meat	Needed for formation of haemoglobin in red blood cells	Deficiency means there is anaemia causing lack of energy, breathlessness; vitamin C helps the absorption of iron
Sodium chloride	Table salt, bread, meat, fish	Needed for formation of cell fluids, blood plasma, sweat, tears	Salt should not be added to any food prepared for babies: their kidneys cannot eliminate excess salt as adult kidneys do; excess salt is harmful in an infant diet

Other essential trace minerals include:
- potassium
- phosphorus
- magnesium
- sulphur
- manganese
- zinc.

A well balanced diet which includes a variety of foods will provide all the vitamins and minerals required for the efficient functioning of the body. It is only when diet becomes restricted in illness or because of food shortages or poor choice of foods that shortages of essential vitamins and minerals will occur.

FIBRE

Fibre in the form of cellulose is found in the fibrous part of plants. It provides the body with bulk or roughage. Fibre has no nutritional value, as it cannot be broken down and used by the body; it is, however, an important part of a healthy diet. Fibre adds bulk to food and stimulates the muscles of the intestine, encouraging the body to eliminate the waste products left after digestion of food.

WATER

Water is a vital component of diet. It contains some minerals, but its role in maintaining a healthy fluid balance in the cells and blood stream is crucial to survival.

A balanced diet

A balanced diet means that the intake of food provides the nutrients that the body needs in the right quantities. There are many nutrients that the body is able to store (fat-soluble vitamins are an example of this) so nutrients can be taken over several days to form the right balance.

A diet which includes a selection of foods is likely to be nutritious. Different combinations of vitamins are found in different foods, so a varied selection of foods will ensure an adequate supply of all the vitamins needed. Offering a variety of foods gives children an opportunity to choose foods they like. It also encourages them to explore other tastes and to try new foods and recipes.

PROPORTIONS OF NUTRIENTS

Children are growing all the time, so they need large amounts of protein to help the formation of bone and muscle. They are also using a lot of energy, so they need carbohydrate in the form of starches which they can use during the day to sustain their activities. In addition they will need adequate supplies of vitamins and minerals.

Suggested daily intakes are as follows:
- 2 portions of meat or other protein foods such as nuts and pulses
- 2 portions of protein from dairy products (for vegans substitute 2 other protein foods from plant sources)
- 4 portions of cereal foods
- 5 portions of fruit and vegetables
- 6 glasses of fluid, especially water.

Although children are small in size they need a considerable amount of food. The chart below shows the number of calories recommended for children and adults. The energy value of food is measured in calories: a medium egg, for example, is about 75 calories. Comparing the requirements of children and adults gives some idea of portion size. A child of 2 to 3 needs roughly half the amount of food, in terms of calories, of an adult.

Age range	Energy requirements in calories
0 to 1 year	800
1 to 2 years	1200
2 to 3 years	1400
3 to 5 years	1600
5 to 7 years	1800
7 to 9 years	2100
Women	2200–2500
Men	2600 3600

The required number of calories for children and adults

Once children are weaned they can eat the same food as adults. More information about early infant feeding and weaning can be found in Chapter 10.

CHECK!

1 Name two sources of first-class protein
2 Name two sources of second-class protein.
3 Why are starches a more valuable source of carbohydrate than sugars?
4 What are the essential differences between saturated and unsaturated fat?
5 What is the advantage of a vitamin being fat-soluble?
6 What is the function of:
   a) Vitamin C
   b) Vitamin D
   c) Vitamin K
   d) Iron
   e) Calcium?
7 Which vitamin helps the absorption of iron?
8 Why is excess salt harmful in an infant diet?
9 What is the essential function of water?
10 What is the best way to provide a balanced diet?

Diets of different groups

Each region or country has developed its own local diet over many years. Diets have evolved based on available foods, which in turn depends on climate, geography, agricultural patterns, as well as social factors such as religion, culture, class and lifestyle. Each diet contains a balance of essential nutrients.

When people migrate, they take their diet with them and generally wish to recreate it as a familiar feature of their way of life. The psychological importance of familiar food should never be overlooked.

RELIGIOUS ASPECTS OF FOOD

For some people food has a spiritual significance. Certain foods nay be prohibited and these prohibitions form a part of their daily lives. Respecting an individual's cultural and religious choices is part of respecting that individual as a whole. It is important for child-care workers to talk to parents and carers about food requirements, especially when caring for a child from a cultural or religious background different from their own.

Religious restrictions may affect the diets of Hindus, Sikhs, Muslims, Jews, Rastafarians and Seventh Day Adventists. Members of other groups may also have dietary restrictions. People are individuals and will vary in what they eat and what restrictions they observe; you should be aware of this when discussing diet with parents or carers. These are some of the restrictions which *may* be observed by different groups.

- Many devout Hindus are vegetarian. The cow is sacred to Hindus and eating beef is strictly forbidden. Alcohol is also forbidden.
- Sikhism began as an offshoot of Hinduism. Some Sikhs have similar dietary restrictions to Hindus. Few Sikhs eat beef and drinking alcohol is not approved.
- Muslim dietary restrictions are laid down by the Holy Quran and are regarded as the direct command of God. Muslims may not eat pork or pork products and alcohol is strictly prohibited. Other meat may be eaten provided it is *halal* (permitted). Healthy adult Muslims fast during the month of Ramadan.
- Jews may not eat pork or pork products, shellfish, and any fish without fins or scales. All meat eaten must have been killed in a special way so as to be *kosher* (fit). Milk and meat may not be used together in cooking.
- Most Rastafarians are vegetarian, but some may eat meat, except pork. No products of the vine, such as wine, grapes, currants, raisins are eaten. Some Rastafarians will only eat food cooked in vegetable oil. Whole foods are preferred.
- Seventh Day Adventists do not eat any pork or pork products.

OTHER DIETARY RESTRICTIONS

- Vegetarians do not eat meat and restrict their intake of other animal products in different ways.
- Vegans do not eat any animal products at all. A vegan diet needs careful balancing if it is followed by children, to ensure that they get the right nutrients to sustain normal growth.

It is not possible to make blanket statements about the diets of different groups, only to suggest possibilities and factors which may be important and which child-care workers may find useful when discussing food and diets with carers.

It is also very important to take account of these points when preparing activities involving food. If you are setting up a baking activity, for example, it would be best to make sure that you use vegetable fats, as these are generally more acceptable. Many more people today are moving towards a vegetarian diet or a diet which restricts the intake of animal products.

Problems with food

Food allergy and food intolerance have received a lot of publicity. Only a small number of reactions to food are true allergic responses, involving the immune responses of the body.

FOOD INTOLERANCE

Food intolerance is a condition in which there are specific adverse effects after eating a specific food. This may be caused by an allergic response or an enzyme deficiency. The removal of foods from a child's diet must be carried out with medical supervision. If the suspected food source is a major source of nutrients, for example milk, then alternatives must be included to make good any deficiency. Conditions such as PKU and coeliac disease require very specialised diets. There is more information about these conditions in Book 1, Chapter 17.

FOOD REFUSAL

Toddler food refusal is common. If the child is of normal body weight and height, is thriving and no medical condition is identified by the doctor, then carers should be reassured. It is important that mealtimes should not become a battle ground. The child should be offered food at mealtimes and allowed to eat according to appetite. Any remaining food should be removed without fuss. The next meal is offered at the usual time and no snacks or 'junk food' given between meals. It is important that the child participates in family meals rather than eating in isolation. Allow the child to feed himself and don't fuss about any mess if he is just learning to do this. The child should see eating as a pleasurable and sociable experience and be encouraged to enjoy mealtimes with the family or in other groups.

FOOD ADDITIVES

Food additives are added to food with the following aim of:
- preserving it for longer
- preventing contamination
- aiding processing
- enhancing colour and flavour
- replacing nutrients lost in processing.

Care should be taken with children's diet because:
- they often eat more foods with additives, for example drinks and sweets
- they are smaller and the amount they take is, therefore, greater in proportion to their size.

Eating should be a sociable experience, with the family or other groups

To reduce additives in the diet:

- use fresh foods as often as you can
- make your own pies, cakes, soups, etc.
- avoid highly processed foods
- look at the labels: the ingredients are listed in order of quantity, with the largest amount first.

E numbers

Permitted food additives are given a number, known as an E number, which label colourings, preservatives and processing aids.

FOOD ADDITIVES AND BEHAVIOUR

Some children may have erratic behaviour after taking, for example, orange squash or coloured sweets, and behaviour improves when the colourings are removed: avoiding the colourings may help. Avoiding additives need not affect the nutritional value of the diet, but any regime which leads to a nutritionally inadequate diet should not be followed. Hyperactivity can only be diagnosed by a paediatrician. Dietary manipulation, for example elimination diets, must be prescribed by a paediatrician and supervised by a dietician. Behaviour and hyperactivity problems are, however, rarely caused solely by food additives. Behaviour was discussed in detail in Chapter 7.

FOOD AND POVERTY

Research has shown that food is one of the first things people cut back on when they are short of money. This can have a serious effect on the nutritional quality of the diet of families managing on a low income.

There may be other problems which contribute to this: cooking facilities may be limited, or impossible if, for example, the family live in bed and breakfast accommodation and much of the food eaten has to be brought in ready cooked. Fuel costs for cooking will also be an important consideration if money is tight. Shopping around for food to get the best bargain or selection may not be possible if bus fares are needed or food has to be carried a long way.

In these circumstances knowing about food and the nutrients which are essential to provide an adequate diet is very important. Help needs to be concentrated on achieving an adequate diet within the budget and ability of the family. Knowing which cheaper foods contain the essential nutrients will enable sensible advice to be offered.

Food safety

Food is essential to good health and survival, but it has to be looked after to avoid contamination with harmful bacteria which could cause food poisoning. Since January 1991 there have been stricter laws about storage and handling of food in shops and restaurants. These laws help to keep food safer and cleaner. Once food has been bought it must be stored safely and prepared hygienically in order to prevent food poisoning.

BUYING FOOD

Check the 'use by' dates. Take chilled and frozen food straight home and use an insulated bag. Make sure you buy from a shop where cooked and raw foods are kept and handled separately.

STORAGE AT HOME

Put chilled and frozen foods into the fridge or freezer as quickly as possible. The coldest part of the fridge must be between 0 ° and 5 °C, and the freezer temperature below 18 °C: use a fridge thermometer to check the temperature. Keep raw meat and fish in separate containers in the fridge and store them carefully on the bottom shelf so that they do not touch or drip onto other food.

IN THE KITCHEN

Always wash your hands well before touching food. Cover any cuts with a waterproof dressing. Wear an apron and tie hair back when preparing food. Avoid touching your nose and mouth, or coughing and sneezing in the food preparation area. Kitchen cloths and sponges should be disinfected and renewed frequently. Disinfect all work surfaces regularly and especially before preparing food.

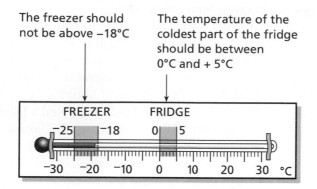

The freezer should not be above −18°C

The temperature of the coldest part of the fridge should be between 0°C and + 5°C

Temperatures for home storage in the fridge or freezer

COOKING

The following guidelines should always be followed when preparing and cooking food:

- defrost food thoroughly before cooking; make sure all food is thoroughly cooked: chicken and meat need special care, and must be cooked through to the centre
- prepare raw meat separately; use a separate board and knife
- cooked food should be cooled quickly and then refrigerated or frozen
- cover any food standing in the kitchen
- eggs should be thoroughly cooked before eating; for babies and small children, cook the eggs until the white and yolk are solid
- cooked food should only be reheated once; reheat until piping hot all the way through
- reheat cooked chilled meals properly
- pregnant women and any one with a low resistance to infection should not eat pate, nor soft cheeses of the Brie or Camembert type.

Children are particularly vulnerable to infection, so it is important to make sure that food is prepared and handled safely. It is also vital that children learn the basic rules about handling food. Always make sure that they wash their hands before eating. If children prepare food as part of a learning activity, the food safety rules should always be followed. Children need to understand why this is important, so that they develop important life skills.

CHECK!

1 What is the best way to reduce additives in a child's diet?
2 What do E numbers label?
3 If you buy chilled or frozen food, what is the best way to transport it?

4 What temperature should the coldest part of the fridge be?

5 Where should you store raw meat and fish?

THINK!

1 Think about all the things you would you be looking for in shops, to ensure that the food you are going to buy is hygienically prepared and handled.

DO!

1 Devise an activity that will involve a group of 5- to 6-year-olds preparing and serving food.

Your plan should:
- be appropriate to the children's level of development
- be consistent with maintaining health and safety
- encourage respect for dietary and cultural differences.

2 Here is part of a label from a tin of baked beans.

Values	Amount/100g
Energy	75 k cal
Protein	4.7 g
Carbohydrate	13.6 g
Fat	0.2 g
Fibre	3.7 g
Sodium	0.5 g

What information does this give you about the nutritional value of the food?

3 Link each food in the chart below with the vitamins and minerals it contains.

Vitamin/mineral	Food
B group	Egg
A	Vegetable oil
C	Carrot
D	Liver
Calcium	Cabbage
Iron	Cheese
E	Pineapple
K	Green vegetables
Fluoride	Milk
Sodium chloride	Water

Store raw meat and fish on the bottom shelf of the fridge

Key terms

You need to know what these words and phrases mean. Go back through the chapter and find out.

Digestion	Amino acid
Unsaturated fat	E number
Nutrient	Unsaturated fat
Fat-soluble vitamin	Calorie
First-class protein	Saturated fat
Second-class protein	Food additive

13 PHYSICAL CARE

This chapter includes:
- **Promoting physical development**
- **Exercise**
- **Rest and sleep**
- **Toilet training**
- **Hygiene: care of the hair, skin and teeth**
- **Clothing and footwear.**

Promoting physical development

The physical development of children from birth to 7 years is discussed in detail in Book 1, Chapter 3.

Babies and young children need a safe yet stimulating environment if they are to grow and develop to their full potential. They need space and encouragement to develop a new skill, and the opportunity to practise and perfect their technique.

A positive atmosphere in which adults praise children's efforts and recognise their achievements will encourage trust and progress. This is why all child-care workers need a thorough knowledge of child development. With this information they can provide the correct environment for the child to progress at their own individual pace.

AGE 1–4

The toddler stage

Many babies are mobile by the time they reach their first birthday. This new found freedom of movement is exciting and should be encouraged, but there is always an element of risk. Babies have no concept of danger and need a watchful adult to ensure their safety. They will fall often, until they can anticipate dangers and avoid obstacles in their path. Their great need to explore and investigate the world should not be prevented, but encouraged in an environment that is safe. They have a desire to find out about everything around them, and an adult who can see the world from the child's point of view will enable this discovery. A safe environment to investigate could be containers with safe, but interesting, contents and not random emptying of drawers. A 'safe' cupboard full of exciting things that may be changed frequently will add to the thrill of discovery and learning.

As the child gets older and their gross motor development progresses, they can run easily, sometimes falling, but less often now. Climbing stairs, jumping, riding a tricycle, gradually beginning to use the pedals are among their achievements.

To stimulate development carers need to provide:

- space
- opportunity
- freedom to learn from experience
- reassurance
- praise
- access to some equipment.

AGE 4–7

The skills learned in the first two years will be perfected as childhood progresses. The hesitant and wobbly runner at 18 months will become the sprinter from 4–7 years. The toddler climbing forwards into a chair will eventually perform increasingly hair-raising stunts on climbing apparatus. Skills are being advanced daily and the need to be given the opportunity to practise continues, for example from riding a tricycle, propelling it with the feet, to riding a bicycle without stabilisers, manoeuvring it around obstacles and using the brakes effectively and safely.

. . . from propelling 3-wheelers with the feet . . .

. . . to controlling a bicycle without stabilisers

When the child has perfected the basic skills of walking, running, climbing their future physical development will depend on the opportunities that are made available to them. Ice-skating, gymnastics, judo, horse-riding, ballet-dancing are some of the activities children may enjoy if they are available to them.

Some physical activities may have an element of cost and it may be expensive to provide lessons, but an increasing number of children do participate in them. Some charitable organisations provide funding for children who are skilled in sport, but whose families cannot afford the cost involved in training.

These activities are not a necessary factor in healthy physical development and available opportunities will depend partly on where the child lives and partly on the financial circumstances of their family. For example, a child living in a snowy country may ski, or a child brought up on a farm may ride a horse. The present interests and hobbies of parents or carers may also have an influence on the type of activity offered to a child.

More commonplace activities are swimming, riding a bicycle, football, but they will all require practice. This will increase confidence, which in turn will encourage progression. As children get better at a particular skill their self-esteem will increase. An interested adult who encourages them to repeat a skill, without forcefulness or disappointment if they do not succeed immediately, will help this process.

Not all children enjoy physical activity or exertion. As they get older and develop other interests, like reading, they may prefer not to take part in outdoor pursuits. Gentle encouragement should be used, but without putting undue pressure on the child to participate. Seeing other children's fun and enjoyment will be more of an incentive than a nagging adult.

Physical development at nursery and infant school

At nursery and infant school the curriculum includes the opportunity for physical pursuits of a wide variety. At nursery outdoor play with tricycles, prams, trolleys, large building blocks, dens, tyres and climbing frames may create an environment for imaginative physical activity. Using music to encourage movement by using the body to interpret the sounds may motivate activity. Group activities may encourage children who lack confidence in themselves.

At infant school opportunities for exercise should include:

- PE, apparatus, dance, music and movement
- football, rounders, throwing and catching, team games, group activities, swimming.

Rainbows, Beavers and other clubs for children will provide the opportunity for physical pursuits. Non-stereotypical activities should be encouraged, such as girls playing football, boys using skipping ropes.

CHILDREN WITH DISABILITIES

When caring for disabled children it is vital to remember that every child is a unique individual with specific needs, which will depend on their own abilities and capacity for independence.

Disabled children may not achieve the level of physical competence expected for their age group, so emphasis must be on an individual programme of stimulation which will enable the child to progress at their own pace within the usual sequence of development. They may spend longer at each stage before progressing to the next. Their present developmental achievements must be compared with their past achievements, so that progress can be assessed and improvement recognised.

Remember that disabled children are children first. Their special/individual needs must be viewed positively as additional needs to those shared with 'average' children. Each achievement should be encouraged and praised so that they develop a high self-esteem. Make the child believe that they are important and are not being compared with other more able children, peers or siblings. Children with disabilities may become frustrated if they cannot achieve a skill quickly, and will require additional, sometimes specialist, help. Adapting the environment to suit their individual needs will help their progress.

PROVIDING A SAFE ENVIRONMENT

Children are the responsibility of the adults who are caring for them. This is often the parents but it may be a nanny, a child minder or playgroup or nursery staff. In the absence of the primary carer the child is their responsibility. It is of prime importance to keep the child safe and in doing so, prevent accidents. (The topic of safety is covered more fully in Chapter 14.)

An accident is something that happens that is not anticipated or foreseen. This definition is certainly misleading, as it gives the impression that accidents are not preventable, but most accidents that occur to children could be prevented with care and thought.

FRESH AIR

All children need regular exposure to fresh air and preferably an opportunity to play outside. If conditions are not suitable for outdoor play – if it is foggy or raining heavily – the play area should be well ventilated to provide fresh air and to prevent a build up of carbon dioxide.

The benefits of fresh air are:

- it contains oxygen (released by plants); breathing in oxygen gives energy and stimulates exercise
- it contains fewer germs than air indoors; germs are killed by the ultra-violet rays in sunshine
- exposure to sunlight causes the skin to produce vitamin D.

Exercise

Exercise is a necessary and natural part of life for everyone. It is especially important for young children who need to develop and perfect physical skills.

All physical exercise strengthens muscles, from a young baby kicking on the floor to a 7-year-old playing football. Encouraging exercise from an early age will lay the foundations for a life-long healthy exercise habit.

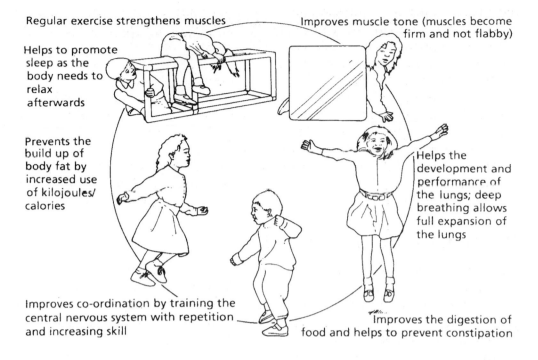

Regular exercise strengthens muscles

Improves muscle tone (muscles become firm and not flabby)

Helps to promote sleep as the body needs to relax afterwards

Prevents the build up of body fat by increased use of kilojoules/calories

Helps the development and performance of the lungs; deep breathing allows full expansion of the lungs

Improves co-ordination by training the central nervous system with repetition and increasing skill

Improves the digestion of food and helps to prevent constipation

The benefits of exercise

It is generally believed that many children do not get enough exercise and will be at increased risk of heart disease and/or other health problems later in life.

Rest and sleep

Rest is necessary after physical exercise, and children will know when to stop their vigorous activity as they begin to feel tired.

The benefits of rest are:
- to allow tissues to recover
- the heart rate will fall
- to allow oxygen to be replaced
- for body temperature to drop
- to allow the CNS to relax
- to take in food if required
- to prevent muscles from aching and becoming stiff after heavy exercise.

Children should exercise regularly to promote their strength, suppleness and stamina, but they must be allowed to rest – this may be relaxation, sleep or just a change of occupation. One of the values of relaxing or of quiet areas in nursery and school is in providing children with the opportunity to rest and recharge their batteries. A book corner, story time, a home corner, soft cushions, relaxing activities can be provided at nursery and at home. Children need not be challenged all the time; it is useful for them to be given toys or activities that are relatively easy and do not require deep concentration to complete.

SLEEP

Everyone needs sleep

Everyone needs sleep but everyone has different requirements. The sleep needs of children will depend on their age and stage of development, the amount of exercise taken and also their own personal needs.

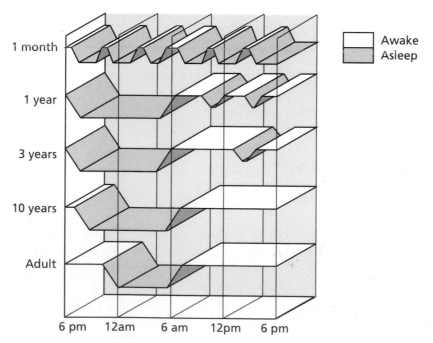

Graph of sleep needs

Sleep is a special kind of rest which allows the body to rest and recuperate physically and mentally. There are two kinds of sleep:

- deep relaxing sleep (DRS)
- rapid eye movement sleep (REM) or dream sleep.

It is generally believed that babies do not dream, but they do have periods of REM, probably when their brains are making sense of all the external stimuli received during the day. Periods of DRS and REM alternate during the sleep period. It is important that periods of REM are completed to awake refreshed. Children who are woken during this period of sleep may be drowsy, disorientated or confused.

Sleep routines

Babies and children need varying amounts of sleep. Some babies may seem to sleep and feed for the first few months, while others sleep very little. Toddlers vary too. Some need a nap morning and afternoon, others need one of these or neither.

Some children wake often at night even after settling late. There is little that can be done apart from following a sensible routine. This will involve

- patience
- not stimulating the child, remaining quiet, calm, not encouraging interaction
- remaining upstairs (do not take the child to where there is any activity)
- encouraging daily exercise
- trying to reduce stress or worries
- being prepared to use the carer's bed may resolve waking in the night.

Bedtime routine

When children need to be at nursery or infant school by 8.45–9 in the morning their bedtime must be early enough to allow for sufficient sleep. Children who share bedrooms or who live in bed and breakfast accommodation may have more distractions and difficulties sleeping, and these may be difficult to overcome.

Social and cultural expectations of children may include letting them stay up later at night. As long as the child is given the opportunity for an adequate amount of sleep it should not create a difficulty.

For successful settling to bed at night it is important to have a regular routine. The same process each night helps the child to feel secure and comfortable and so aids sleep. Children need a period of relaxation before going to sleep, and should never be threatened with bed as a form of punishment. This can result in difficulties at bedtime. A suggested routine is as follows:

- a family meal at 5–6 p.m., about 2 hours before bedtime: this is a chance to talk about the day's events. Babies and toddlers enjoy this social occasion too
- playtime: with siblings and carers, this is time for individual attention
- bathtime: fun, play, relaxation, learning hygiene routines; talking about worries, experiences; this should be one-to-one if possible
- drink if required

■ story time: preferably in bed, after saying goodnight to other family members and cleaning the teeth; storytime should be an opportunity for a cuddle, and to snuggle up in bed preparing to sleep

Story time should be an opportunity for a cuddle, and to snuggle up in bed preparing to sleep

■ sleep, in a comfortable, warm bed with the light out or night light on if the child requests it.

Avoid loud noises coming from conversations or the TV which might distract from sleep. This is not always possible and will depend on the housing situation.

Using a familiar routine and reassurance that carers are nearby may encourage children who are unwilling to go to bed to settle more willingly.

CHECK!

1 How can children be encouraged to progress in physical skills?
2 What facilities for physical play should be available in a nursery?
3 How can disabled children be encouraged in physical development?
4 What are the benefits of fresh air?
5 Why is exercise important?
6 What are the two types of sleep called?
7 How can children be encouraged to have a sensible sleep routine?

THINK!

1 Think about why children may or do not get enough exercise.
2 Think about what sort of exercise is required to maintain good health.

1 Write a report describing how you think that children can be encouraged to take more exercise.
2 Research playground games: ask older friends and relatives what sort of games they played at school. What sort of physical exercise did children have:
   a) 20
   b) 30
   c) 40
   d) 50
   e) 60 years ago?
   Ask people you know. Elderly relatives usually love to talk about their child-hood antics!
   Compare these activities with evidence a) from your own experience, and b) from observing children that you know.
3 Research and investigate exercise programmes at your local or placement nursery or infant school. Do you think that they are adequate?

Toilet training

There are many different theories of when and how to train babies and children in the use of potty and toilet. Some people report that their children were 'trained' before the first birthday. These are the exception and not the rule! There are wide variations in this area of development, as in all others.

A child will only become reliably clean and dry by the age of 2 to 3 years, at whatever age the potty is introduced. There does not seem to be any point in rushing this skill. It is much more easily achieved if it is left until the child is 2 years at least, unless they show an interest earlier.

GENERAL GUIDELINES

- The child must be aware of the need to use the toilet or potty. The CNS must be sufficiently developed for the message that the bowel or bladder is full to be understood by the brain. (See Book 1, page 77). Babies of 12–18 months may know when they are soiled or wet, but are not yet able to anticipate it.
- They must have sufficient language to tell their carer, verbally or with actions, that they need to go.
- Too much pressure at an early age can put the child off the idea completely and create a 'battleground'.
- Wait until the child is ready.
- Make training fun! Carers should be relaxed and not show displeasure or disapproval about accidents which will certainly happen. The child may be more upset than the adult and deserves understanding.
- Provide good role models. Seeing other children or adults use the toilet will help the child to understand the process.

- In theory bowel control comes first: the child may recognise the sensation of a full bowel before that of a full bladder. However, most carers report that children are dry earlier than they are clean. This may be because children urinate more often than they have their bowels open, so have more practice.
- Have a potty lying around for a long time before it is used, then it will become familiar and children can sit on it as part of their play.
- Watch for signs of a bowel movement and offer the potty, but do not force it. If it is successful then congratulate the child and show them how pleased you are.
- Training is easier in warm weather when children can run around without nappies or pants. They can become aware of what is happening when they urinate or have their bowels open.

BEDWETTING (ENURESIS)

Enuresis is often a hereditary tendency and is particularly common in boys. If it begins after a long dry period it may be due to an infection of the urinary tract or to a stressful event, for example a new baby, moving house or school or the death of a relative or friend. Regression in this area may also be caused by illness.

Children usually become dry at night of their own accord. Accidents are common and should be treated with understanding and not displeasure. There is no need for concern about occasional accidents unless the child is upset. Seeing a sympathetic doctor or health visitor should help.

SOILING (ENCOPRESIS)

Soiling may be caused by an objection to using the potty or toilet that grows to an aversion, and the child withholds the motion until they can relieve themselves elsewhere. Soiling may be due to an emotional disturbance, or it may cause one. Children with this difficulty need very sensitive treatment. It can be resolved, often with the help of the health visitor and/or GP.

CHECK!

1 At approximately what age are children reliably clean and dry during the day?
2 What is enuresis?
3 What factors may contribute to enuresis?
4 What is encopresis?

THINK!

1 Think about what advice you would offer to a parent who approached you with concerns about toilet training.

Toilet training: two points of view

1 Make a wall display for a day nursery giving general guidelines in a visually interesting way for toilet training. The display must be eye-catching to encourage parents or carers to read it.

Hygiene: care of the hair, skin and teeth

You should refer to the section *Care of the skin* in Chapter 10.

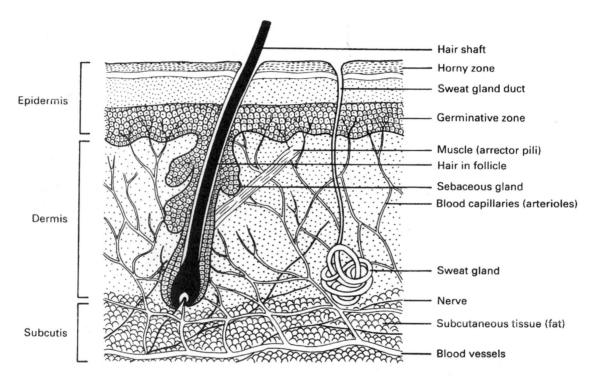

Layers of the skin

All children need adult help and supervision in their personal hygiene requirements. Good standards of hygiene in childhood are important for the following reasons:

- they help to prevent disease
- they increase self-esteem and social acceptance
- they prepare children for life by teaching them how to care for themselves.

To understand the importance of hygiene it is valuable to understand the functions of the skin and hair. The structure of the skin is shown in the diagram above.

FUNCTIONS OF THE SKIN

The skin performs the following functions:

a) protection
   - of underlying organs
   - against germs entering the body
b) sensation: the skin is the organ of touch, and conveys sensations of hot, cold, soft, hard, etc.
c) secretion of sebum, an oily substance, which:
   - lubricates the hair
   - keeps the skin supple and waterproof
   - protects the skin from moisture and heat.
d) the manufacture of vitamin D, from exposure to ultra violet rays from the sun; vitamin D which is necessary for healthy bone growth. (Black children may need a supplement in the winter as their skin does not easily make vitamin D.)
e) sweat: the skin excretes sweat and this:
   - gets rid of some waste products
   - helps to regulate the temperature when the body is hot.

Because the skin has so many important functions and because it is the first part of the body to come into contact with the environment, it must be cared for adequately. This does not mean obsessive cleaning of the skin: too much cleaning can be as harmful as too little because it may make the skin dry and sore and also wash away sebum, which protects it.

- Wash the face and hands in the morning and before meals.
- Wash hands after going to the toilet and after messy play.
- Keep the nails short by cutting them straight across. This will prevent dirt collecting under them.
- A daily bath or shower is necessary with young children who play outside and become dirty, hot and sweaty. Dry them thoroughly, especially between the toes and in the skin creases to prevent soreness and cracking.
- Observe the skin for rashes and soreness. If treatment is prescribed it must be followed.
- Black skin needs moisturising. Putting oil in the bath water and massaging almond oil into the skin afterwards helps to prevent dryness.
- If a child does not require a daily bath, a thorough wash is good enough. Remember to encourage children to wash their bottoms after the face, neck, hands and feet.
- Hair only needs to be washed once or twice a week unless it is full of food or the residue of messy play! Avoid using a hairdryer every time the hair is washed as this can damage the hair.
- Rinse shampoo out thoroughly in clean water. Conditioners may be useful for hair that is difficult to comb.
- Black curly hair needs hair oil applying daily to prevent dryness and hair breakage.
- Skin needs protecting from the sun to prevent burning and the associated

A daily bath is necessary for active toddlers playing outside

risks of cancer. Use a sunblock or high factor sun cream and monitor the length of time in the sun. Black skin needs the same protection as pale skin. The benefits of good hygiene are:

- clear, glowing skin and shiny hair are a sign of good health
- the child looks attractive and feels well, and develops a positive self-image
- washing is a tonic; children feel healthy as a result
- infection is prevented (it can spread from child to child from dirty hands and nails)
- health is maintained
- good habits give a pattern for life
- it allows the skin to perform its functions
- treats skin problems, for example eczema, sweat rash; itchy, sore skin can prevent sleep and make the child irritable and restless. This may affect all-round development.

ENCOURAGING INDEPENDENCE IN HYGIENE

There are several ways in which carers can encourage a child to develop independence in personal hygiene:

- provide positive role models
- establish caring routines that encourage cleanliness from early babyhood
- make hygiene fun: use toys in the bath, cups and containers, sinkers and floaters

- provide the child with their own flannel, toothbrush, hairbrush, etc. that they have chosen themselves
- allow the child to wash themselves and participate at bath time. Let them brush their hair with a soft brush and comb with rounded teeth
- provide a step so that they can reach the basin to wash and clean teeth
- make haircuts fun too: some barbers and hairdressers specialise in children's hair.

TEETH

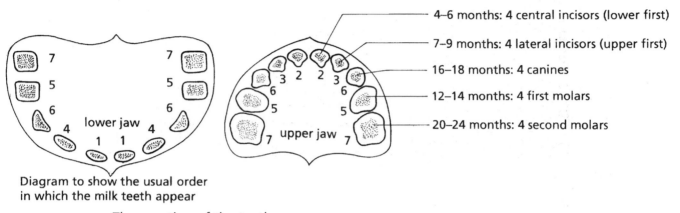

4–6 months: 4 central incisors (lower first)

7–9 months: 4 lateral incisors (upper first)

16–18 months: 4 canines

12–14 months: 4 first molars

20–24 months: 4 second molars

Diagram to show the usual order in which the milk teeth appear

The eruption of the teeth

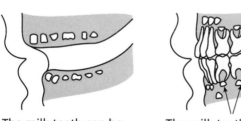
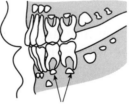
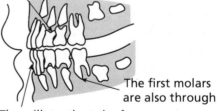

The roots of the remaining milk teeth are beginning to disappear

The first molars are also through

The milk teeth can be seen developing inside the jaw

The milk teeth are all through. The permanent teeth are developing underneath

The milk teeth at the front of both jaws (the incisors) have been replace by permanent teeth.

Development of the teeth

Teeth may appear at any time during the first two years of life. It is usually expected that they will begin to erupt during the first year but this is not necessarily so. They usually come through in the same order as shown in the illustration, but variations may occur. The first 20 teeth are called the 'milk teeth', and they will usually be complete by the age of 3 years. From 5–6 years these teeth begin to fall out as the adult teeth come through. There are 32 permanent teeth, and the care they are given in childhood will help them to last a lifetime.

Care of the teeth

Provide a soft toothbrush for a baby to use and become familiar with. It is not necessary for babies to have teeth to begin oral (mouth) hygiene. They will enjoy playing with the brush, and as they get older, will put it in their mouths to suck it and to rub their gums. Give them the opportunity to watch adults and siblings clean their teeth. When the first tooth does appear, try to clean it gently with a small, soft brush. If the baby objects do not force her to have the tooth or teeth cleaned – make it a game and increase her confidence. Teach older children how to clean their teeth. A dental hygienist will be able to offer professional assistance – the dentist will arrange this. Ensure that cleaning the teeth becomes a habit: in the morning after breakfast and after the last drink or snack before bed. Cleaning the teeth after meals should be encouraged, but this may not always be possible.

Diet

Encourage healthy teeth and prevent decay by providing a healthy diet that is high in calcium and vitamins and low in sugar. Avoid giving sweet drinks to babies and children, especially in a bottle or soother; this coats the gums and teeth in sugar and encourages the formation of acid which dissolves the enamel on the teeth. Sugar can penetrate the gum and cause decay before the teeth come through. This is common in babies and children who are frequently offered sweet drinks.

Children will probably demand sweets. Give them after a meal and then encourage them to clean their teeth. Do not offer sweets and sugary snacks between meals, as this will encourage decay. If you do need to feed a child between meals, provide food that needs to be chewed and improves the health of the gums and teeth, like apples, carrots and bread.

Fluoride

Fluoride in the water supply has been proven to strengthen the enamel on the teeth, and so prevent decay. In areas where the fluoride content is low, drops can be given daily in drinks. Fluoride toothpaste also helps to prevent decay.

The dentist

Visit the dentist regularly. A baby who attends with an adult, and then has her own appointments, will feel more confident about the procedure. Prepare children for their dental appointments by explaining what will happen and participating in role play. *Never* pass on any adult feelings of terror, fear or anxiety about the dentist.

Clothing and footwear

Toddlers and children work hard at their play, and this will mean that they get dirty. Although they are often washed for their health and comfort they will

Toddlers will inevitably get dirty when they play

soon be dirty again. The attraction of a muddy puddle, digging soil and exploring the sandpit will see to that! This is all natural and should be encouraged. Children should not be pressurised into keeping clean or the spontaneity and excitement of play will be lost.

CLOTHING

Clothing must be comfortable and loose enough for easy movement but fitted well enough to prevent loose material from catching and hindering movements. It should be able to be easily washed; children *do* get dirty. This should be expected and not disapproved of.

Clothes should have fasteners that a child can reasonably manage, for example large buttons, toggles, velcro and zips.

Underwear
- Cotton is preferable, to absorb sweat and increase comfort.
- When babies are in nappies, all-in-one vests prevent cold spots.

General clothing
- Trousers or shorts are best for both sexes when a child is crawling and falling. Dresses often get in the way of active play.
- Stretch track-suits are ideal.
- Dungarees, except when the child is learning to use the toilet, as they are difficult to remove and replace.

- T-shirts, cotton jumpers.
- Add extra, light layers when it is cold.

Coats
- A showerproof, colourful anorak with a hood is warm and easily washed. Extra underlayers can be added when the weather is very cold.
- Waterproof trousers and wellingtons enable happy puddle splashing.

Pyjamas
- Use all-in-one suits without feet, with correctly sized socks.

Footwear
The bones of the feet develop from cartilage, and are very soft and vulnerable to deformity if they are pushed into badly fitting shoes or socks. A child may not complain of pain because the cartilage will mould into the shape of the shoe.

Shoes should not be worn unless it is absolutely necessary, and not indoors. Walking barefoot in the house is preferable, partly because babies and children use the toes to balance, and floors can be like skating rinks for a baby or child wearing socks alone. If floors are cold or damp, socks with non-slip soles can be worn. Shoes are not necessary until a child will be walking outside, when they protect the feet and preserve warmth.

Feet grow 2–3 sizes each year until the age of 4. The primary carer is responsible for making sure that footwear fits correctly. This should be done by regularly checking the growth of the feet. They must be checked every 3 months by an expert trained in children's shoe fitting. Both the length and width are important.

Shoes should:
- protect the feet
- have no rough areas to rub or chafe the feet
- have room for growth
- have an adjustable fastener, for example a buckle or velcro
- be flexible and allow free movement
- fit around the heel
- support the foot and prevent it from sliding forwards.

Socks must be of a size to correspond to the size of the shoe. Stretch socks should be avoided.

CHECK!

1 What are the functions of the skin ?
2 What particular care should be given to black skin?
3 What are the benefits of good hygiene?
4 How can independence be encouraged in hygiene routines?
5 How many 'milk teeth' are there?
6 How can healthy teeth be encouraged?

7 What type of clothing is most suitable for a toddler?

8 When are shoes necessary?

9 On average, how many sizes do feet grow in a year until the age of 4 years ?

10 How often should children's feet be measured by an expert ?

THINK!

1 Think about how you can make care of the skin, teeth and hair fun. Remember how you were taught to take responsibility for your own personal hygiene. You may want to use some of the ways that were successful with you, or you may decide to adopt an entirely different approach with the children you care for.

DO!

1 Plan a suitable wardrobe for a child between 1–4 years. Take into account the seasons, the child's age and stage of development, laundering, etc. Give reasons for your choices of clothing, including their advantages.

2 Plan a hygiene routine for a young child that includes all aspects of care related to the child's needs and development.
Include the following:
- encouraging independence during bathing and dressing.
- sleeping requirements
- opportunity for rest and exercise
- stimulation
- safety factors
- awareness of the needs of the family.

Key terms

You need to know what these words and phrases mean. Go back through the chapter and find out.

Deep relaxing sleep	Sebum
Rapid eye movements	Sweat
Bedtime routine	Hygiene
Toilet training	Milk teeth
Enuresis	Fluoride
Encopresis	

14 *SAFETY*

Anticipating accidents

Children are born with no awareness of danger. They are totally dependent on their carers for protection and survival. Carers need a sound knowledge of child development to be able to anticipate when an accident may occur due to a child's increasing physical skills or curiosity. For example, a baby of 4 to 5 months may seem quite safe lying on the sofa, until the day she can roll over and off onto the floor. Or the young baby sitting on a carer's knee as they drink a cup of tea may seem to have no interest or curiosity about the cup or its contents until the day their co-ordination allows them to grab the cup and scald themselves.

Babies and children are constantly changing from day to day. It may be surprising when they do things for the first time, but their increasing abilities should be expected. Carers should anticipate and avoid dangerous situations. Children have a right to this level of care.

PROTECTING FROM ACCIDENTS

Babies and toddlers cannot remember what they have been told from one moment to the next. Saying *No!* as they crawl towards the open fire may stop their progress for a moment, but they will soon be off again. They are not being naughty or disobedient. They are naturally curious and need to investigate. They have lots of energy and will keep trying until they succeed. This is usually encouraged by adults, so babies will be confused and upset when they are discouraged from an unsafe situation, for example trying to pull at that tempting wire hanging from the kitchen worktop, or emptying kitchen cupboards, or grabbing a pan handle when it is on the hob. The adult carer must try to make all situations safe, while leaving children space to explore.

As children get older and their memory develops, their awareness of what is dangerous increases. They will begin to remember what hot feels like, that it hurts, and they will avoid touching the oven door or radiator. They are beginning to protect themselves. As they mature they may begin to protect

Children love to explore

other, younger toddlers, giving them some of the benefit of their own experience.

It is still necessary to provide a balance between protecting the child from danger yet allowing them the space and opportunity to explore and develop at their own pace to their full potential. Achieving this balance will require an adult to provide a safe environment for exploration. The home, the nursery, the car, the school, the playground must be as child-safe as possible. A watchful adult presence is always necessary.

ACCIDENTS

Accidents are the greatest cause of death in children over 1 year old. Most accidents happen at home, and 1- to 4-year-olds are most at risk. Look at the following statistics:

- 3 children die every day as the result of an accident
- 120 000 children are admitted to hospital every year as the result of accidents
- 3 000 000 children attend casualty departments for accidental injuries every year
- every year 1 in 5 children needs medical treatment after an accident.

THINK!

1 Why should 1- to 4-year-olds be most vulnerable at home? Think about their development and write down as many dangerous situations as you can, that may be encountered at home.

COMMON FACTORS IN ACCIDENTS

All carers are human, and there may be times when they are less vigilant than others, but when caring for children constant awareness is essential. Children may take more risks when adults are distracted, or when they have seen other children do dangerous things. The following paragraphs summarise some of the situations in which accidents may occur.

Stress

When adults or children are worried or anxious they may be less alert or cautious. Carelessness creates dangerous situations.

Haste

When late for school or an appointment, anyone may take less care in keeping safe; we may, for example, rush across the road.

Tiredness

Tiredness makes everyone less alert. Adults may be pleased that children are quietly playing which allows them to rest. They may be unaware that the garden gate is open, or that the children have wandered onto the balcony of the flat.

Remember that when children are unusually quiet in their play they have probably found something which fascinates them. Check that they are not playing with a dangerous object or in a potentially dangerous situation.

Under-protection

Children who are not supervised by caring adults are more likely to have accidents. They have not been made aware of dangers and are allowed to play in hazardous situations.

Over-protection

Children who are so protected that they are not allowed to explore are less likely to be aware of danger when they are left alone. They may be determined to do something usually disallowed.

Preventing accidents

The successful prevention of accidents depends largely upon the five areas outlined below.

ROLE MODELS

The most important way of reducing risk is by setting a good example to children. Children copy adult actions so adults have a responsibility to teach them how to be safe in, for example crossing the road, wearing a seat belt, closing the door.

THINK!

1 Think of as many ways as you can of being a good safety role model to a child.

MODIFYING THE ENVIRONMENT

Make sure that the home, and other areas used by children, are as safe as possible, while still allowing them to become independent and learn for themselves

EDUCATION

Children need to be educated about safety. Many national campaigns, for example Play it Safe, Green Cross Code, Stranger Danger, have aimed at increasing awareness of safety issues. Children can be taught how to avoid dangers and how to cope if a hazardous situation occurs. Adults too need educating in these areas: this means child-care workers, teachers, parents, health professionals and those who design environment areas such as shopping centres, parks or roads.

PRODUCT SAFETY

All equipment should be safe for use with children and preferably approved for safety and display, for example, the BSI kitemark, European standards markings, the BEAB Mark of Safety (see page 139).

LEGISLATION

Pressure on local and national government may encourage them to make and enforce laws which support the prevention of accidents and the promotion of safety.

Safety at home

DO!

Before reading this section, look around your home, room by room.
1 Make a list of all the potentially dangerous items.
2 Make a list of all the accidents that could occur if a young child lived with you.
3 How could you prevent these accidents from occurring?

Everyone is relaxed at home, and may feel safe because they are at home. This is clearly not true. It is interesting to note that most home accidents occur during the summer months, especially July. 1- to 4-year-olds are most at risk because they are mobile and want to explore, but they cannot yet anticipate danger; accident figures indicate that boys are more at risk than girls. Causes and ways of preventing home accidents are given below under the relevant headings.

FIRE

House fire is the commonest cause of death by fire. Death usually results from inhaling poisonous fumes given off from furniture. The risk of fire must be reduced because:

- a child could cause a house fire
- children may burn themselves even if they do not cause a house fire.

Prevention

- Reduce the source of fire, for example do not leave matches in children's reach, restrict smoking, use a fireguard (it is illegal to leave a child under 12 in a room with an open fire), avoid using chip pans, store petrol and other flammable (burnable) materials correctly.

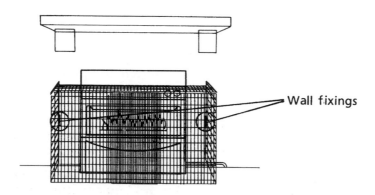

Wall fixings

- Reduce the flammability of materials such as nightdresses and soft furnishings.
- Restrict the possible spread of fire by the use of fire doors (which should always be kept closed), fire extinguishers and fire blankets.
- The use of an early warning system such as a smoke alarm will give the extra minutes needed to escape from a fire. All houses should have at least one, especially if children live there.

FALLS

Half of all domestic accidents involving children are due to falls. 20 children die each year after falling. Toddlers are most in danger. Some dangerous situations are:

- a baby in a baby bouncer or carrycot placed on a high surface such as a table or bed.
- the baby himself placed on a high surface
- toddlers in a house with unguarded stairs, open unprotected windows, balconies or bunk beds.

Prevention

- Never leave babies unattended on a high surface; lie them on the floor instead.
- Use stairgates at the top and bottom of stairs, to prevent babies and toddlers from entering the kitchen unattended, or getting out of the back or front door.

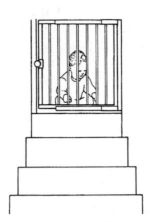

- Teach children to use the stairs safely, how to crawl up and down with supervision. This will increase their confidence and reduce fear. It should help to prevent a fall if the stairs are accidentally left unguarded. Ensure that banister rails are close enough to prevent a young child climbing through.
- Use childproof window locks or latches.
- Move furniture away from windows so that children will not be so tempted to climb up.
- Avoid baby walkers. These are very dangerous and cause many accidents. Babies do not need them; they will learn to walk when they are ready.
- Use reins in the pram, pushchair, highchair and supermarket trolley.

- Place garden climbing equipment on safe surfaces such as grass or wood chippings.

BURNS AND SCALDS

Burns and scalds occur most commonly to babies and toddlers The causes may be:
- the bathwater too hot
- hot drink spilling onto the child
- pulling the kettle flex
- hot fat from cooking or chip pan
- contact burns from fires, radiators, irons, etc.
- playing with matches.

Prevention
- Use a playpen if you are cooking and prevent toddlers entering the kitchen with a safety gate.
- Use a coiled kettle flex.
- Use a cooker-guard and turn pan handles inwards.
- Do not keep matches in the house.
- Use non-flammable clothing.
- Teach children the dangers of fire.
- Keep children away from bonfires and fireworks, except at safe, public displays.
- Put cold water in the bath first.

CHOKING

50–60 children die each year as the result of a choking accident. It is the largest cause of accidental death in children under 1 year. At 6 months babies can grasp objects and put them in their mouths to explore them. Small objects such as marbles, Lego, peanuts, sweets, buttons, bottle and pen tops must be kept out of their reach.

Prevention
- It is the responsibility of the carer to remove all potentially dangerous items from the child's reach.
- Dummies must meet safety standards with holes in the flange, in case it is drawn to the back of the throat.
- Never leave small items lying around at home.
- Do not use toys with small parts that are unsuitable for young children.
- Do not give the child peanuts, nor have them available.
- Do not allow the child to play when they are eating.

SUFFOCATION

Suffocation occurs when the airways are covered and the passage of air to the lungs is obstructed. Hanging and strangulation will also cut off the air supply.

Prevention

- Some household items are dangerous for babies and young children:
  plastic bags
  cords around the necks of clothing
  pillows.
- Never prop feed a baby (i.e. do not prop the bottle so that the baby sucks without being held).
- Make sure that there are no jagged edges on the cot or pram which could trap the clothing and strangle the baby as he moves.
- Do not use babynests, unless the baby is actually being carried in one.
- Avoid using quilts with young babies under 1 year.
- Warn older children of the dangers of ropes, strings, and dangerous places such as old fridges, freezers, cupboards that could trap them inside.

CUTS

Cuts are usually caused by ordinary items such as glass, sharp knives or tin cans; there are also dangers from items such as gardening equipment, or broken windscreens, windows, etc.

Prevention

- Keep knives out of reach.
- Use plastic drinking cups and bottles.
- Use safety glass in doors or cover glass with safety film.
- Put stickers on large glass areas such as patio doors, so that it is obvious when they are closed; it is much safer to board up low-level glazing such as this.

ELECTRICITY AND ELECTROCUTION

The most likely cause of electrocution in the home is toddlers sticking objects into electrical sockets. Electrical equipment in a bathroom can cause death and it is against the law to have any sockets there other than those for shavers or electric toothbrushes.

Faulty electrical appliances are lethal.

Prevention

- Use safety sockets, to prevent investigation with small fingers or objects.
- Use circuit breakers, which will instantly cut off the electricity supply when there is a short circuit.
- Switch sockets off when not in use.
- Do not use a hair dryer or any other electrical equipment in the bathroom.
- Check all electrical equipment for safety, for example check for worn flexes.

POISONING

About 2000 children each year are admitted to hospital after taking a poisonous substance. 2- to 3-year-olds are most at risk. They are exploring the environment, but cannot yet distinguish tastes. At this age there may be easy access to poisons, such as adult medicines, bleach or cleaning fluids. There may also be dares from other children.

Prevention
- Use child-resistant containers.
- Close all containers after use.
- Store medicines in a high, preferably locked cupboard. If there is no lock use a child-proof latch.
- Put child-resistant locks on all cupboards
- Do not store dangerous substances in the cupboard under the sink. Find a safer storage area.
- Keep chemicals in their original containers. Do not store them in old drink bottles or jam jars that may look attractive to young children.
- Prevent children eating berries or seeds from the garden or park.

CHECK!

1 Why is it important for adults to be aware of safety when working with young children ?
2 What is the greatest cause of death in children over 1 year of age?
3 When are accidents most likely to happen?
4 Give four general ways that adults can prevent accidents.
5 Where do most accidents take place?
6 How can fires be prevented?
7 Which children are most at risk of falling?
8 What may cause burns and scalds?
9 How can the home be adapted to reduce the risk of burns?
10 How can choking accidents be prevented?

THINK!

1 Try to see the world from a child's viewpoint. Crawling on the kitchen floor will help you to see the hazards that may look so interesting to a child.

DO!

1 Research the occurrence of accidents at home to children who attend your placement.
2 With the permission of your placement supervisor, send a questionnaire home with the children.

2 Display the results visually to show the age at which accidents have occurred and the scene of the accident. This could be part of a display about safety.

3 Complete a project about road safety. Include research about the incidence of accidents involving children as pedestrians and as car passengers. Suggest methods of ensuring the safety of children on the roads.

4 Prepare a topic within your placement to increase awareness about road safety. You could invite speakers in to talk to the children about various aspects of safety, and/or arrange suitable visits.

Key terms

You need to know what these words and phrases mean. Go back through the chapter and find out.

Accidents

Safety legislation

Flammable

Suffocation

15 CHILDHOOD ILLNESSES AND AILMENTS

Disease transmission

Disease is a condition which arises when something goes wrong with the normal working of the body. As a result the child becomes ill. Signs that a child is ill and has a disease include:

- raised temperature
- headache
- sore throat
- rashes on the skin
- diarrhoea.

Other possible signs of illness are a lot of crying, being irritable, behaviour that is unusual. Possible signs of illness are always more worrying and significant in a baby or very young child.

Organisms which cause disease are called *pathogens*. The most important pathogens are bacteria, viruses and some fungi. The everyday name for pathogens is germs. Pathogens get into the body mainly through the mouth and nose and sometimes through cuts on the skin. Once they are inside the body they multiply very rapidly. This is the *incubation period* and can last for days or weeks depending on the type of pathogen. Although the person is infected during the incubation period, they only begin to feel ill and have signs of the infection at the end of the incubation period.

Pathogens work in different ways when they infect the body. Some attack and destroy body cells, others produce poisonous substances in the bloodstream. The intense activity of the pathogens produces a lot of heat; one of the signs of infection by pathogens is that the child's temperature goes up.

HOW DISEASES SPREAD

The ways by which diseases are spread are by droplets in the air, by touch, by food and water, animals and cuts and scratches.

Droplets in the air

When you cough , sneeze, talk and sing, tiny droplets of moisture come out of your nose or mouth. If you have a disease these droplets will be swarming with pathogens. If they are breathed in by another person the disease can be spread to them. Colds (caused by viruses) spread rapidly in this way.

Touch

It is possible to catch some infectious diseases by touching an infected person, or by touching towels or other things used by that person. The skin disease impetigo (caused by bacteria) is spread in this way. Another skin disease, athlete's foot (caused by a fungus) can be picked up from the floors of changing rooms and showers.

Food and water

The urine and faeces of an infected person will contain pathogens. Drinking water may be contaminated if sewage gets into it. Food and drinks can be contaminated if they are prepared or handled by a person with dirty hands, or if the food preparation area is dirty. This is why hand-washing after visiting the lavatory and before handling food is so important. Food poisoning (caused by bacteria) easily spreads in this way, especially in places where lots of children play and eat together, such as nurseries.

Animals

Pathogens are brought on to food by animals like flies, rats, mice and cockroaches. Other diseases are spread by animals which suck blood; an example of this is malaria.

Cuts and scratches

Pathogens can enter the body through a cut or other injuries to the skin. An example of this is the tetanus bacteria and the hepatitis virus.

Immunity

When pathogens do enter, the body does not just sit back and let them take over. White blood cells work to try to destroy the invading bacteria or viruses. The white cells identify the invading pathogens as a foreign substance and begin to make antibodies. Antibodies make the pathogens clump together so that the white cells can destroy them by absorbing them – the process of phagocytosis.

It may take some time for the white cells to make enough antibodies. This may give the pathogen enough time to multiply so that the child shows signs of having the disease. Eventually the white cells make enough antibodies to destroy the pathogens and the child recovers from the illness. If the same pathogen attacks again some time later, the white cells quickly recognise it and

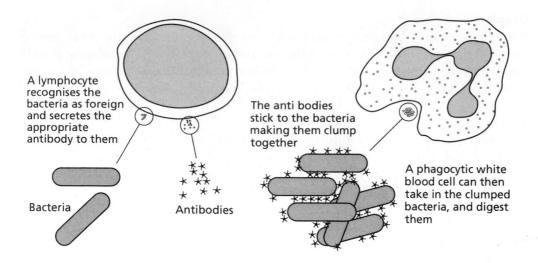

Phagocytosis: how white cells destroy bacteria

make large quantities of antibody and the pathogen is destroyed before it has chance to multiply. The child is immune to that pathogen and the disease.

ACTIVE IMMUNITY

Having a disease and recovering from it is one way of becoming immune to it. This is *active immunity*, because the white cells make the antibodies. Active immunity is also acquired by having a vaccination. Some vaccines, the BCG vaccine for tuberculosis, for example, contain bacteria which have been weakened. When they are injected into the body they are too weak to multiply, but the white cells can identify them as foreign cells and begin to make antibodies. Immunity to the disease is then acquired.

PASSIVE IMMUNITY

Another type of immunity is *passive immunity*. Here the antibody is put into the blood ready-made. Breast fed babies acquire immunity to diseases because there are antibodies in breast milk. Passive immunity does not last indefinitely, because the antibodies gradually disappear from the blood. Active immunity lasts much longer because the white cells have learnt to make the antibody.

Infectious diseases

The following chart lists some of the diseases child-care workers are likely to meet.

Disease	Incubation period	Signs to look for	Care
Chicken pox: viral infection	14–16 days	Begins with general signs of feeling unwell, maybe a slight temperature; spots appear first on the chest and back and then spread; red at first but become fluid-filled blisters; they eventually dry off into scabs which drop off; spots come in successive crops and are very itchy	Give plenty to drink, keep the child as comfortable as possible, with baths, loose comfortable clothes and calamine lotion to ease the itching
Diphtheria: bacterial infection	2–6 days	General signs of being unwell, difficulty with breathing; classic sign of diphtheria is white membrane forming across the throat and restricting the airway; toxins produced by the bacteria can damage the heart and brain	Requires prompt medical treatment with antibiotics and admission to hospital
Gastroenteritis: bacterial or viral infection spread by direct contact or eating infected food or water	Very variable: 1–14 days; viruses affect more quickly	Child is generally unwell, with severe vomiting and diarrhoea; babies and young children quickly show signs of dehydration, with dry mouth and skin, decreased urine output; anterior fontanelle (Book 1, page 5) in small babies sinks down	Call the doctor, initial treatment in hospital may be necessary; keep the child cool and comfortable; give drinks of water very regularly; oral rehydration solutions may also be given
Measles: viral infection	7–12 days	Begins with signs of bad cold and cough; child gradually becomes more unwell and miserable with raised temperature and sore eyes; before rash appears on the skin white spots can be seen inside the mouth; when rash appears spots are red and rash is blotchy; rash usually starts behind the ears and quickly spreads downwards to rest of the body	Child may be very unwell; call the doctor; in addition to any medical treatment, give rest and plenty of fluids; eyes may need special attention and gentle bathing; keep mouth clean and moist; watch for signs of ear infection

(Continued overleaf)

Disease	Incubation period	Signs to look for	Care
Meningitis: inflammation of the membrane covering the brain; can be caused by bacterial or viral infection	2–10 days	It is important to recognise meningitis early as it develops very rapidly; usually begins with high temperature, headache, vomiting, confusion, irritability; later signs may develop, pain and stiffness in the neck, dislike of the light	Get medical help early; treatment and care in hospital will be required
Mumps: viral infection	14–21 days	Generally unwell; pain and tenderness around the ear and jaw, uncomfortable to chew; swelling starts under jaw and up by the ear, usually on one side of the face, followed (though not always) by the other	Keep the child comfortable and give plenty to drink; doctor may advise analgesic (such as paracetamol) to ease soreness; rest is necessary as rare complication in boys is inflammation of the testes
Poliomyelitis: viral infection which attacks the nervous system causing muscle paralysis	5–21 days	Becoming suddenly unwell, with headache, stiffness in the neck and back, followed by loss of movement and paralysis; maybe difficulty with breathing	Initial hospital care, followed by rest and rehabilitation
Rubella (German measles): viral infection	14–21 days	Begins like a mild cold, but often child does not feel unwell; rash appears first on the face, then spreads to the body; spots are flat and only last for about 24 hours; glands in the back of the neck may be swollen	Children with rubella often do not feel unwell; give plenty to drink; if a pregnant woman gets rubella, there is a risk of damage to her baby; keep the child away from anyone who is pregnant or likely to be; if the child was with anyone who is pregnant before you knew about the illness let them know; any pregnant woman who has had any contact with rubella should see her doctor urgently

(Continued on facing page)

Hepatitis , A   2-6 wks   fever, nausea, lassitude,
                                headache, Jaundice
Exclusion 7 days after onset
of Jaundice and until
physically well.

Illness	Incubation period	Symptoms	Treatment
Scarlet fever: bacterial infection	2–6 days	Begins with child suddenly feeling unwell, with sore throat, temperature, feeling sick; tongue looks very red, cheeks are flushed, throat looks red and sore, with white patches; rash starts on the face and spreads to the body	Make sure child rests and drinks plenty; doctor may prescribe antibiotics; observe for complications, such as ear and kidney infections
Tetanus: bacterial infection; bacteria found in soil, dirt and dust, enter the body through cuts, scratches and other wounds	4–21 days	Tetanus attacks the nervous system, causing painful muscle spasms; muscles in the neck tighten and the jaw locks	Any cuts, etc. must be properly cleaned; immunisation kept up-to-date; immediate hospital treatment needed for suspected tetanus
Tuberculosis (TB): bacterial infection	28–42 days	Persistent coughing, weight loss, further investigation shows lung damage	Initial period of treatment in hospital may be required; specific antibiotics given, rest and good quality diet essential
Whooping cough (pertussis): bacterial infection	7–14 days	Begins like cough and cold; cough usually gets worse; after about 2 weeks coughing bouts start; long bouts of coughing and choking are exhausting and frightening, as coughing can go on for so long that child finds it hard to breathe and may be sick; sometimes there is a whooping noise as child draws in breath after coughing; coughing bouts can continue for several weeks	Call doctor who may prescribe antibiotics; child will need lots of support and reassurance, especially during coughing bouts; encourage child to drink plenty; may be necessary to give food and drink after coughing bouts, especially if child is being sick; possible complications: convulsions, bronchitis, hernias, ear infections, pneumonia and brain damage

Note   Rashes look different on different people. The colour of the spots may vary and on black skin rashes can be less easy to see. If you are doubtful, check with the doctor, especially if the child is showing other signs of illness. Some infectious diseases can be prevented by immunisation (see Chapter 11 for more information on this).

Common childhood illnesses

COLDS

Children get many colds because there are many different cold viruses and young children are getting each one for the first time. As they grow up they build up immunity and get fewer colds. Colds are caused by viruses, not bacteria, so antibiotics will not help. There are things you can do to help the child breathe more easily: keep the nose clear and use a menthol rub or decongestant capsule. Make sure the child has plenty to drink, and give light, easily swallowed food.

COUGHS

Most coughs, like colds, are caused by a virus. If a cough persists or the chest sounds congested, a doctor should be consulted. Most coughs are the body's way of clearing mucus from the back of the throat, or from the air passages in the lungs. The cough therefore serves a useful purpose and should be soothed rather than stopped. Honey and orange or lemon in warm water or a bought cough mixture will help.

DIARRHOEA

Young babies' stools are normally soft and yellow and some babies will soil nearly every nappy. If you notice the stools becoming very watery and frequent, with other signs of illness, consult the doctor. Young babies who get diarrhoea can lose a lot of fluid very quickly, especially if they are vomiting as well. This can be very serious. Call the doctor and in the meantime give as much cooled boiled water as you can. Use a teaspoon if the baby is reluctant to suck and try to give some water every few minutes. Diarrhoea in older children is not so worrying, but maintain the fluid intake. If the diarrhoea persists for more than two or three days, consult the doctor.

EAR INFECTIONS

Ear infections often follow a cold. The child may be generally unwell, pull or rub the ears or there may be a discharge from the ear. There may be a raised temperature. The child may complain of pain, but small babies will just cry and seem unwell or uncomfortable. If you suspect an ear infection it is important that it is treated promptly by the doctor to prevent any permanent damage to the hearing.

SORE THROAT

Sore throats are caused, like colds, by viruses. The throat may be dry and sore a day or so before the cold starts. Sometimes a sore throat is caused by tonsillitis, and the throat is red and sore with white patches on the tonsils, which are enlarged. The child may find it hard to swallow and have a raised temperature with swollen glands under the jaw. If there is a raised temperature, consult the doctor. Meanwhile give plenty of clear drinks.

TEMPERATURES

As you know from studying this chapter, a raised temperature is a sign that pathogens have entered the body and are multiplying. If a baby has a raised temperature and/or other signs of illness, always consult the doctor as soon as possible. With older children, contact the doctor if the temperature remains high or if the child has other signs of illness. It is important to bring the temperature down. Do not wrap a baby up; take off a layer of clothing and let older children wear light clothes. Give plenty of cool drinks, little and often. The doctor may order paracetamol to help lower the temperature.

THRUSH

Thrush is a fungal infection. The fungus forms white patches in the mouth, usually on the tongue and the inside of the cheeks and lips. If you try to rub off the fungus it leaves a red sore patch. A baby may also have a sore bottom because the thrush has infected the skin in the nappy area. Consult the doctor who will give the specific treatment to clear up the infection. Thrush is spread because feeding equipment is not properly sterilised and handled. It can also be passed on from an infected adult.

VOMITING

All babies will bring up some milk from time to time. If the baby is vomiting often or violently and/or there are other signs of illness, contact the doctor. Babies can lose a lot of fluid if they vomit frequently. Maintain the fluid intake, but stop giving milk and give clear fluids as often as possible.

CHECK!

1 List all the signs you can think of that would indicate that the child has an infection.
2 What are the organisms called which cause disease?
3 In what different ways are diseases spread?
4 What are the two main types of immunity?
5 Name two waterborne infections.
6 What are the signs of measles?
7 Why is rubella particularly dangerous to pregnant women?
8 What are the signs of meningitis?
9 Why is it important to act quickly if a baby has diarrhoea?

1 Think of all the situations in the day when a child might be at risk of getting an infection.

2 Think of all the general safeguards that people use to protect themselves from infection.

DO!

1 Write a paragraph to describe how active immunity is acquired.

2 You are a nanny looking after a child of 5 who has measles; write a plan of care for one day.

Infestations

Parasites obtain their food from humans and are likely to affect all children at some time. Common parasites which infest children include:

- fleas
- head lice
- ringworm
- scabies
- threadworms.

FLEAS

Fleas are small insects. They cannot fly, but jump from one person to another. The type of flea which feeds on human blood lives in clothing next to the skin. When it bites to suck blood it leaves red marks which itch and swell up. Fleas lay their eggs in furniture and clothing to be near to humans and their food. Cleanliness is very important; regular washing of clothes and bedding will get rid of the eggs. Sometimes children are sensitive to fleas which normally live on cats and dogs. Animals need to be treated regularly to prevent this problem.

HEAD LICE

Head lice are small insects which live in human hair, near to the scalp, where they can easily bite the skin and feed on blood. Many children get head lice; they catch them by coming into contact with someone who is already infested. When heads and hair touch the lice simply walk from one head to another. The lice lay eggs, called nits, close to the scalp and cement the eggs firmly to the hair. Nits look like specks of dandruff, but when you try to remove them they are firmly attached to the hair. The first sign of head lice is usually an itchy scalp.

If a child has head lice, the condition must be treated straight away. Treatment is an insecticide lotion available from the chemist, clinic or doctor.

Follow the instructions carefully and treat the whole household. The lotion kills the lice and nits, but the nits are not washed off. To remove dead nits you need to use a tooth comb which is obtainable from the chemist. Lice are discouraged if the hair is regularly brushed and combed. It is good practice to check children's hair regularly for signs of infestation.

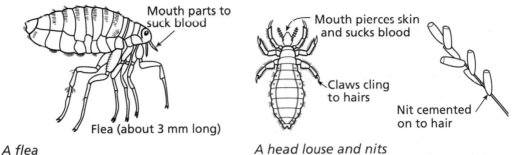

Mouth parts to suck blood

Flea (about 3 mm long)

A flea

Mouth pierces skin and sucks blood

Claws cling to hairs

Nit cemented on to hair

A head louse and nits

RINGWORM

Ringworm is a fungus which can be caught from animals. It is seen as a raised red circle with a white scaly centre. It is very itchy. Ringworm patches can occur on the body and on the scalp. Contact the doctor who will prescribe the specific treatment, usually an antibiotic cream.

SCABIES

Scabies is caused by a tiny mite, *sarcoptes scabiei*, which burrows under the skin, causing intense itching. The mites spend their lives feeding on the skin and laying their eggs. It may be possible to see the burrows, or red raised spots which are very itchy. Scratching may cause redness and infection. Scabies is mostly seen on the hands between the fingers, on the wrists and sometimes in the armpit and groin. The mites crawl from one person to another. The doctor will prescribe a lotion to kill the mites and eggs. All the bedding and clothing will need to be washed and all family members treated.

THREADWORMS

Threadworms are small white worms that look like pieces of cotton. They live in the bowel and can be seen in the stools. Threadworms come out of the bowel at night to lay their eggs around the bottom. This causes itching and when the child scratches, eggs are transferred to the fingers and under the nails. Later the child will lick their fingers and eggs are swallowed, to hatch and develop in the bowel, perpetuating the cycle.

The doctor will prescribe the specific treatment. Everyone in the household needs to be treated, keep their nails short and wash their hands well after using the lavatory and before eating. Close fitting pyjamas may help to stop the child scratching at night.

1 What is a good way to discourage headlice?
2 How is ringworm caught?
3 What signs might lead you to suspect that a child has scabies?
4 Where are threadworms seen?
5 What are nits?

DO!

1 Look at the ways in which disease can be transmitted. Can you suggest and describe three hygiene routines that will help to prevent infection?
2 Plan an activity which will help children aged 5 and over to learn how infection is spread.
3 Plan a display that you could put in the parents' and carers' area to give information about head lice.

Key terms
You need to know what these words and phrases mean. Go back through the chapter and find out.

Pathogen	Passive immunity
Incubation period	Vaccine
Antibody	Toxin
Active immunity	Parasite

16 CARING FOR SICK CHILDREN

Caring for sick children at home

Babies and children need to be with their main carer when they are ill. Unless the doctor suggests that the child stays in bed, they may feel less isolated if they come downstairs. Here they can see and hear what is going on and a bed could be made up, for rest, on the settee. Some children may need the quiet and comfort of bed and in this case the carer and other adults should try to spend as much of the time as possible with them.

PHYSICAL CARE

The child should be kept clean and comfortable. Change clothes frequently and make sure they are loose and made of absorbent material. If the child is staying in bed, give an all-over wash if a bath is not possible. Straighten up the bed, smooth the sheets and pillows and wash the hands and face and comb the hair at regular intervals.

FOOD AND DRINK

Drinking is important. Offering a variety of drinks may encourage an unwilling child to drink more. Appetite may be affected by illness so do not worry about food for the first day or so unless it is wanted; after this, try to find ways of making food tempting.

ROOM TEMPERATURE

Make sure the room is kept warm and well ventilated (not too hot) day and night.

MEDICINES

The following points are important to note in the giving of medicines.
- Only give a child medicines prescribed or advised by the child's doctor.

Giving medicine

- Medicines need to be given at the right time and in the right dose (quantity); check the with the instructions on the label each time the medicine is given.
- If a course of medicine is prescribed it is very important to finish the full course. This must be done even if the child seems to be better, so that the full benefit is obtained.
- When a medicine is prescribed ask about any possible side effects. If you think the child is reacting badly to a medicine (for example with a rash or diarrhoea) stop giving it and tell the doctor.
- Never use medicines prescribed for someone else.
- Aspirin should not be given to children.
- Keep all medicines in a locked cupboard if possible.
- Do not keep prescribed or out-of-date medicines.

TAKING A TEMPERATURE

Thermometers which you hold on the child's forehead show the skin temperature, not body temperature; to take an accurate temperature it is best to use a mercury thermometer.

First shake down the mercury in the thermometer. Hold the child on your knee and tuck the thermometer under the armpit next to the skin. Leave the thermometer there for about three minutes; it might help to read a story while you do this.

A normal temperature taken under the tongue is 37 °C; taken under the arm, it is 36.4 °C.

ACTIVITIES

A carer should give time for games, stories, company and comforting the sick child. Children will need activities which are not too difficult or needing lots of concentration. They may like to return to activities and games which they enjoyed when they were younger.

Taking a temperature under the arm

Sick children are easily tired and need plenty of rest. They may not manage to concentrate for long and may want you to do things for them that they did quite capably when they were well.

CHECK!

1 When giving medicines to children, what two important things should be checked?
2 What is a normal temperature taken under the arm?
3 What is a normal temperature taken under the tongue?
4 Why is it important to finish the full course of a medicine which the doctor has prescribed?
5 If a sick child has no appetite, what is the best thing to do?

DO!

1 Write a plan of care for one day for a child aged 3 who is recovering from a severe stomach upset.

Children in hospital

PREPARATION

A large number of children have to go into hospital at some stage in their lives; many go into hospital as emergency admissions so it is important that all children get to know about hospitals. Children often see ambulances and play with toy ones and this will give an opportunity to talk about hospitals. You may pass the hospital in the car or on the bus and can point out the building. There are lots of books about hospitals that can be used, so you do not have to wait until the child is going to be admitted before making them familiar with hospitals – this familiarity will help if a child does have to go in to hospital with little or no warning.

A large number of children have to go into hospital at some stage in their lives

PLANNED ADMISSIONS

Despite general preparation, the prospect of hospital admission can be frightening for the child and the parents or carers. Planned admissions have the advantage of contact with doctors and nurses in the out-patients department. Visits to the ward may be arranged before admission. A hospital booklet especially for children is an important source of information. It may contain pictures of children or a familiar toy such as a teddy participating in hospital activities. It will also have pictures of things that a child is likely to see, like a thermometer or stethoscope.

PREPARING AT HOME

At home the child can be helped to understand what will happen by playing at hospitals. A few days before admission the child should be told clearly and honestly what will happen. Any questions should be answered as truthfully as possible in a way which the child can understand. The child should be assured that parents or carers will be able to arrange to stay overnight and visit whenever possible. How much a child can be told or will understand will depend on their age. Children may enjoy packing and unpacking their case, choosing favourite toys to bring into hospital, especially if they have a cuddly or toy which they like to hold. Any special name for these things should be mentioned to the ward staff.

IN HOSPITAL

Positive reminders

Continuing links with home are important even when a child has parents or carers who are resident or visit frequently. There are ways to provide children with reminders of home:

- familiar possessions: clothes, toys, cuddlies
- a photograph for the child's locker
- something familiar belonging to the mother or carer
- letters and cards, to be put up where the child can see them.

Emotional reactions

Children's reactions to being in hospital will be affected by the severity of their illness. The acutely ill child may have little awareness of their surroundings; the less ill child will react sensitively to the environment. The two factors which most affect the child's feelings are age and degree of dependence on parents or carers. Babies and pre-school children are most secure if the parent or carer is with them for most of the time; 4- to 8-year-olds are beginning to be independent but need a lot of reassurance. They need to have a parent or carer with them, particularly during the more stressful parts of their hospital stay.

Children who are separated from their parent or carer during a stay in hospital may show all the signs of acute distress. These are described more fully in Book 1, Chapter 14, *Separation and loss.*

Play in hospital

Any severe anxiety may have short-term or longer lasting effects on a child's emotional development. Anxiety associated with being in hospital must be anticipated, recognised and reduced to a minimum. Play can be a valuable way of doing this and there are a variety of opportunities, some of which are outlined below:

- in the community: parent and toddler groups, playgroups and primary schools can provide play, a hospital box, toys and books; children can be encouraged to act out their experiences, both in home corner play, and through topics such as 'People who help us'; visits from the school nurse, health visitor or other health personnel will be helpful familiarisation for children. NAWCH, The National Association for the Welfare of Children in Hospital, provides information for parents and children about local facilities
- out-patients: play should be available in out-patients, and children attending can be encouraged to participate by attractive and interesting provision; this helps to reduce their own anxiety level and that of their parents
- in the ward: when settling in, familiar favourite toys and treasured objects should always be brought in to the ward.

Planning play

Sick children need to play. but they may not make the effort or have the ability to create suitable play activities for themselves. As mentioned in the section on caring for sick children at home, concentration may be lacking, they may tire easily and they may regress and revert to a former level of behaviour.

Sick children may lack concentration and tire easily

A variety of play needs to be offered; some children because of their previous experience may need support to play and be messy. Those who are immobile will need individual play. The child should be able to take part fully in the activity. The best play builds on the familiar, fits the child's abilities and stimulates with some thing new.

THE CHILD CONFINED TO BED

Supine
Lying supine means that vision is restricted. Mirrors can help here, and pictures, posters and mobiles will make the area above the child's head more interesting. Books, listening to stories, tapes, and talking and some board games will be possible, but using the arms for all activities in this position is very tiring.

On the side
If the child has to lie on her side, then activities with play people, animals, board games, trains are possible.

Prone
In prone more activities are possible, especially if the child is supported on a special frame. The child can then paint, read or play board games.

Sitting up

Children may be confined to bed but able to sit up, for example if they are on traction. They may have lots of energy which can be released through clay and dough play or a hammering activity.

The child with an intravenous infusion (IV)

An IV may limit mobility but not confine the child to bed. When the IV is set up care is taken not to use the dominant arm. This leaves the more skilful hand free for play. Wherever possible move the child to where the activities are going on. Suitable activities will include painting, board games, small toys, any thing that does not require two hands. If in doubt, try it out one-handed yourself first.

The child needing intensive care

Very ill children may show little interest in play but it is still important to continue visual and aural stimulation. Singing, reading, mobiles, pictures and talking to the child about everyday things are very important. A favourite comfort object needs to be in sight, even if it cannot be held.

The child requiring isolation

A child being nursed in a cubicle may see little of other children. Any visitors, usually adults, may have to wear gowns and masks. As a result the child will need the carers to spend much more time in the cubicle initiating and joining in with the play. Toys and games will have to stay in the cubicle. Washable toys and water play will be especially useful.

The ward playroom

Many children's wards and departments have their own playrooms with a qualified child-care worker, who will provide play to meet the needs of the children who use it.

Children with life-threatening or terminal illness

The death of a child seems to be more difficult to accept than the death of an adult. Many people feel that children, with all their future before them, are a far greater loss than an adult who may have already lived a full and useful life. The death of a child today, when there are so many ways of preventing death, is far more of a tragedy than in the days when many children died in infancy.

A CHILD'S PERCEPTION OF DEATH

Children have many experiences of death in a broad sense. Loss and separation are also a part of many of their experiences. How they think about these things depends on how the adults close to them react and on the explanations they give. Death is often a subject which is not spoken about and the thought is pushed away, when the need is to think through ideas in order to be able to answer children's questions. The idea of death is complex and is built up over many years. The child's understanding will be limited by:

- previous experience
- language development
- grasp of the concept of time
- intellectual development.

Children who are dying often have very clear images fears and concerns about death. Adults may say that a child does not know, but many children do realise they are dying and the crucial difference is whether they have the chance to express their feelings or not. To say that a child does not talk about death could mean that the child has had no chance to talk, usually because the adults are finding this too difficult.

The young child, under 7, thinks that death is reversible, a state of sleep or separation, from which the person could return. Perhaps the main fear for the young child who is dying is thinking about separation and going into a darkness where there is no one familiar to give love and comfort. Children will express their fears in different ways; they may want close physical comfort and someone to listen and talk to them. At other times they may express their fears in anger. Their anger can often be directed at the person they love and trust the most. This can often be very hard for loving parents and carers to understand, but it is an indication of the child's feelings of trust in them.

ADULT REACTIONS TO THE DEATH OF A CHILD

Parents' emotions affect the care they give to their dying child and to the rest of the family. Frequently parents experience a range of emotions:

- initial shock: parents and carers may suspect that their child has a life-threatening illness, but the confirmation of this will produce the reactions of shock, disbelief, numbness and panic; they may not take in any of the explanations and afterwards may say that no one explained
- confusion: this is a common reaction; one reason for it is that suddenly parents or carers lose the role they thought they had, that of bringing up a child
- fear: part of the confusion is because of a gripping physical, emotional fear; there is a feeling of being trapped and being unable to cope with the unknown
- anger: this arises from the feelings of unfairness that the child is dying; the feelings of anger are often very powerful and it can take very little to trigger them off
- guilt: parents and carers often take the death of a child as a punishment for something they have done, but this is often unrelated to the child's illness.

STAYING IN THE FAMILY

Children with terminal illness very rarely die in hospital. Families are supported so that they can care for their child at home. Each family can decide upon their own plan of care in consultation with the care team. The family can be in frequent contact with the home-care nurse who acts as the consultant to the family in providing care for their child. During the home visits home-care nurses also provide emotional support to the child's family. Although families are apprehensive about their child dying at home, good support and a feeling of being in control in familiar surroundings will often create the best and most comfortable circumstances for all the family.

CHECK!

1 In what ways can you raise children's awareness of hospitals?
2 What are the advantages of a planned admission to hospital?
3 List some of the ways in which children might express their fear of hospital.
4 What is the role of the home-care nurse?

THINK!

1 Think of all the fears that a 5-year-old might have if left alone in hospital.

DO!

1 Plan two activities for a 6-year-who has one arm out of action because of an IV in place.
2 It is Monday morning and children aged from 3 to 10 will be admitted for their operations tomorrow. You are in charge of the play room. Decide what activities you will set out to encourage the children to come in and participate. Give reasons for your choices.

Key terms
You need to know what these words and phrases mean. Go back through the chapter and find out.
Dose
Prone
Supine
Regress

THE SOCIAL AND LEGAL FRAMEWORK AND THE FAMILY

This chapter includes:
- **The family**
- **Similarities between families**
- **Differences between families**
- **Partnership arrangements**
- **Family breakdown**
- **Family size**
- **Changing roles within the family**
- **Working with children and their families**
- **Alternative forms of care.**

The family

Children are totally dependent at birth. They become independent during childhood. To survive and develop during this period of dependency, they need care, security, protection, stimulation and social contact.

CARE AND PROTECTION: THE ALTERNATIVES

Large children's homes, sometimes called orphanages, used to exist in Britain. In these children whose parents were dead or unable to care for them were cared for in large groups. This type of institutional children's home no longer exists in Britain, but does still exist in some parts of Europe.

Occasionally people live together in communes. Adults share tasks and bring up their children collectively. This arrangement was popular among a small minority of people in the 1960s and 70s.

Some people in Israel live on kibbutzim. A kibbutz is a place where people live and work together for the economic benefit of the whole community. Children are cared for together, in units separate from their parents, leaving parents free to use their time and energy for work.

The family is by far the most common environment for bringing up children, both in Britain and other countries. The family is probably the most common arrangement for child care because it is the most practical way to meet both children's and parents' needs.

THINK!

1 Can you think of any advantages and disadvantages of the different types of child-care arrangements described above?

WHAT IS A FAMILY?

It is surprisingly difficult to define what a family is, but it can be said that
- all families have things in common
- all families are different.

One very general definition is 'a group of related people who support each other in a variety of ways, emotionally. socially and or economically'

DO!

1 Think of your own idea of what a family is, and then write it down. Try to share your ideas with others.

pg23 Working with Parents

WHY STUDY THE FAMILY?

Family life, in some form, is basic to the experience of most children. The family has a strong influence on every aspect of a child's life and development. For this reason we need to:
- understand the importance of the family to children's development
- know the particular family background of the children in our care
- understand the possible influences and effects of different family circumstances on children.

An extended family (page 245) enables children to develop a variety of caring relationships

Similarities between families

The family has certain functions (things it does for its members). Families all perform similar functions, but have different traditional ways of carrying them out. These functions are socialisation, practical care and emotional, social and economic support.

SOCIALISATION

Families provide the basic and most important environment in which children learn the culture of the society of which they are a part. The family consciously and unconsciously teaches children the main aspects of any culture. These are:
- values (beliefs that something is right)
- norms (rules for behaviour)
- a shared language.

Peers, schools and the media have a strong influence as children grow older, but children learn the foundations of culture within the family (see Book 1, Chapter 10, *An introduction to emotional and social development*).

PRACTICAL CARE

The family is very effective in providing practical day-to-day care for its dependent members: children, those who are sick or have disabling conditions and those who are old. Caring for people outside the family is much more expensive, and often less effective.

EMOTIONAL AND SOCIAL SUPPORT

Families perform a very important role. They give a baby a name and initial position in society. (When we hear of an abandoned baby we immediately wonder who the child is and where the child comes from.) The family gives us an identity, a sense of belonging, and a feeling of being valued. A child's family is able to provide a positive feeling of worth that is fundamental (basic and very important) to healthy emotional development. It meets the basic need for love and affection, company and security. In a busy and crowded life, people are less likely to find this support outside their family where contacts are more impersonal. Foster care, (i.e. a substitute family) is now routinely provided in Britain for children who lose their families. This is because family life is regarded as very important for emotional and social well being.

ECONOMIC SUPPORT

The extent of economic support varies between cultures. The family is still an economic unit. However, in Britain and other European countries, family members are no longer totally dependent on each other for survival. The state now provides an economic safety net (for example social security benefits) which prevents the starvation and destitution of the past.

DO!

1 Write in your own words what families commonly do for their members.

Differences between families

Although there are many similarities between families, there are many variations in their structure and size. These differences can significantly affect the lives of children.

THE NUCLEAR FAMILY WITH TWO PARENTS

This is a family grouping where parents live with their children and form a small group. They have no other relatives living with them or close by. This type of family has become increasingly common in modern societies like Britain. People tend to move around for work or education and leave their family of origin (the one they were born into) behind. In countries where people work on the land, they are much more likely to remain near their family of origin.

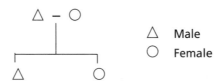

A nuclear family

Social and cultural variations in nuclear families
Nuclear families are more common in higher socio-economic groups, among those employed in managerial, administrative and professional jobs (such as running businesses, teaching or the law). These families are more likely to move for education and employment. Higher incomes make this possible and worth doing. In some nuclear families parents have developed a system of sharing family responsibilities. This is called a democratic system, because they share earning money, child care and domestic jobs.

Life in a nuclear family
Children who grow up in a small nuclear family:
- may experience close relationships within the family
- receive a lot of individual attention.
- have more space and privacy.

They may, however:

- feel a sense of isolation
- experience intensity of attention from parents
- have fewer people to turn to at times of stress
- suffer if their parents have no support system to care for them at times of illness or need.

THE NUCLEAR FAMILY WITH ONE PARENT

The term 'one-parent family' is used to describe the variety of families with dependent children that are headed by a lone parent. Of these roughly 10 per cent are headed by men, 90 per cent by women. Of the women about 60 per cent are divorced or separated, 23 per cent are single and 7 per cent widowed.

Social and cultural variations in one-parent families

The incomes of most lone parents are lower than those of most two-parent families. Many receive state benefits and their life style involves little spare money for luxuries. The publicity given to the Family Support Agency has focused attention on the government's attempts to make fathers more financially responsible for their families following separation.

A minority of lone parents are affluent (well off). They are more likely to be lone parents who are divorced or separated. Their incomes enable them to work and to afford day care for their younger children.

An increasing number of children (one in every eight) is born in Britain to women who are not married. A high proportion is within lower socio-economic groups. Single mothers are less likely to work, as their income would not enable them to pay for child care. Many live on income support. Both they and their children are vulnerable at times of difficulty (such as illness) if they do not have an extended family to support them.

Women of African–Caribbean origin have a tradition of single parenthood. This was one of the results of slavery in the Caribbean, where the nurturing of children by their fathers was forbidden. In some families subsequent high unemployment rates both in the West Indies and in Britain has perpetuated this tradition of low involvement by fathers. African–Caribbean families therefore tend to be matriarchal (women are important and dominant).

Life in a one-parent family

Children who grow up in a one-parent family:

- may establish a close, mutually supportive relationship with the parent they live with.
- may maintain a close relationship with their other parent and his or her family.

However they may:

- have experienced a period of grief and loss when their parents separated (see Book 1, Chapter 14, *Separation and loss*)
- lose contact with their other parent

- experience lower material standards than children in a two-parent family.
- have less adult attention at times when their parent is coping with practical and emotional difficulties.

THE EXTENDED FAMILY

An extended family extends beyond parent(s) and children to include other family members, for example grandparents, uncles and aunts. A family is usually referred to as extended when its members:
- live either together or very close to each other
- are in frequent contact with each other.

Many people who live at a distance from their relatives gain a great deal of emotional support from them but distance makes practical support difficult. When an extended family includes only two generations of relatives such as uncles, aunts and cousins, it is referred to as a joint family.

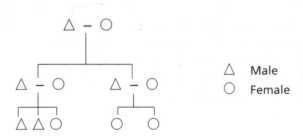

△　Male
○　Female

An extended family

Social and cultural variations in extended families

People in lower socio-economic groups involved in semi-skilled or manual jobs are less likely to move for work or education. This means that they are more likely to be part of a long-established extended family system. In white working-class families there is a tradition of women staying close to their mothers. A matriarchal system is common. Roles within the family are likely to be divided with men traditionally the bread winners and women in charge domestically, although they may also work outside the home.

Families who came originally from India, Pakistan and Bangladesh have maintained a tradition of living in close extended families. Many came from rural areas where this was traditional. Their cultural and religious background also places a strong emphasis on the duty and responsibility to care for all generations of the family. These extended families are usually patriarchal (men are dominant and make the important decisions). On marriage a woman becomes a part of her husband's family and usually lives with or near them.

Families whose origins are in Mediterranean countries such as Cyprus and Italy also tend to have a strong extended family tradition. Family members

Greece
T.V
programme

frequently meet together for celebrations. Daughters tend to stay close to their mothers on marriage, but the man has considerable authority in the family.

Life in an extended family
Children who experience life within an extended family:
- have the opportunity to develop and experience a wide variety of caring relationships
- are surrounded by a network of practical and emotional support.

However they may
- have little personal space or privacy
- feel they are being observed by and have to please a large number of people
- have less opportunity to use individual initiative and action.

THE RECONSTITUTED FAMILY

The reconstituted, or reorganised, family is an increasingly common family system as many parents divorce and remarry. It contains adults and children who have previously been part of a different family. The children of the original partnership usually live with one parent and become the step-children of the new partner and step-siblings of the new partner's children. Children born to the new partnership become half-siblings. Such families vary in their size and structure, and may be quite complicated!

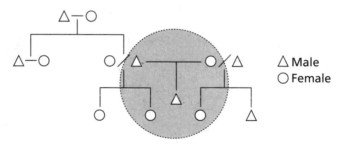

A reconstituted family

Social and cultural variations in reconstituted families
Reconstituted families are more common among people who are more likely to accept divorce: these may include those who have no religious beliefs, and Protestant Christians. Moslems do not forbid divorce, but are committed to family life and divorce is less common.

Reconstituted families are less common amongst people who have a strong belief in the family and who disapprove of divorce, usually because their religious doctrines are against it. These include Hindus, Sikhs and Roman Catholics to whom marriage is sacred and should not be dissolved.

Life in a reconstituted family

This can be a positive experience for a child because:

- their parent may be happier, more secure and have greater financial resources
- the child gains a parent and possibly an extended family.

However they may:

- have difficulty relating to a step-parent and step-brothers and sisters
- have to compete for attention with children of their own age
- feel a loss of attention because they have to share their parent
- have to accept the birth of children of their parent's new relationship.

CHECK!

1 What is the difference between a nuclear, extended and reconstituted family?

DO!

1 Draw a diagram of your own family tree and show whether it is nuclear, extended or reconstituted.
2 Consider the points made above about life in different families and compare it with your experiences.

Partnership arrangements

Adults have a wide variety of arrangements for partnerships. These provide different care environments for children. They include:

- monogamous marriage between heterosexual partners (one partner of each gender); this is still popular in Britain, although the rate of marriage has declined since the 1960s
- polygamy, the marriage of a person of one gender (usually a man) to a number of others (usually women) at the same time; it is illegal to enter into this arrangement in Britain, where it is called bigamy. It has been very common in other countries, especially with Moslem cultures
- serial monogamy, a term used to describe a series of partners over a period of time, each followed by divorce or separation
- cohabitation, in which partners live together without the legal tie of marriage; this is increasingly common in Britain where about 30 per cent of partners cohabit; although many marry their partner later, especially when they have children. This arrangement is now acceptable among many social groups who would have previously seen it as a disgrace; some people, including Asian families, continue to be against it
- homosexual partnerships, especially between women, are increasingly viewed as an acceptable base for the rearing of children. As recently as the early 1980s women who left their husbands to live with a woman often lost the

custody of their children; such an arrangement was thought unsuitable. In June 1994 two women from Manchester became the first lesbian couple to be made the joint legal parents of the child of one of them. This was made possible by The Children Act (1989) that enables parental responsibility to be shared by a range of people. All the research carried out so far since the 1960s shows no differences in the social and emotional development of children of lesbian and heterosexual partnerships, or to their gender orientation.

THINK!

1 In what ways do you think that the different partnership arrangements outlined above make any fundamental difference to a child's experience and development?

Family breakdown

Marriage is a legal contract between two people. It places on partners certain duties to behave reasonably and to support each other. It also gives certain rights to both partners, including the right to live in the marital home and to have equal parental responsibility for their children. The sole grounds for divorce following the Divorce Reform Act (1969) is the 'irretrievable breakdown' of a marriage. The evidence that can be used to prove breakdown is:

- adultery
- unreasonable behaviour
- desertion for two years
- partners living separately for two years and agreeing to a divorce
- partners living separately for five years.

The breakdown of the partnership between parents is experienced in a similar way by children, whether their parents are legally married or not. The possible effects of separation and loss are described in Book 1, Chapter 14.

An unmarried father has no legal rights over his children following separation, unless he has acquired parental responsibility (see Chapter 19, *Understanding child protection*).

When a partnership breaks down, there can be disagreements between parents about where a child should live and how often each parent should see the child. In such a dispute, parents can apply to the court for a variety of orders under the Children Act (1989). This Act replaces orders that previously concerned custody and access with four new orders known as Section 8 orders, plus a Family Assistance order. These four orders are:

- a Residence order, stating who the child is to live with; it can be made in favour of more than one person and state how much time the child should spend with each person

- a Contact order, requiring the person with whom the child lives to allow the child to have contact with the person named on the Order; parents, grandparents and other family members may apply for this if they are being denied contact with a child
- a Prohibited Steps order, applied for if someone objects to something that a parent is doing concerning a child; the order aims to restrict the way that a person exercises their parental responsibility, whether they can take a child abroad, for example
- a Specific Issues order, aiming to settle disputes about a child's care and upbringing; it can make a specific order, for example, concerning education or medical treatment.

The Family Assistance Order aims to provide short term help to a family who cannot overcome their disagreements concerning their children following separation.

DO!

1 Make a study of the rise in the rate of divorce in the past 150 years and explore the reasons for this.

THINK!

1 Why is it important that child-care workers know of any orders that relate to children in their care?

CHECK!

1 Name five kinds of partnership arrangements.
2 What are Section 8 orders?

Family size

The average number of dependent children per family in Britain is now about two. This has gradually fallen since the middle of the last century when it was about six. There are many reasons for this change. The most significant are:
- the increased availability of contraception and legal abortion
- a rise in the standard and cost of living, together with the fact that children are more expensive to support because they start work later
- changes in women's roles, attitudes and expectations; many women regard child rearing as only a part of their lives and want to do other things as well.

Although the average family has two children, there are of course families with more. Children from large families have some differences in their life experiences. Research shows that on average their life chances are not as good as children from small families.

Many children grow up in families where they are the only child. These children are more successful, but there are possible social disadvantages for them.

DO!

Pair up with another

1 Carry out some research of your own: talk to someone who is a member of a large family, and someone who is an only child. Record the positive and negative aspects of their experience and any ideas you have.
2 Think of any particular needs that only children, and those from large families, might have when they start school. Describe some activities that you could provide to meet these children's differing needs.

Changing roles within the family

DOMESTIC ROLES

There is evidence that, in families across a range of social and cultural groups in Britain, the traditional role of male as provider and bread winner, and female as carer and homemaker, have changed. Men are increasingly involved in the care of their young children, and women are more likely to work outside the home. Research shows, however, that women still have the major responsibility for either doing or organising domestic work.

DO!

1 Carry out some research of your own: interview an older member of your family and find out differences between the tasks that men and women do now compared to those in the past. Write an account of your results.
2 Talk to someone from a cultural background different from your own and compare the roles of men and women in their family.

WOMEN AND WORK

Nearly half the workforce in Britain is female. Although an increasing number of women with dependent children work outside the home, the younger their children are, the less likely they are to work either full- or part-time. This probably reflects the absence of affordable child-care provision for young children. In some European countries there is a much higher level of provision and a much higher proportion of mothers working outside the home.

DO!

1 Try to find out some facts and figures about female employment and child-care facilities in other European countries.

The effects of parents working

When both parents of young children work outside the home they have to make some arrangement for the care of their children. A range of different alternatives is outlined in Chapter 1. Current research shows that children's needs can be met if they are provided with good substitute care.

DO!

1 Write a description of what good substitute day-care provision should provide in order to meet the all-round developmental needs of young children.

Children's needs can be met if they are provided with good substitute care

Working with children and their families

There are some important points for anyone working with children and their families to remember:

- the family forms a central part of any child's life
- children come from a variety of family types and structures
- each child's family is important and meaningful to that individual child
- we tend to be very self-centred in our view of families, seeing our own family as 'normal', and others as 'different'

- in order to respond positively to the children in their care child-care workers need to understand and accept different family types
- stereotyping and judgmental attitudes concerning families must be avoided.

IMPROVING WORKING PRACTICE

- Try to increase your awareness and understanding of different family patterns. You can do this by observing people, talking to them, reading books and articles, watching programmes on the television and videos. It is important to be open and willing to learn.
- Inform yourself of the family circumstances of each child in your care. Remember that confidentiality is essential, both in what you say to others and how you keep records.
- Assess the individual needs of each child. This is the only way that you can ensure equality of opportunity for each child. People who say that they 'treat all children the same' are denying them equality by not recognising and providing for their differences.
- Plan the best way to meet these needs by providing appropriate care and activities.

Alternative forms of care

Under the Children Act (1989) local authorities have a responsibility to provide a range of services to safeguard and provide welfare for 'children in need' in their area (see Chapter 1). They can do this by providing advice, assistance and services to families. They may also do this by looking after children full-time, in foster homes or community homes.

LOCAL AUTHORITY CARE

Provision of accommodation

Sometimes the most appropriate help a local authority can give a family is to provide accommodation for a child under a voluntary arrangement with the child's parents. This might be offered:

- to give parents respite (a break) from looking after a child who is difficult to care for
- when a family situation makes it very difficult for parents to meet the needs of a child, through illness or severe family problems.

Parents may have their children back home at any time under this voluntary arrangement, and are encouraged to have regular contact with them.

Children in care

Local authorities aim to keep children and parents together, and to promote the care of children within their own families. There are, however, situations when children's welfare can only be protected by removing them from their family or placing them under compulsory supervision within it. To do this the authority must obtain a court order. These orders include:

- an Emergency Protection order
- a Child Assessment order
- a Supervision order
- a Care order.

These orders are described in Chapter 22. An Education Supervision order places a school-age child under the supervision of the local authority if the court decides that the child is not attending school properly.

Types of care

A local authority will provide the type of care for a child that is most appropriate to the child's needs. The type of care is not necessarily linked to whether the child is being provided with accommodation voluntarily or is the subject of a care order. Children may be placed in foster homes, residential children's homes, or in some circumstances, with adopters.

Foster care

Foster parents are people from all backgrounds who are recruited by a local authority to take children into their homes for short or longer periods of time. They can be single or married couples. They are interviewed at length concerning their suitability to look after children; they need a range of qualities to meet the demands of looking after children whose behaviour may be disturbed by their life experiences. They may also have contact with the children's parents.

Once the foster parents are approved they are paid a weekly allowance for children placed with them. Foster care is now considered the most appropriate form of substitute care for children who cannot be with their families.

Residential care

Residential care is the term used to describe children's homes, often referred to as community homes. They usually consist of small units, often ordinary houses within the community. They are staffed by residential social workers. They are generally considered to be unsuitable for the care of young children, except in special circumstances; they are more likely to be used to accommodate older children, larger families, or to assess children's developmental needs.

Adoption

Adoption is a legal process whereby the parental rights and responsibilities for a child are given up by one set of parents and taken on by another. Adoption must be arranged through a recognised adoption agency and an order made in court. All local authorities must provide an adoption service. Adopters go through a similar interview and selection process as foster parents. In recent years the number of babies placed for adoption has declined enormously, from 2649 in 1979 to 895 in 1991. Many adoptions now involve older children.

Children have a right to make their wishes known at an adoption hearing. The current trend is towards open adoption, where some form of contact between a child and their birth parents or relatives is maintained. Attention is also given to the need to place children in families of the same ethnic origin.

THINK!

1 What qualities do you think foster parents need?
2 Why is foster care considered to be the most suitable form of substitute care for young children?
3 Why is residential care considered to be less suitable than fostering?
4 Why do you think there are now fewer babies available for adoption?
5 In what circumstances may adoption be more suitable for a child than long-term foster care?

DO!

1 Find out more about foster care and adoption from your local authority social services department.

Key terms
You need to know what these words and phrases mean. Go back through the chapter and find out.

Functions of the family	Reconstituted family
Monogamous	Section 8 orders
Cohabitation	Foster care
Nuclear family	Adoption
Extended family	

---

18 SOCIAL ISSUES

> **This chapter includes:**
> - What is society?
> - The individual and society
> - The effect of the individual on society
> - The effect of society on the individual
> - Personal and social pressures and problems
> - Sources of social disadvantage and pressure
> - Differing responses to pressures and problems.

What is society?

The following statement was made in 1987 by Margaret Thatcher, the then Prime Minister of Britain: 'There is no such thing as Society. There are individual men and women, and there are families.' This statement has since been commented on by many people.

On the other hand many people believe that society does exist. They perceive that individuals and families do not live in isolation, but are strongly affected by the social and legal environment within which they live.

Society can be described as people living together within a framework of laws and customs that have been created and shared by them over a period of time. Society provides the social, cultural, economic and physical environment for people's lives.

A MULTI-CULTURAL SOCIETY

A multi-cultural society is one that includes a variety of cultural groups who have differing customs and rules. This can provide a varied and positive social environment. Sometimes the customs of one group become known and adopted by another group. In this way people's lives are enriched. A simple example of this in Britain is the enjoyment by many people of the traditional foods of different cultural groups.

For a multi-cultural society to work positively and be of benefit to all its members it is essential that:
- certain laws are shared and respected by all
- there is mutual acceptance and tolerance of differences in customs
- no group has, or is thought to have, more power, status and resources than another.

1 Can you think of instances when the sharing and tolerance mentioned above does not happen in Britain?

A multi-cultural society can provide a varied and positive social environment

DO!

1 Talk about Margaret Thatcher's statement and decide what you think it means. Do you believe that something called 'society' exists outside and beyond individuals and families and that 'society' affects them and is affected by them?

The individual and society

THE LEGAL FRAMEWORK

Britain, like every democratic society, has a set of laws. These have been passed in parliament by elected representatives and apply to everyone. They form a framework of rules that cover the rights citizens have to be treated fairly and equally. They include an outline of a citizen's:

- rights to certain services

- right to protection from harm
- duties to behave in certain ways
- penalties and punishments the individual will incur if they break the law.

SOCIALLY DEVIANT BEHAVIOUR

The term 'deviant' is used to describe behaviour that is socially different. Behaviour comes to be regarded as deviant by some if they consider that the actions of others are not what they expect or find desirable and do not follow the rules of the group.

There are two main types of deviant behaviour:

- illegal: this behaviour is criminal and carries legal sanctions to punish and prevent it; it includes violence, vandalism, stealing and drug dealing
- legal: this behaviour may either be disapproved of or tolerated; it includes dressing and behaving differently, New Age travelling (the government wants to make this illegal), prostitution.

The media is often very powerful in labelling certain groups as deviant and suggesting that they are responsible for society's problems. The way that travellers are portrayed is an example of this. Deviance does not necessarily result in poor parenting. Some parents whose behaviour is socially different meet the needs of their children very well. Some life styles, however, may leave children more vulnerable to neglect.

THINK!

1 Think of some behaviour that is illegal. Have you ever done anything illegal, like breaking the speed limit, or using materials at work for your own purposes?
2 Can you think of some behaviour that is regarded by many as deviant but is legal?
3 There are many personal and social explanations for deviant behaviour; try to think of some of these.
4 What kinds of deviant behaviour might affect a family's ability to care for their children? What kinds might have no effect?

The effect of the individual on society

SOCIAL ACTION

Individual members of any society can significantly affect the society in which they live. They can do this by taking social action directed at other people or groups in society. They can do this in a variety of ways.

Throughout history individual politicians, social reformers, those in business, industry and the media have brought about changes to society and people's lives. On a smaller scale some people work hard in their local communities. They give time and energy through different organisations to contribute to the lives of the people around them. Others contribute to the richness of society by participating in everyday events within their local schools and community groups. Some members of society accept their position and use their energy simply to cope with their own lives and with their families.

Sometimes people perceive that they have a worse position in society than others, but they do not accept their situation passively. They want to achieve a better position. They sometimes join together to fight what they see as an unfair system. The Trades Union movement grew out of this perception. People may use legal means to achieve this, (like marches and strikes) or they may feel justified in taking illegal action (suffragettes who were trying to win the vote did this).

In many societies there are people who believe, rightly or wrongly, that the system is against them achieving success or equality. They believe they are discriminated against and denied access to the things that are valued by society as a whole. They do not believe that they can achieve anything either by positive group action or legal means. They take destructive action either against themselves (for example through drug addiction) or against individuals or groups (for example through crime) or against society as a whole (for example by terrorism).

THINK!

1 Try to think of other examples of social action by people that illustrate each of the categories described above.

The effect of society on the individual

SOCIETY AND SOCIO-ECONOMIC STATUS

A person's socio-economic status or position (often referred to as their social class) is determined by the structure of the society they live in. In Britain people's status is usually decided by the type of work they do, in other words their occupation. Manual work is of lower status and is usually paid less than non-manual work.

The government uses six socio-economic categories that place people according to the occupation of the head of their household. The categories are labelled as follows:

- 1: professional and higher administrative (for example lawyers, accountants, doctors, large company directors)
- 2: intermediate professionals and administrative (for example teachers, managers, librarians)
- 3NM: non-manual skilled workers (for example clerks, policemen, sales representatives, office clerks)

- 3M: skilled manual workers (for example electricians, miners, train drivers, printers)
- 4: semi-skilled manual workers (for example postmen, farm workers, telephonists)
- 5: unskilled manual workers (for example labourers, cleaners, refuse collectors, porters).

The government uses these categories and carries out research into different aspects of people's lives. It makes links between social class and life experiences and chances. Such research shows for example that those from higher groups are more likely to survive infancy, have better health and live longer.

DO!

1 Work out the category of the following occupations: the Director of Education, a teacher in a primary school, a nursery nurse, a school secretary, a builder, a cook, a cleaner.

SOCIAL MOBILITY AND EQUALITY OF OPPORTUNITY

The test of how far a society gives equality of opportunity to its members is how easy it is for anyone to move upwards to a higher status, for example from Group 5 to Group 1. In a 'closed' society (for example the caste system in India, and in feudal Britain) people are ascribed (given) a role and position in society at birth and can never move from this. In an 'open' society people are able to move from one social position to another. They can do this through the education system, their job and by marriage.

The extent to which children can move from their social position of birth depends on the relative openness of a society. In Britain there are still many people who find it less easy to be successful and upwardly mobile. This includes those from the lowest socio-economic groups and those who commonly experience prejudice and discrimination. Equal opportunities policies are designed to overcome this.

DO!

1 Find out which groups of people in Britain are less likely to be successful.
2 Discuss this with others and suggest some reasons why it happens.
3 Find out what is stated in the equal opportunities policy of your place of work.
4 Suggest ways that an equal opportunities policy can be carried out in practice in a nursery or school environment.

CHILDREN AND SOCIAL MOBILITY

Children initially take the social status of their family of birth. The day-care and education system provides them with a real opportunity to broaden their experience and, if they wish, to change their social position as adults. The attitudes of their family of origin are very important in determining whether children make use of opportunities offered them.

The strong influence of family background is obvious when the government publishes the examination results of individual schools. With slight variations, the children from schools that are in areas where more families are from higher socio-economic groups achieve higher results than children from schools in areas where most families are from lower socio-economic groups.

THINK!

1 The publication of examination results illustrates that children from lower socio-economic groups tend on average to do less well academically at school. Can you think of any reasons for this? (See Book 1, Chapter 11, *Socialisation*.)

Personal and social pressures and problems

All adults are likely to face some kind of difficulty, problem or pressure in their lifetime. If they are parents their children will probably be affected in some way by their experiences.

Some problems are referred to as 'personal' when their cause lies very close to the circumstances of an individual person's life. Examples of personal problems are difficulties with or loss of relationships, bereavement, mental and physical ill-health. Other problems are referred to as 'social' when they are caused mainly by the way the social and physical environment is organised. Examples of social problems are urban decay or rural decline, racial and social discrimination, poverty, unemployment, bad housing, homelessness.

There are often close links between social and personal problems; the experience of social problems often causes personal problems. For example unemployment may cause stress, worry and feelings of uselessness; these can lead to anxiety, depression and ill health.

DO!

1 Write down other links that may exist between the experience of social and personal problems; explain the links.

Sources of social disadvantage and pressure

People can be described as disadvantaged if they do not have the equal opportunity to achieve what other people in society regard as normal.

POVERTY

Lack of money is usually a major problem for people. A family are considered to be living in poverty if their income is less than half the national average weekly wage. This is called the poverty line. A Department of Social Security report published by the government in 1994 revealed that 14 million people in Britain were living below the poverty line; four million of them were children. This is three times the number recorded in 1979.

Poverty is now accepted by most people to be relative. This means that people are considered to be poor 'if their resources fall seriously short of the resources commanded by the average individual or family in the community' (Peter Townsend, *Poverty in the United Kingdom*, 1979). In the past in Britain there were many people living in absolute poverty, that is they did not have 'enough provision to maintain their health and working efficiency' (Seebohm Rowntree, *Studies of Poverty in the City of York*, 1899).

DO!

1 There are many references to poverty in sociology and social policy books. Read some of these so that you understand clearly the ideas of absolute and relative poverty.

The main causes of poverty are low wages or living on state social security benefits. The people who are most likely to be poor are those who are:

- unemployed
- members of one-parent families
- members of black and other minority groups
- sick or incapacitated
- elderly
- low paid.

The effects of poverty on the family

Poverty can affect every area of a family's life. There may not be enough money for a nutritious varied diet, adequate housing, transport, household equipment, toys. It can cause stress, anxiety, unhappiness and lead to poor physical and mental health. People are limited in their ability to go out, to entertain others, and to have outings or holidays. Family relationships can become strained.

People are aware through the media, especially television, that others have a much higher standard of living. This can result in a feeling of hopelessness and of being outside the main stream of society. An 'underclass' of people, who have no hope, can form.

Many people experience the poverty trap: if they are receiving state benefits, they find that by earning a small amount more they lose most of their benefits and become worse off. They are trapped in their position.

UNEMPLOYMENT

Unemployment has been high since the late 1970s. It sometimes falls only to rise again. At present there is little immediate hope of achieving full employment. Unemployment has affected every section of the population, but some people are more vulnerable to it than others. These are:

- people without skills or qualifications, and manual workers
- young and old people
- women
- people who generally suffer discrimination in society; these include people from ethnic minority groups, people who have disabilities
- those who have suffered mental illness or have been in prison.

The effects of unemployment on the family

Unemployment can have profound effects on individuals and families. Those experiencing long-term unemployment are more likely to be living in poverty and suffering its effects. They may also have feelings of shame, uselessness, boredom and frustration that can affect their mental and physical health. Family relationships can become strained, and provide an unhappy or even violent environment for children. Whole communities can become demoralised and run down.

DO!

1 Find out what the current level of unemployment is and how this has varied in recent years.
2 Find out who can and cannot register as unemployed.

INADEQUATE HOUSING

Despite the fact that there has been a massive slum clearance and rebuilding programme since the 1950s, many people still live in accommodation that is damp, overcrowded and unsuitable for children. Some of the high-rise flats that were built to rehouse people in the 1950s and 1960s were very badly built. They contributed to a wide range of personal and social problems. Many of them have since been demolished, although they still remain in some urban areas.

There are obvious links between people being poor and living in poor housing conditions. Those who have money buy accommodation that suits their needs. Those who are poor have to take anything that is available to them.

The effects of inadequate housing on the family

Damp, inadequate and dangerous housing can lead to bad health, illness, accidents, the spread of infection, and poor hygiene. It is difficult to improve broken down houses or keep them clean. Adults may blame each other, feel depressed and worried. This, together with lack of play space, creates an unsuitable environment for children to grow up in.

1 Write down the disadvantages to a young family of living in a poorly maintained high-rise block of flats.

HOMELESSNESS

There is a national shortage of accommodation at affordable prices. This is caused in part by the government's policy of giving council tenants the right to buy their houses, while not allowing councils to use the money from sales to build more houses. Private owners are reluctant to let accommodation to families because legislation makes it difficult subsequently to evict them. There is a growing number of homeless people; they mainly become homeless when:

- their relatives are unwilling or unable to continue to provide them with accommodation
- they are evicted for mortgage or rent arrears
- their marriage or partnerships break up.

The majority are:

- young
- either single or with young families
- on low incomes.

The local authority has a legal duty to accommodate homeless families. The shortage of accommodation means that an increasing number are placed in temporary bed and breakfast accommodation (see Chapter 1). The conditions for families in bed and breakfast hotels are totally unsuitable. The accommodation can often be overcrowded, dangerous and unhygienic. There is usually a lack of cooking, washing and other basic amenities. There is little privacy or play space. People often suffer isolation from family and friends. In addition their access to education, health and other services is disrupted. Families can spend several years in this type of accommodation.

The effects of homelessness on the family

Living for a long period in cramped and unsatisfactory conditions can have a very bad effect on family relationships between adults and children. Parents who experience this degree of stress in their everyday existence may have little energy to provide more than the basic necessities for children. The lack of play space leads to children being under-stimulated and having little access to fresh air and exercise. Their development can be affected in every area. The provision of day care can be of great value for children living in bed and breakfast accommodation.

1 Write down the five developmental areas as headings. Under each heading, list the needs that a child has in each area. In another column write down the reasons that these needs may not be met if a child is living in bed and breakfast accommodation.

2 Describe how a day-care centre can help the whole family.

The provision of day care can be of great value for children living in bed and breakfast accommodation

RACIAL DISCRIMINATION

Race is difficult to define, but the term is used to describe a group who share some common biological traits. Ethnic groups are people who share a common culture. Ethnic minority groups are smaller than the majority group in their society.

There are many ethnic groups in Britain. Some attract little attention, for example the many people of Italian, Polish and Irish origin who live in some parts of Britain. The groups that receive the most attention are those who are noticeable because their culture, dress or skin colour make them stand out, particularly those of African-Caribbean, Indian, Pakistani and Bangladeshi origin. They are commonly referred to as black and/or Asian.

The Race Relations Act (1965) made it illegal to discriminate against people because of their race in employment, housing, and the provision of goods and services. In 1976 the Commission for Racial Equality (CRE) was given greater powers to take people to court for both direct and indirect discrimination.

Indirect discrimination occurs when people are treated, either intentionally or unintentionally, less favourably than others.

Patterns of migration

Historically the pattern of migration (movement to and from the country) in Britain has been that:

- there has been a steady flow of people emigrating (leaving)
- there have been noticeable waves of people immigrating (coming in).

Overall the numbers have more or less balanced each other.

THINK!

1 Try to think of ways in which children and their parents may suffer indirect discrimination in a school.

The problems faced by ethnic minority families

Ethnic minority families, particularly those that are very visible, experience discrimination, prejudice and intolerance, stereotyping and scapegoating as part of their everyday life. Black and Asian people experience discrimination particularly in:

- employment: they are more often found in low-status, low-paid jobs with less chance of promotion and more shift work than white people; black people are also more vulnerable to unemployment and poverty
- housing: differences between ethnic groups are very noticeable; Asian families have tended to buy, but usually the cheapest houses in inner city areas; African-Caribbeans are more likely to live in poorer council accommodation
- racial harassment and attacks: there has been an alarming rise in racial attacks in Britain, some resulting in death; the experience of this can be devastating for an individual and a family. The police are introducing programmes to counteract racism amongst police officers and to encourage a policy of quicker response to racist attacks.

DO!

1 Find out and write down a definition of discrimination, prejudice, intolerance, stereotyping and scapegoating.
2 Carry out some research into patterns of migration in Britain. Find out when and why people have immigrated to, and emigrated from, Britain. You will find references to this in GCSE sociology books. Write your conclusions in your own words.
3 Find out some more detailed information about the differences in life chances between people from different ethnic groups.

THE URBAN ENVIRONMENT

Many of Britain's inner cities are characterised by environmental pollution and decay, lack of playspace and higher crime rates. They have attracted a lot of publicity in recent years. This has resulted in a number of government and voluntary funded schemes aimed at improving the environment and the quality of people's lives. The success of these initiatives is varied, partly because of the difficulty of knowing exactly what the problems are.

Britain's inner cities have suffered a loss of population in recent years. Many people have moved from urban centres to the suburbs for gardens and cleaner air. This has been helped by the development of public and private transport. There has also been a loss of industry and employment opportunities in inner cities, and poor planning has contributed to impersonal environments and decay.

In most cases therefore, those who have material resources choose not to settle in the centre towns, but live on the outskirts. This leaves a concentration of people with fewer resources, including those experiencing:

- poverty, unemployment and housing stress
- physical and mental illness
- discrimination because of their ethnicity or disability
- social isolation, being members of one-parent families
- family problems including violence and abuse.

There are also more people involved in crime, drug abuse and prostitution.

In addition, demands on the health and social services tend to be higher, and because of this the quality of these services tends to be poorer.

One way of understanding inner city problems therefore is through the idea of 'multiple deprivation'. This emphasises the fact that urban deprivation is not a single problem, but a number of problems concentrated in one area.

The effects of the urban environment on the family

It is important to remember that an urban environment is not necessarily a negative experience for all residents. There are many people who live happy and fulfilled lives and who rear their children successfully in urban centres. Deprivation is, however, more common than in suburban areas. The lives of some children and their development may be adversely affected in a variety of ways by living in such an environment.

DO!

1 Write down how children's development can be affected if their family are experiencing 'multiple deprivation'. Give the reasons for your suggestions.

THE RURAL ENVIRONMENT

Much less publicity is given to the problems faced by families in rural areas. Britain has a proportionally smaller rural population than many European

Many of Britain's inner cities are characterised by environmental pollution, decay and lack of playspace

In most cases those who have material resources choose not to settle in the centre of towns, but live on the outskirts

countries. Some people who live in rural areas are supported by a high income and this buys them desirable housing, land and private transport. Others, for example farm workers, have incomes well below the national average. They may suffer from poverty and unemployment and all the effects that this can bring. They can find housing and transport very difficult to obtain.

The effects of a rural environment on the family

Families living in a rural environment can be subject to similar pressures to those of an urban family if they are on low incomes. The following question will help you to think more about this.

DO!

1 Write down the possible difficulties and disadvantages that may be faced by a family with a low income in a rural environment.

Differing responses to pressures and problems

One of the dangers of describing social problems and people's responses to them is that not all people respond to them or are affected by them in the same way. It can be puzzling that some people cope with pressures and others do not. We can only say that people may respond to, or might be affected in a certain way. Differences in responses can partly be explained by:

- how severe, intense and long-term the pressure is: many people cope reasonably well with short-term pressures in every day life, but are more tested by those that are long term and severe
- differences in the resources that people have to cope with life.

RESOURCES

Resources are the practical, social and emotional sources of help and strength that people have in varying degrees to help them to cope with life, and bring up their families. Some people have fewer resources to cope with everyday life than others. This means that:

- at times of stress and difficulty they are very vulnerable and can be overwhelmed
- they are less able to protect their children from pressures and problems
- they may at times be unable to provide adequate care for their children (this does not mean, however, that they are irresponsible or lack affection for their children).

Practical resources

Practical resources include reserves of money, material assets, managing skills, mobility.

Lack of practical resources

The stress caused by social conditions such as poverty, unemployment or poor housing may affect the capacity of a person to care for their children either temporarily or permanently. People who have no savings, who worry constantly about money and who endure poor environmental conditions probably experience a higher level of stress in their everyday lives than those who have no such worries.

Social resources
Social resources include a supportive family, friends, a close social network, being a member of a group.

Lack of social resources
People experience social isolation when they have no close family or friends to care about them. It means there is no one to share troubles and anxieties with. There is a saying 'A trouble shared is a trouble halved'. Parents who have warm and caring personal relationships, and have the support of others, may be better able to cope at times of stress and difficulty.

Emotional resources
Emotional resources include having had the experience of stable and caring relationships, having high self-esteem, the ability to cope with stress and frustration, being able to recognise and deal with extreme feelings and having a positive view of life and the ability to trust and give.

Lack of emotional resources
A range of personal issues such as low self-esteem, mental ill health, difficulties with relationships, bereavement, illness, incapacity or other previous life experiences may affect people's emotional resources. These issues can profoundly affect a person's view of life and make them vulnerable to stress. This may in turn affect parenting skills.

DO!

1 Describe how social pressures and a lack of resources can affect the healthy development of a child.
2 Explain how a nursery can help to meet the all-round needs of a child and help to compensate for any disadvantage the child may experience.

HELP AVAILABLE

There are many statutory, voluntary and private organisations that can help people at times of need. These are described in Chapter 1 of this book.

Key terms

You need to know what these words and phrases mean. Go back through the chapter and find out.

Society	Personal and social problems
A multi-cultural society	Social disadvantage
Socially deviant behaviour	Absolute and relative poverty
Socio-economic status	The poverty trap
Equality of opportunity	Ethnic minority groups
Social mobility	Migration

19 UNDERSTANDING CHILD PROTECTION

> **This chapter includes:**
> - **Child protection, history and the law**
> - **Child protection and the rights of children and parents**
> - **Understanding child abuse.**

Child protection, history and the law

The unkind treatment by some adults of children has occurred throughout history. The novels of Charles Dickens paint a vivid picture of the lives of some children in 19th century Britain. In *Oliver Twist*, for example, Dickens shows how cruelty and harsh punishment were both common and acceptable. Many children had to work long hours; they were often beaten and neglected.

The Earl of Shaftesbury was one of the people in the 19th century who initiated a series of social reforms that improved the lives of children. Laws passed since then have increasingly recognised the right of children to have their basic needs met and to be protected from abuse. The most recent child protection law to be passed was The Children Act (1989).

The novels of Dickens paint a vivid picture of the lives of some children in 19th century Britain

RECENT HISTORY

By the 1960s most people thought that the ill-treatment of children was a thing of the past. Whenever cases came to light people thought that they were exceptional. There was an apparent lack of awareness that abuse was still taking place. There remained also a commonly held belief that no one should interfere with the rights of parents over their children, especially the right to punish them. Consequently, the law still failed to protect children.

However, during the 1960s, some doctors and social workers began to develop a new awareness of abuse. They took a close interest both in the injuries that they observed in children and the explanations that carers gave for their children's injuries. They asked questions to try to find out whether some injuries were really accidental. As a result they began to discover more and more cases of abuse. In 1962 Dr CH Kempe wrote about 'The battered child syndrome'. This drew attention to the problem of 'non-accidental injury' of children by their carers both in the USA and Britain. During the 1970s and 1980s awareness increased of a range of signs that might indicate deliberate injury to children. Awareness of the occurrence and signs of sexual abuse was also increasing during this time.

CHECK!

1 Why did most people In Britain in the 1960s think that the ill-treatment of children was a thing of the past?

DO!

1 Find out about some of the ways that children were ill-treated in the past.
2 Indicate which of these no longer happen and suggest why they do not.

Child protection and the rights of children and parents

The Children Act (1989) is a major piece of legislation. Previous laws, passed over many years, overlapped and were sometimes inconsistent. This caused confusion and difficulty. The Children Act aims to provide a consistent approach to child protection by both bringing together and changing previous laws.

There was also a concern that recent law had gone too far and could be used too easily to take rights and responsibilities away from parents. This was thought to be neither in the interests of children nor parents. One of the main aims of the 1989 act was therefore to balance the *needs and rights of children* and the *rights and responsibilities of parents*.

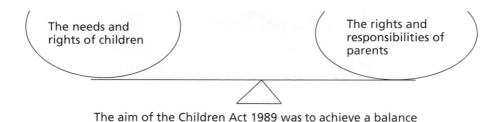

The aim of the Children Act 1989 was to achieve a balance

The Children Act (1989)

THE NEEDS AND RIGHTS OF CHILDREN

The way that children are brought up varies a great deal between different social groups and cultures. For example, some groups are traditionally more indulgent towards children while others are more strict. The Children Act (1989) values and acknowledges these differences. However, the act recognises that all children have certain needs that are universal: this means that all children have these needs, whatever their culture, ethnic origin, social class or family background, and are entitled to have them met. These are the basic developmental needs:

- the need for physical care and protection
- the need for intellectual stimulation and play
- the need for emotional love and security
- the need for positive social contact and relationships.

All children have certain rights; these include the right:

- to have their needs met and safeguarded
- to be protected from neglect, abuse and exploitation
- to be brought up in their family of birth wherever possible
- to be considered as an individual, to be listened to and have their wishes and feelings taken into account when any decisions are made concerning their welfare.

THE RIGHTS AND RESPONSIBILITIES OF PARENTS

Parents' rights

In the past parents had the right of ownership of their children. This right, supported by the law, allowed parents to do more or less as they wished with their children. The law has gradually changed. It now limits parents' rights and powers, but gives them the right to be involved throughout any child protection process as long as this is consistent with the welfare and protection of the child. The law includes the idea that parents also have certain duties and responsibilities towards their children.

All children have the right to be brought up in their family of birth wherever possible

Parents' responsibilities

The Children Act uses the phrase *parental responsibility* to sum up the collection of duties, rights and authority that parents have concerning their children. The idea of parental responsibility is a principle that is at the centre of the Children Act (1989). The law does not say precisely how adults should exercise their parental responsibility; it recognises that there is a great variety of ways that they can do this. It emphasises that parents have a duty to care for their children and raise them 'to moral, physical and emotional health'. In this way the law imposes minimum standards for the care of children and protects their welfare. The 1989 act recognises that parents are responsible towards their children for the following:

- caring for and maintaining them
- controlling them
- making sure that they receive proper education.

Parents also have the authority to:

- discipline them
- take them out of the country
- consent to medical examination and treatment.

DO!

1 Using the outline above, write in your own words the everyday things that parents have a responsibility to do for, and provide for, their children.

The following groups have parental responsibility:

- married partners
- separated or divorced parents; their responsibility is legally unaffected by the separation
- an unmarried mother.

The following may acquire (gain) parental responsibility:

- an unmarried father, but he does not have it automatically; he must either make formal 'parental responsibility agreement' with the mother, or he may apply to court for an order that gives him parental responsibility
- people who are appointed as guardians if a child's parents die
- carers, following an adoption order, or a residence order
- a local authority, when a court makes a care order or an emergency protection order (see Chapter 22, *Child protection procedures*).

Parents do not now lose parental responsibility for their children (except when they are adopted). They continue to have responsibility even if a court order is made that removes a child from their care.

Understanding child abuse

Despite the passing of legislation that makes clear both children's rights and parents responsibilities, children are still neglected and abused. Child-care workers need to understand why this may happen.

THINK!

1 Can you think why it is important to try to understand why child abuse still occurs?

THE IMPORTANCE OF UNDERSTANDING

It is important to develop an understanding of child abuse, firstly because understanding is necessary for a professional approach to carers. Unless we understand at least some of the factors that contribute to any case of child abuse we may be in danger of behaving unprofessionally towards a carer and not treating them with consideration. This professional approach includes:

- being considerate, caring and understanding
- having a non-judgmental attitude towards others
- not stereotyping individuals or groups of people
- respecting confidentiality appropriately.

Child-care workers are increasingly involved in working with parents. *Partnership with parents* is one of the principles of the Children Act. The act recognises that parents are individuals with needs of their own and are entitled to help and consideration. They are also entitled to be involved in decisions affecting their children (see Chapter 3, *Working with parents*).

A second reason for the importance of developing an understanding of child abuse is that it helps in planning for the future. There are many factors that contribute to parents being abusive to their children. Understanding why abuse occurs increases the ability to understand a carer's needs and to predict the prognosis (the most likely outcome) of working with a carer. The ability of a parent to respond to the support you give may determine whether the parent is allowed to continue to care for their children.

DO!

1 Describe a professional response to child protection.

WHY DOES ABUSE OCCUR?

Research shows that abuse does not occur entirely at random, but is more likely to happen in some situations than others. There is a wide variety of predisposing factors (factors that exist in people's lives that make them more prone to abusing their children). Abuse is usually the result of a series of these factors occurring together. In each case there will be a different combination of factors. The relative importance of each of them will also vary.

The danger in trying to understand abuse is that it might lead to a prediction that if certain characteristics are present abuse will happen, or that all people with those characteristics will become abusers. This is not so. Nevertheless it is possible to look at certain factors, a combination of which is usually present in many cases of abuse. These factors enable us to recognise, understand and work with families where there is a higher risk of abuse. They can be described as *predisposing factors.*

PREDISPOSING FACTORS

Predisposing factors in cases of abuse may include an adult's personality and background, some kind of difficulty and stress in the adult's life or environment and factors relating to the child.

An adult's personality and background
A combination of the following characteristics has been noticed in abusing parents (remember that non-abusing parents may also have these characteristics):
- immaturity: some people have not developed a mature level of self-control in their reactions to life and its problems. Faced with stressful situations an adult may react strongly as a young child might
- having low self-esteem: some people have a very poor self-image; they have not experienced being valued and loved themselves. If they are struggling to care for a child they may feel inadequate and blame the child for making them feel worse about themselves
- an unhappy childhood where they never learnt to trust others: parents who

have experienced unhappiness in childhood may be less likely to appreciate the happiness that children can bring to their lives. They do not have a good role model to create a happy and caring environment for their children

- difficulty in experiencing pleasure: an inability to enjoy life and have fun may be a sign of stress and anxiety. This person may also have problems in coping with the stress of parenting and gain little pleasure from it
- unsatisfactory relationships where they may be experiencing sexual or other difficulties: difficulties in relationships can form an underlying base of stress and unhappiness in a person's life. It may form a general background of neglect or violence within which there is little respect for the individual
- being socially isolated: parents who have no friends or family nearby have little or no support at times of need; they have no one to share their anxieties with, or to call on for practical help
- having a fear of spoiling the child and a belief in the value of punishment: some people have little understanding of the value of rewards in dealing with children's behaviour; they think that responding to a child's demands will inevitably spoil the child. They are more likely to leave a child to cry and not to be warm and spontaneous in their reactions to them
- a belief in the value of strict discipline: there are many variations in parenting styles, family structures and relationships; these are not necessarily better or worse than each other. They meet the needs of children in different ways. Some styles of discipline use punishment (both physical and emotional) rather than rewards. This is more likely to lead to abuse if other factors are present
- not seeing children realistically: this involves having little or no understanding of child development and the normal behaviour of children at different stages; such adults are more likely to react negatively to behaviour that causes them difficulty, rather than accepting it as normal. They may inappropriately punish young children for crying, wetting themselves, having tantrums or making a mess
- being unable to empathise with the needs of a child and to respond appropriately: some people have difficulty in understanding the needs of children; they may react negatively when children make their needs known and demand attention
- having been abused themselves as children: these parents may have a number of unmet needs themselves and are therefore less likely to be able to meet the needs of a dependant child; they have also had a poor role model for parenting and family life
- have experienced difficulties during pregnancy and/or birth, or separation from their child following birth: difficulties during pregnancy and childbirth and early separation can result in a parent being less positive towards a child; faced with their children's demands they may be less able to cope. They may lose their temper more quickly and resort to violence more easily (this is covered in Book 1, Chapter 13, *Bonding and attachment*).

Difficulty and stress in the adult's life and environment

Stress may be short- or long-term (sometimes referred to as acute or chronic). It may have many causes. The experience of stress drains people's energy and leaves them with fewer resources available to cope with meeting the demands of children. Some factors that create stress are:

- personal problems: these include a range of personal pressures such as loss of relationships, bereavement, physical and mental ill health; the experience of these can weaken a person's ability to cope (as previously mentioned, it does not mean that they are irresponsible or lack affection for their children)
- social problems: the stress caused by social conditions such as poverty, unemployment or poor housing may affect the capacity of a person to care for their children; people who have constant money worries and who have to endure poor environmental conditions probably experience a higher level of stress in their everyday lives than those without such worries. This can provide a general background of unhappiness. This may be significant if it is experienced in combination with other factors outlined here.

Factors relating to the child

Although none of the following factors necessarily lead to a child being abused, significant factors may include:

- a crying child: most people can sympathise with the stress created by a child who cries a lot; when a carer is tired, and other factors are present, the stress brought about by crying can make a child vulnerable to abuse
- anything that interferes with early bonding or attachment between carer and child: there is much evidence that a carer is more likely to abuse a child when the attachment is weak rather than strong; it is for this reason that modern antenatal and postnatal care aims to keep parents with their babies and thus encourage the development of a strong bond between parent and child
- a child who is less pleasing to the carer or who does not meet parents expectations: this could be because the child is difficult to feed or care for, or is sickly and unhealthy; it includes children with disabilities who are statistically more vulnerable to abuse. The child may not be the gender the parents wanted; this may be very significant to parents for a variety of reasons
- some children are felt by their carers to be more difficult to care for at a specific stage of development: some people find babies particularly demanding and difficult, others have more difficulty caring for toddlers or older children
- some children 'invite' abuse: these children have learned that the only attention they get is abusive; they learn to bring about certain negative reactions in their carers because this is preferable to having no attention at all.

It does not necessarily follow that people who lack resources will abuse or neglect their children. In the majority of families they do not. The factors above can, however, help us to understand the different types of stress that may be present in any parent's life and may contribute to abusive situations.

Most people can sympathise with the stress created by a child who cries a lot

DO!

1 Write briefly and in your own words about the factors in an adult which increase the risk of abuse.

2 Read the following case study. It is a fictitious story of a child who was abused.

J is the third daughter of Mr and Mrs M. Mrs M. is 24 years old, Mr M is 10 years older than his wife. Mr M travels a great deal for his work and frequently spends several nights away from home at a time. This makes Mrs M jealous and unhappy. They live in an area where nobody seems to have much to do with their neighbours. Mrs M sees very little of her family who live in the next town. She was unhappy at home as a child; her parents frequently argued and fought, and so she felt pleased to get away when she married. Although her husband's family lives nearby, she seldom sees them as they disapproved of their son's marriage. Mrs M has never been very good at managing money or the house and her husband blames her for this; it worries her a great deal. Before J was born her parents very much wanted a boy. Her two sisters are 2 and 4 years old. Mrs M had high blood pressure during her pregnancy; as a result of this J's birth was induced four weeks before term. During the birth she showed signs of fetal distress; because of this a normal delivery was not possible and J was born by Caesarian section under general anaesthetic.

Mrs M was discharged from hospital two weeks before J. She found it very difficult to visit her during this time. When she came home J was very unsettled and cried a lot. She took a long time to take her feed and the doctor diagnosed colic. In recent weeks J's mother has seen both her health visitor and doctor several times and reported a series of minor ailments in the infant. Finally Mr M took the baby to the local casualty department following a long feeding session. J's body was bruised and she was unconscious.

3 With reference to the family described above, write down the specific factors relating to this adult and child, and the stresses that made abuse more likely to occur.

4 Write two short case studies of your own:
   a) about a family where there are little or no predisposing factors for abuse
   b) about a family where, because of the presence of certain factors, there appears to be a higher risk of abuse occurring.

Key terms

You need to know what these words and phrases mean. Go back through the chapter and find out.

The needs of children	Professionalism
The rights of children	Partnership with parents
The rights of parents	Predisposing factors
Parental responsibility	Higher risk

20 TYPES OF CHILD ABUSE

> **This chapter includes:**
> - Physical abuse and injury
> - Additional indicators of physical abuse
> - Neglect
> - Failure to thrive
> - Emotional abuse
> - Sexual abuse
> - Ritual and organised abuse
> - Disabled children and abuse.

Physical abuse and injury

Physical abuse involves someone deliberately harming or hurting a child. It covers a range of unacceptable behaviour, including what may be described, by some, as physical punishment. It can involve hitting, shaking, squeezing, burning, biting, attempted suffocation, drowning, giving a child poisonous substances, inappropriate drugs or alcohol. It includes the use of excessive force when carrying out tasks like feeding or nappy changing.

Physical abuse also includes Munchausen's Syndrome by Proxy. Munchausen's Syndrome describes a condition where a person presents themselves to medical staff for treatment of an illness that they do not have. They seek gratification from the subsequent medical attention, medical tests, care and treatment that they receive. Munchausen's Syndrome by Proxy therefore indicates that the sufferer receives gratification from the illness, symptoms, treatment, dependency and resultant need for care of others, including children. A recent case highlighted the damage to children that a sufferer from this condition can inflict.

CHECK!

1 What is physical abuse?
2 What does it include?

THINK!

1 Are some forms of physical punishment abusive?
2 Families differ in their attitude to and use of physical punishment. Are these differences based on culture, religious beliefs, socio-economic group?

INDICATORS OF PHYSICAL ABUSE

Responsibility for diagnosing child abuse rests with GPs and consultants. However, working with young children, you may be in a unique position to notice the signs and symptoms (indicators) of child abuse.

Bruises

70 per cent of abused children suffer soft tissue injury, for example bruises, lacerations, weals. The position of the bruising is important: bruises on cheeks, bruised eyes without other injuries, bruises on front and back shoulders are less likely to occur accidentally, as are diffuse bruising, *pinpoint haemorrhages* and finger tip bruises. Bruises occurring frequently or re-bruising in the same position as old or faded bruising may also be indicators of abuse.

The pattern of bruises may also be an indicator: bruises reflecting the cause, for example finger tip, fist or hand-shaped bruising. Bruises incurred accidentally do not form a pattern.

It is very important that *mongolian spots* (see Chapter 9) are not confused with bruises. They should not arouse suspicion of abuse. Mongolian spots are smooth, bluish grey to purple skin patches, often quite large, consisting of an excess of pigmented cells (melanocytes). They are sometimes seen across the base of the spine (*sacrum*) or buttocks of infants or young children of Asian, Southern European and African descent. They disappear at school age.

Diagnosis of child abuse is by health care professionals: it is rarely made on the basis of physical indicators alone and may depend on prompt referral to appropriate professionals.

Burns

Around 10 per cent of abused children suffer burns, but only 2 per cent of these are burnt non-accidentally. Examples are cigarette burns, especially when clear and round and more than one, and burns reflecting the instrument used, for example by placing a heated metal object on the skin.

The pattern and position of scalds can be significant, for example a 3-year-old child with scalds on her feet that are spread like socks. This would imply that the child was placed in hot water and probably held there.

Fractures

In diagnosing non-accidental injury the following would be significant to a doctor:
- the age of the child; immobile babies seldom sustain accidental fractures
- X-rays revealing previous healed fractures of differing ages
- the presence of other injuries
- the explanation given by child or carer (see *Additional indicators*, page 285).

Head, brain, eye injuries

Head, brain or eye injuries may indicate that a child has been swung, shaken, received a blow or been hit against a hard surface. The result may be a small fracture or bleeding into the brain (*subdural haematoma*). A small outward sign of head injury accompanied by irritability, drowsiness, headache, vomiting or head enlargement should be treated with urgency, as the outcomes can include brain damage, blindness, coma and death.

Internal damage

Internal damage, caused by blows, is a common cause of death in abused children.

Poisoning

Any occurrence of poisoning needs to be investigated.

Other marks

Other indicators of abuse may be bites, outlines of weapons, *bizarre markings*, nail marks, scratches, abrasions, a torn *frenulum*. (The frenulum is the web of skin joining the gum and the lip. Damage in a young child usually results from something being forcibly pushed into the mouth, such as a spoon, bottle or dummy. It hardly ever occurs in ordinary accidents. This damage may be associated with facial bruising.

CHECK!

1 How could a subdural haematoma and a torn frenulum be caused non-accidentally?
2 Where would you expect bruising to occur on a child's back if they had been picked up and shaken?

THINK!

1 What might you suspect if you saw this pattern of bruising on a small child's face?

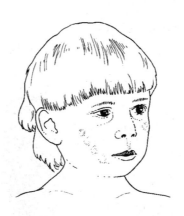

RECORDING THE INDICATORS OF ABUSE

If you have noticed the indicators of abuse, your responsibility may also include describing and recording them for referral to, and liaison with, appropriate professionals. Records need to be accurate and dated and should clearly distinguish between direct observation and what you are told by others (hearsay). The position of the injury, including any pattern, should be recorded as well as the nature of the injury. Physical indicators may be recorded onto a diagram of a child's body to make the position clear and accurate and to avoid misunderstanding.

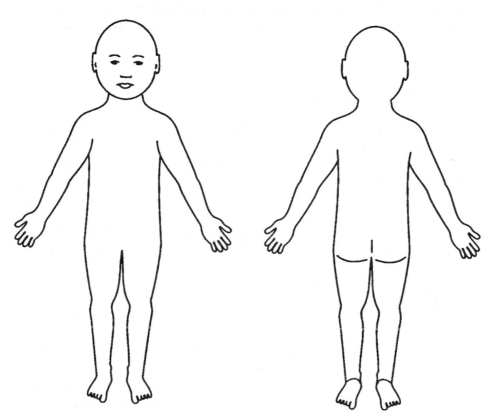

Physical indicators may be recorded onto a diagram of a child's body

All staff in an establishment need to use similar methods of recording and to share the responsibility of this task. Before you are in a position to notice possible indicators of abuse, find out who to report to in the establishment (the *designated staff member*). They, or a senior colleague, should always be informed immediately in an appropriate way.

Make sure that you are clear about the rules in your establishment concerning information sharing and *confidentiality*, and the circumstances under which these may be breached. Remember, if you are unsure about something you have seen or heard, discuss it with the designated person or a senior member of staff. Do not keep it to yourself.

1 Why is it important, in any establishment, to record all accidents and injuries sustained by children?
2 During childhood most children sustain some injuries accidentally. For each of the indicators outlined above, ask yourself if it is likely that the injury was caused non-accidentally.

DO!

1 Find out who is the designated person for child abuse in your workplace.
2 Design a method of recording all accidents and injuries sustained by children in your workplace.

Additional indicators of physical abuse

Physical indicators alone may be insufficient to diagnose child abuse. They should, therefore, always be considered alongside other factors. The presence of the following additional indicators increases the likelihood that injuries were sustained non-accidentally; they should be recorded alongside the physical indicators. Some of these additional indicators highlight the need to keep accurate, up-to date-records:

- an explanation by the parent or carer that is inadequate, unsatisfactory or vague, inconsistent with the nature of the injury, considering the age or stage of development of the child
- an unexplained delay in seeking medical attention, or seeking treatment only when prompted by others
- a series of minor injuries to a child which may in themselves have satisfactory explanations
- a history of child abuse or neglect of this child or other children in the family
- the existence of certain parental attitudes, such as a lack of concern, remorse or guilt over an accident, blaming others or the child for the injury, denying there is anything wrong or self-righteously justifying the infliction of injury during punishment. For example, if a child aged $3^1/_2$ was found to have belt marks on his buttocks and lower back, and on being questioned the carer said 'He deserved it. I warned him if he was cheeky once more I'd thrash him. Smacking does no good at all these days.'

CHECK!

1 Describe the additional indicators of neglect.

THINK!

1 A 6-week-old baby, with a fractured arm, is said by the carer to have 'just

woken up with her arm like that this morning.' Why would you suspect non-accidental injury?

BEHAVIOURAL INDICATORS

In seeking to recognise physical abuse the following behaviour in an injured child will be significant. This behaviour should be recorded in order to consider it alongside physical and additional indicators, but it cannot be said to prove the existence of abuse:

- fear and apprehension: professionals working with abused children have described a particular attitude or facial expression adopted by abused children and labelled it *frozen awareness* or *frozen watchfulness*. This describes a child constantly looking around, alert and aware, (vigilant), while remaining physically inactive (passive), demonstrating a lack of trust in adults
- inappropriately clinging to, or cowering from, the carer
- unusually withdrawn or aggressive behaviour (a change in behaviour may be particularly significant)
- the child's behaviour in role play situations, including their explanation of how the injury occurred.

CHECK!

1 Describe the possible behavioural indicators of physical neglect.

THINK!

A 2-year old child often comes to the day nursery with fresh bruises on his arms and upper body. His mother explains these are the result of minor accidents while playing.

1 What might lead you to suspect that the child was being non-accidentally injured?
2 Explain how you would respond to the mother immediately.
3 Describe the procedure you would work through within the establishment, include how and what you would record.

Neglect

Neglect involves persistently failing to meet the basic essential needs of children, and/or failing to safeguard their health, safety and well-being.

Neglect involves acts of *omission*, that is not doing those things that should be done, such as protecting children from harm. This contrasts with other types of abuse that involve acts of *commission*, that is doing those things that should not be done, for example beating children.

To understand neglect you need to know about children's basic essential needs and their rights. See *The needs and rights of children*, page 273.

We will consider neglect under three headings: physical, emotional and intellectual, although in practice these areas will often overlap.

1 What is neglect?

PHYSICAL NEGLECT

Physical neglect involves not meeting children's need for adequate food, clothing, warmth, medical care, hygiene, sleep, rest, fresh air and exercise. It also includes failing to protect, for example leaving young children alone and unsupervised.

EMOTIONAL NEGLECT

Emotional neglect includes refusing or failing to give children adequate love, affection, security, stability, praise, encouragement, recognition and reasonable guidelines for behaviour.

INTELLECTUAL NEGLECT

Intellectual neglect includes refusing or failing to give children adequate stimulation, new experiences, appropriate responsibility, encouragement and opportunity for appropriate independence.

CHECK!

1 Describe three types of child neglect.

THINK!

1 Think about how families differ in their standards of care.
 a) Are these standards based on culture, socio-economic group or intelligence?
 b) Are they related to external forces such as poverty and inadequate housing?

INDICATORS OF NEGLECT

The following signs and symptoms may be observed and should be recorded accurately and dated:
- constant hunger, voracious appetite, large abdomen, emaciation, stunted growth, obesity, failure to thrive (see overleaf)
- inadequate, inappropriate clothing for the weather, very dirty, seldom laundered clothing
- constant ill health, untreated medical conditions, for example extensive persistent nappy rash, repeated stomach upsets, chronic diarrhoea
- unkempt appearance, poor personal hygiene, dull matted hair, wrinkled skin, skin folds
- constant tiredness or lethargy

- repeated accidental injury
- frequent lateness or non-attendance at school
- low self-esteem
- compulsive stealing or scavenging
- learning difficulties
- aggression or withdrawal
- poor social relationships.

It is important to remember, however, that behavioural indicators may be due to causes other than neglect. For this reason you need to be aware of the background of children in your care. Diagnosis will not be on the basis of behavioural indicators alone. Possible medical conditions that may account for the physical indicators observed will need to be ruled out.

CHECK!

1 Describe the indicators of neglect.

DO!

Read the following case study and answer the questions that follow.

Rachel, aged 2, attends an expensive private day nursery. Her parents, both solicitors, drop her off at 8 o'clock from Monday to Friday and are usually the last to pick her up when the nursery closes at 6. On a number of occasions they have been as late as 7 o'clock. Rachel is underweight for her age, unable to manage solid food and prefers a bottle. She takes little interest in the activities of the nursery, preferring to sit alone sucking a toy and rocking rhythmically.

Her mother explains that Rachel was premature, and has never put on much weight, but that her husband's side of the family are all small anyway. Both parents resent being questioned about their child and offer extra payment, to cover the staff's inconvenience, when they are late to collect Rachel.

1 Write a list of the indicators of neglect described in the case study.
2 Describe the kind of on-going records that should be available to confirm each indicator of neglect in this case.
3 Write a description of a child you have known to be physically neglected.
4 Why may the carers of the child you have described be neglecting their child's needs?

Failure to thrive

Failure to thrive describes children who fail to grow normally for no organic reason. Some children are small because their parents are small. Others have a medical condition causing lack of growth. Children may be referred to paediatricians because of concern about growth. Growth charts (percentile charts) are used in the assessment of such children.

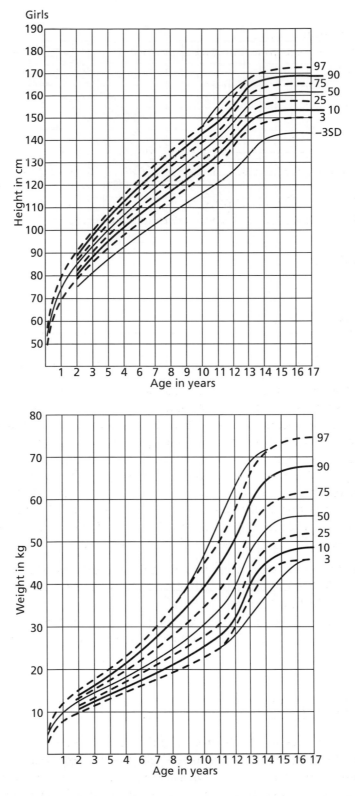

Percentile charts showing (top) height and (below) weight gain in girls up to the age of 17

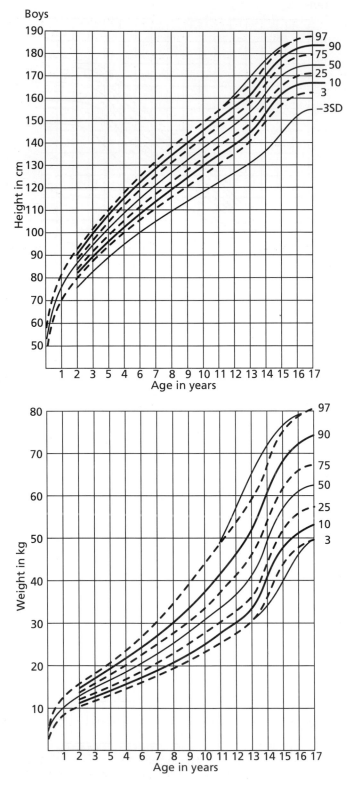

Percentile charts showing (top) height and (below) weight gain in boys up to the age of 17 years

As a rough guide, any child falling below the bottom line on the graph (*the third percentile*) should be admitted to hospital for investigation. If in hospital, with no specific treatment, the child gains weight at more than 50 grams a day, it is likely that the quality of care has been poor. Most children admitted to hospital for medical reasons tend to lose weight.

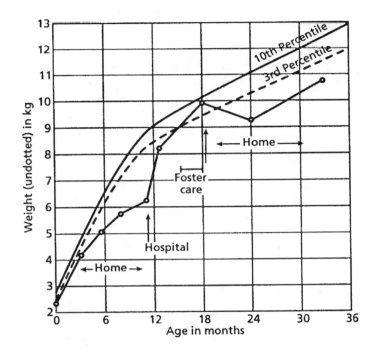

Chart showing a child's weight changes during stays in hospital, foster care and home

The chart shows the changes in a child's weight when he was in hospital and foster care from the time spent at home.

CHECK!

1 What is 'failure to thrive'?

THINK!

1 What would be your role as a child-care worker in the completion of percentile charts?
2 What factors would you need to consider when completing such charts?
3 How could you ensure that the chart was completed accurately?
4 What might be the results of completing such charts inaccurately?

5 Using the chart above, explain what happens to this child's weight in hospital, foster care and at home.

6 What might lead you to suspect that this child was being neglected?

7 In the case study of Rachel (page 288) above, how might a diagnosis of neglect be made?

Emotional abuse

Failing (omitting) to meet the needs of children in any area of their development will cause emotional damage. In addition it is possible to commit acts of emotional abuse. This occurs when children are harmed by constant threats, verbal attacks, taunting and or shouting.

Emotional abuse includes the adverse effect on children's behaviour and emotional development as a result of their parent or carer's behaviour, including their neglect and or rejection of the child. This category is only used in circumstances where it is the only or main form of abuse.

Children may fail to thrive as a result of emotional neglect or abuse as well as of physical neglect. Children who are neglected are more likely to be victims of other forms of abuse such as emotional, sexual or physical.

DO!

Read the following case study and answer the questions that follow.

The Wilson family

The Wilson family live in a well-maintained detached house in an expensive suburb. They have two children, James aged 6 and Sarah, 4. Sarah is small for her age with a thin pale face. She looks sad and wary of adults.

The nursery staff are concerned about Sarah, who seems to be failing to thrive and lacks confidence. Since starting nursery some three months earlier, she has been reluctant to join in structured activities and tells nursery staff that she is no good at anything.

When nursery staff invite the family in for an informal chat Mrs Wilson constantly compares Sarah unfavourably with her brother, who looks on smugly and agrees with everything his mother says. Mr Wilson doesn't speak directly to Sarah at all, treating her as if she does not exist. In conversation with the staff he refers to her as 'just like her mother'.

The story unfolds, that Sarah was premature, difficult to feed, did not put on weight, was slow to learn and happy to be left alone to lie in her cot. Mrs Wilson often left her there as James was a rewarding child and demanded a lot of attention. Mr Wilson was away a great deal when Sarah was a baby.

Mrs Wilson made no effort to protect Sarah from the negative comments she was making and said repeatedly to her that she was useless and hopeless, compared to her brother. James referred to Sarah as 'the dummy.' Mr Wilson said he couldn't understand what all the fuss was about, as she was only a girl.

1 Write down the indicators of neglect in this case.
2 Describe how Sarah was being emotionally abused.
3 After reading Chapter 21, *Responding to child abuse*, describe the possible short- and long-term effects on each aspect of Sarah's development.
4 How could staff in the nursery help to alleviate the effects of neglect or abuse?
5 How might the family be encouraged to adopt a different attitude towards Sarah?
6 Describe the roles of other professionals who may become involved with this family.

Sexual abuse

Sexual abuse is 'the involvement of dependent, developmentally immature children and adolescents in sexual activities that they do not fully comprehend and are unable to give informed consent to, or that violate the social taboos of family roles' (Kempe (1978). An example of a social taboo of family roles might be incest.

Victims of sexual abuse include children who have been the subject of unlawful sexual activity or whose parents or carers have failed to protect them from unlawful sexual activity, and children abused by other children. Sexual abuse covers a range of abusive behaviour not necessarily involving direct physical contact. It often starts at the lower end of the spectrum, for example exposure and self-masturbation by the abuser, and continues through actual body contact such as fondling, to some form of penetration.

CHECK!

1 According to Kempe's definition, what is sexual abuse?

THINK!

1 What does it mean to violate the social taboos of family roles?
2 What does informed consent mean?
3 Why does Kempe include the phrase 'fully comprehend'?
4 What does a range or spectrum of sexual abuse mean?

DO!

1 Write down a definition of sexual abuse in your own words.
2 Find out what sexual activities are unlawful.

WHO ARE THE VICTIMS OF SEXUAL ABUSE?

Child sexual abuse is a universal phenomenon. It is found in all cultures and socio-economic groups. It happens to children in all kinds of families and communities. It is untrue that it is only found in isolated rural communities.

Both boys and girls experience sexual abuse. As far as we know many more girls are abused than boys. There have been reported incidents of children as young as 4 months old being sexually abused.

Both men and women sexually abuse children. It is becoming clear that the majority of children who are sexually abused know the identity of the abuser. They are either a member of their family, a family friend or a person the child knows in a position of trust, for example a teacher or a carer.

CHECK!

1 What does 'Child abuse is a universal phenomenon' mean?

THINK!

1 What are the implications of the fact that the majority of children who are sexually abused know the identity of the abuser?

HOW WIDESPREAD IS SEXUAL ABUSE?

The prevalence of sexual abuse is largely unknown as it is under-reported and we are dependent on estimates. In a study of college students 19 per cent of women and 9 per cent of men reported having been sexually abused as a child. Out of 3000 respondents to a recent survey by a teenage magazine 36 per cent said they had been subjected to a sexually abusive experience as a child.

CHECK!

1 What is sexual abuse?
2 What percentage of people are abused?
3 Who are the victims of sexual abuse?
4 Is the abuser likely to be known to the child?

THINK!

1 Why is sexual abuse under-reported?
2 What are your feelings about child sexual abuse?
3 How could your feelings affect your attitude towards abusers and the victims of abuse?

INDICATORS OF SEXUAL ABUSE

Early recognition of the indicators of sexual abuse may prevent progression, by the abuser, from less to more abusive acts. If sexual abuse is not recognised in the early stages, it may persist undiscovered for many years.

CHECK!

1 Why is early recognition of the indicators of sexual abuse so important?

THINK!

1 Why may sexual abuse persist for many years, undiscovered, if it is not recognised in the early stages?

Physical indicators

The following are physical indicators of sexual abuse:

- bruises or scratches to the genital and anal areas, chest or abdomen
- bites
- blood stains on underwear
- sexually transmitted diseases
- semen on skin, clothes or in the vagina or anus
- internal small cuts (lesions) in the vagina or anus
- abnormal swelling out (dilation) of the vagina or anus
- itchiness or discomfort in the genital or anal areas.

In addition there are signs that are specific to either boys or girls:

in boys:

- pain on urination
- penile swelling
- penile discharge.

in girls:

- vaginal discharge
- *urethral inflammation, urinary tract infections*
- *lymph gland inflammation*
- pregnancy.

CHECK!

1 Ensure you understand all the medical terminology in this section, for example: lesions, dilation, urination, urethral inflammation, urinary tract infection, lymph gland inflammation, penile discharge.

Behavioural indicators

There may be no obvious physical indicators of sexual abuse, so particular attention should be paid to behavioural indicators. The following should be recorded accurately and discussed with the designated person in your establishment or a senior member of staff:

- what the child says or reveals through play with dolls with sexual characteristics, genitals, etc. (*anatomically correct dolls*)
- over-sexualised behaviour that is inappropriate for the age of the child; being obsessed with sexual matters; playing out sexual acts in too knowledgeable a way, with dolls or other children; producing drawings of sex organs such as erect penises; excessive masturbation
- sudden inexplicable changes in behaviour, becoming aggressive or withdrawn

- showing behaviour appropriate to an earlier stage of development (*regression*)
- showing eating or sleeping problems
- showing signs of social relationships being affected, for example becoming inappropriately clingy to carers; showing extreme fear of, or refusing to see, certain adults for no apparent reason; ceasing to enjoy activities with other children
- saying repeatedly that they are bad, dirty or wicked (having a poor *self-image*)
- acting in a way that they think will please and prevent the adult from hurting them (placatory), or in an inappropriately mature way (*pseudo-mature behaviour*).

CHECK!

1 Describe:
   a) the behavioural indicators
   b) the physical indicators
   of sexual abuse.

DO!

1 Read the following case studies. In each case decide whether the behaviour may be an indicator of sexual abuse or not.

2 Explain what influenced your decisions.

Claire
During play in the nursery, Claire, 3 $^1/_2$, is observed to be preoccupied with bed-times and bathtimes. She places dolls, a teddy and herself into these situations again and again over a period of two weeks. She also acts out being smacked in the bath.

Rangit
When a group is asked to draw themselves for a display, Rangit draws himself with a huge penis and testicles, stating 'Boys have willies, girls have holes instead.'

Helen
Helen indicates that she is sore in the vaginal area. She has spent the previous weekend with her grandfather. Her grandfather was convicted of sexual abuse of the child's mother years ago.

Raymond
Raymond has been displaying over-sexualised play with other children. One 3-year-old boy states he is frightened of Raymond because he keeps asking him to hide and play 'sucking willies'.

Kearan and Liam
Kearan and Liam were playing together in water; both were lying naked on their stomachs. A staff member heard a lot of giggling and saw the boys doing

press-ups in the water. When asked what they were doing, one boy said 'We're growing our tails'. Both boys had erections.

Ritual and organised abuse

The media have reported a number of incidents of ritual or organised abuse. The definition used by professionals for this is organised abuse; it often contains bizarre elements which may, or may not, link with satanic practices. Ritual abuse is probably not very common.

CHECK!

1 What is ritual abuse?

Disabled children and abuse

All that has already been written about abuse applies to disabled children, including those with learning difficulties. However, some children are particularly vulnerable to all forms of abuse and have special need for protection.

WHY ARE DISABLED CHILDREN MORE VULNERABLE?

Some offenders abuse children because they are particularly attracted to their dependency. This, combined with society's negative attitude to disabled people, may increase the risk of disabled children, and those with learning difficulties, being abused. In addition disabled children:
- receive less information on abuse and may be less likely to understand the inappropriateness of it
- are often more dependent on physical care for longer and from different people; this increases their vulnerability
- may receive less affection from family and friends and so be more accepting of sexual attention
- may be less likely to tell what has happened (*disclose*) because of communication difficulties, fewer social contacts, isolation and the fact that they are generally less likely to be believed
- may have an increased desire to please because of negative responses generally, including rejection and isolation
- may lack assertiveness, vocabulary or skills to complain appropriately
- may find it difficult to distinguish between good and bad touches
- are likely to have low self-esteem and feel less in control
- are likely to have less choice generally, therefore less opportunity to learn whether to choose to accept or reject sexual advances.

Read the following case study and answer the questions below.

The Steadman family

Wayne, 7, has learning difficulties. He is looked after regularly by Philip, a long standing friend of Mr and Mrs Steadman. They believe it is good for Wayne to meet older people and are glad of a break when Philip has Wayne to stay at his flat or minds him at home while the Steadmans go out.

Philip has been sexually abusing Wayne for a year. It started with Philip asking Wayne to show him his penis but has now progressed to mutual masturbation and oral sex. Philip gives Wayne sweets and tells him not to tell his parents or else he won't let Wayne stay up to watch TV with him.

Wayne tells a friend at school that he gets sweets from Philip and is allowed to stay up late watching TV if he lets Philip play with his 'willy'. Wayne's friend doesn't understand and asks Wayne to show him what Philip does.

The boys are discovered in the library corner at school and asked to explain what they are doing. Wayne explains, but asks the staff not to tell his mother because she will be cross with him for staying up late.

1 Describe how Wayne was being abused.
2 What indicators of sexual abuse may have been evident in this case?
3 After reading the section *The effects of abuse* in Chapter 21 (page 303), describe the possible short- and long-term effects on Wayne of this abuse.
4 How could staff in school help to alleviate the effects of abuse?
5 Why was Wayne particularly vulnerable to abuse?
6 After reading the section *Prevention and protection* in Chapter 21 (page 308), explain how Wayne could have been helped to protect himself and how the abuse could have been prevented.

Key terms

You need to know what these words and phrases mean. Go back through the chapter and find out.

Munchausen's Syndrome by Proxy	Third percentile
Pinpoint haemorrhages	Developmentally immature
Mongolian spots	Informed consent
Sacrum	Social taboos
Bizarre markings	Urethral inflammation
Frenulum	Urinary tract infections
Subdural haematoma	Lymph gland inflammation
Designated person	Anatomically correct dolls
Confidentiality	Obsessed
Behavioural indicators	Over-sexualised behaviour
Frozen awareness/frozen watchfulness	Regression
Compulsive stealing	Pseudo-mature behaviour
Failure to thrive	Self-image

21 RESPONDING TO CHILD ABUSE

Introduction

Working with young children provides both the opportunity and the responsibility to recognise signs and symptoms (*indicators*) of abuse. In addition to this important role in the early recognition of child abuse, you will need to develop additional skills in situations where abuse is both suspected and confirmed.

Children may tell you or show you they are being abused and you will need to handle *disclosure*. You may also *observe* and *monitor* abused children. This work may include recording your findings for *referral* to other agencies and professionals, and in order to *liaise* with staff in the establishment, parents and carers.

Working with abused children will also involve helping to alleviate the effects of abuse and managing difficult behaviour. All these skills, in relation to child abuse, are considered in this chapter.

Working with abused children may also mean having regular contact with their families, including those members who commit abuse. To practise in a professional way it is essential to recognise your own reaction to child abuse issues, and to put the needs of children and their families before your own needs.

The physical and emotional stress of working in these situations should be acknowledged and provision made to receive support. Emotional support can come from being part of a team with good working relationships, and being able to talk about and share your feelings with appropriate people. Many of the skills required in these situations can be learned and developed during practice, supervised by experienced professionals.

THINK!

1 What special skills do you need to work with abused children and their families?

2 What sort of stresses are you likely to experience?

3 Why is emotional support so important?

4 How can you make provision to receive support?

Dealing with disclosure

In any day-care setting it is possible that children will tell you they are being abused; in other words they will *disclose*, in a full and open way. Alternatively they may, through words or behaviour, hint that abuse may have taken place; in other words they will disclose in a partial, hidden or indirect way. This may happen at inappropriate or pressured times and in awkward situations. You will need to be prepared to respond sensitively and appropriately, both immediately, at initial disclosure, and later on.

This section deals with initial response. For information on follow up, see Chapter 22, *Child protection procedures*.

RESPONDING TO DISCLOSURE

It is not possible to write down exactly what to do when children tell you they have been, or are being, abused. The points below are only guidelines. You will need to draw on your communication skills and adapt your approach according to the age and stage of development of the child.

- Listen and be prepared to spend time and not hurry the child. Use active listening skills. Do not interrogate them and avoid using questions beginning why, how, when, where or who.
- Do not ask leading questions, putting words into children's mouths, for example 'This person abused you, then?'
- Reassure them truthfully. Tell them they are not odd or unique; you believe them; you are glad they told you; it is not their fault; they were brave to tell; you are sorry it happened.
- Find out what they are afraid of, so you know how best to help. They may have been threatened about telling.
- Be prepared to record what the child tells you, as soon as possible, comprehensively, accurately and legibly, with the date of the disclosure.
- Let the child know why you are going to tell someone else.
- Consult your senior (designated person), your agency's guidelines, or if you are working in isolation, for example nannying, an appropriate professional you think will be able to help. This may be a social worker, a health visitor, a police officer, or an NSPCC child protection officer.
- Seek support with your personal emotional reactions and needs from an appropriate colleague or professional.

Do not attempt to deal with the issue by yourself. Disclosure is a beginning, but by itself will not prevent further abuse.

Listen and be prepared to spend time and not hurry the child

THINK!

1 What communication skills do you need to handle disclosure of child abuse?
2 How can you practise these skills in safe conditions?
3 What does a child have to lose by disclosing?
4 What might be the impact of disclosure on other family members?

DO!

1 Check your establishment's procedures for handling disclosure.
2 Talk to staff who have been involved in handling disclosure.
3 Consider your own need for practical training in the skills required to handle disclosure.

Observation and monitoring

In order to recognise and understand the effects of abuse, skills in observation, monitoring and recording are vital. These skills, useful in the early recognition of abuse, can also be used to monitor progress or regression in each aspect of children's development. Careful monitoring can highlight the long-term effects of abuse on individual children, and enable staff to work out plans to alleviate these effects and to monitor their success.

Monitoring is particularly important where progress is slow or erratic, and it is easy to think no progress has been made. It is also important in cases where re-abuse is suspected.

All observations and assessments, including for example percentile charts, need to be recorded regularly and accurately, and dated in order to provide documented evidence for all those involved with the child.

Referral and liaison

Child abuse should never be dealt with exclusively by one person. Recent trage-dies highlight the importance of inter-agency co-operation and the need for different professionals to work closely together.

In your establishment you need to know:

- the designated person responsible for child abuse
- who you are directly responsible to
- the roles and responsibilities of the team of people involved with the child, and when to refer to other professionals inside and outside the establishment.

Team work involves liaison, sharing of information and planning. The following guidelines are important when providing information to other professionals about child abuse.

Information should be relevant, accurate and up-to-date. It should also be within your role and responsibility to supply, and provided within agreed boundaries of confidentiality and according to the procedures of the setting.

Requests for reports on incidents, disclosures or suspicions of child abuse should be responded to promptly. Reports should clearly distinguish between directly observed evidence, information gathered from reliable sources and opinion. It should be presented to the appropriate person in the form and at the time requested. It is very important that the report remains confidential and is stored securely.

THINK!

1 For each of the following professional groups think about what information is most likely to be required, and for what purpose:
- social workers
- NSPCC child protection officers
- police officers
- health visitors
- play therapists.

DO!

1 Find out the procedures of your work place with regard to:
a) rules and limits of confidentiality for supply of information to others
b) arrangements for the security of any documents retained relating to child abuse
c) the rights of parents to access information held within the setting or passed to other professionals
d) how and when it is possible to share such information with parents.

The effects of abuse

As with any trauma, children's reactions to abuse vary. Being subjected to abuse can affect all aspects of children's development: physical, intellectual and linguistic and emotional and social. Perhaps the most significant effect of abuse is the long-term damage to children's self-esteem or self-respect, damage which may persist into adult life. To be abused is to be made to feel worthless, misused, guilty, betrayed. Children's feelings may be translated into observable behaviour patterns.

Martin and Beezley (1977) drew up a list of characteristic behaviour of abused children, based on a study of 50 abused children. The behaviour patterns may also be regarded as indicators of abuse:

- impaired capacity to enjoy life: abused children often appear sad, preoccupied and listless
- stress symptoms, for example, bedwetting, tantrums, bizarre behaviour, eating problems
- low self-esteem: children who have been abused often think they must be worthless to deserve such treatment
- learning difficulties, such as lack of concentration
- withdrawal: many abused children withdraw from relationships with other children and become isolated and depressed
- opposition or defiance: a generally negative, unco-operative attitude
- hypervigilance, or frozen awareness or watchful expression (see *Indicators of physical abuse* in Chapter 20, page 282)
- compulsivity: abused children sometimes feel or think they must carry out certain activities or rituals (sets of activities) repeatedly
- pseudo-mature behaviour: a false appearance of independence or being excessively 'good' all the time or offering indiscriminate affection to any adult who takes an interest.

Children's reactions can be summarised as either 'fight or flight'. They may respond by becoming aggressive and anti-social (fight), or by becoming withdrawn and over-compliant (flight).

Alleviating the effects of abuse

The effects of abuse do not generally make children appealing. Abused children may be very difficult to like. Often they do not attract the love and affection they so desperately need. Alleviating the effects of abuse requires a professional response that puts the needs of children before your own. Caring for abused children may provide you with a deep sense of satisfaction, but they are not there to provide this for you. Love and affection should be offered to even the most unattractive, unresponsive personalities. Abused children need consistent caring adults they can rely on, who will provide unconditional love and affection.

IMPROVING THE SELF-IMAGE

In order to help abused children you need to have a good understanding of the development of self-image or self-concept. You will need to contribute to the development of a positive self-image, and enhance children's self-esteem. How you do this in practice will vary according to their age or stage of development. For a thorough understanding of this topic, read Chapter 12 in Book 1, *The development of self-image and self-concept*. The guidelines listed there as Twenty golden rules are repeated here for convenience.

TWENTY GOLDEN RULES

1   From the earliest age, demonstrate love and give children affection, as well as meeting their all round developmental needs.
2   Provide babies with opportunities to explore using their five senses.
3   Encourage children to be self-dependent and responsible.
4   Explain why rules exist and why children should do what you are asking. Use 'do' rather than 'don't' and emphasise what you want the child to do rather than what is not acceptable. When children misbehave explain to them why it is wrong.
5   Encourage children to value their own cultural background.
6   Encourage children to do as much for themselves as they can, to be responsible and to follow through activities to completion.
7   Do not use put-downs or sarcasm.
8   Give children activities that are a manageable challenge. If a child is doing nothing, ask questions to find out why. Remember that they may need time alone to work things out.
9   Give appropriate praise for effort, more than achievement.
10 Demonstrate that you value children's work.
11 Provide opportunities for children to develop their memory skills
12 Encourage children to use language to express their own feelings and thoughts and how they think others feel.
13 Provide children with their own things, labelled with their name.
14 Provide opportunities for role play.
15 Give children the opportunity to experiment with different roles, for example leader, follower.
16 Provide good flexible role models with regard to gender ethnicity, and disability.
17 Stay on the child's side! Assume they mean to do right rather than wrong. Do not presume on your authority with instructions such as 'You must do this because I'm the teacher and I tell you to', unless the child is in danger.
18 Be interested in what children say; be an active listener. Give complete attention when you can and do not laugh at a child's response, unless it is really funny.
19 Avoid having favourites and victims.
20 Stimulate children with interesting questions, that make them think.

ENCOURAGING EXPRESSION OF FEELING

Abused children benefit from involvement in activities that enable and encourage them to express their feelings in an appropriate, acceptable way. Those who work with abused children need to understand the link between feelings and behaviour. They need to be able to see beyond presenting behaviour to children's underlying feelings, and to respond to these rather than to the unacceptable behaviour they may demonstrate.

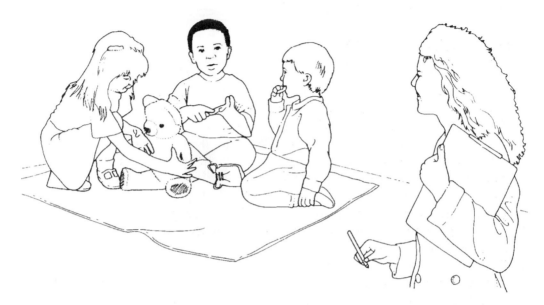

Observation skills are invaluable

Observation skills are invaluable in this respect. Information from observations should be carefully recorded and available to all those involved with the care of an abused child. It is not always possible to be certain about children's feelings. The behaviour observed should always be recorded as well as what you think the child was feeling (the evaluation or interpretation).

PLAY THERAPY AND THE USE OF ANATOMICALLY CORRECT DOLLS

Some abused children will need expert professional counselling or play therapy in order to alleviate the effects of abuse. This may be with a child psychologist, a psychiatrist, a counsellor or a play therapist. You may be involved in liaising with these professionals. Under their direction you may be involved in the use of anatomically correct dolls with children who have suffered sexual abuse.

Use of the dolls can be helpful because they:
- ease the anxiety involved in discussing sexual matters for the adults as well as the children

- act as an ice breaker to get discussion going, possibly by establishing names for describing the sexual organs and their characteristics
- appeal to a wide age range of children.
- maintain a child-oriented atmosphere
- give the child permission to discuss sexual matters and understand what is natural.

The use of anatomically correct dolls may ease the anxiety involved in discussing sexual matters

The dolls can be used to:
- give children an opportunity to act out, through the dolls, their feelings about what has happened to them
- educate children about sexual matters generally
- describe and demonstrate the events involved in the abuse
- facilitate group or individual play therapy sessions, involving other family members.

They may also be used to encourage, to enable disclosure in the investigation of suspected abuse and to obtain evidence of actual abuse. In these contexts their use may be videoed.

PARTNERSHIP WITH PARENTS OR CARERS

Part of your responsibility may include working with parents. Your aim will be to enhance, not undermine, the relationship between abused children and their parents or carers. Support and encouragement should be given to parents or carers to motivate them to copy (emulate) good methods and practices in relation to their child, rather than to judge and alienate them.

It may be necessary to help particular children to develop positive relationships with their parents or carers. This role will require sensitivity and a real understanding of the importance of the relationship between parent or carer and child. It will require a genuine commitment to partnership with parents.

CHECK!

1 What are the uses of anatomically correct dolls?
2 What are their possible benefits?

THINK!

1 Why may abused children be difficult to like?
2 Why do abused children desperately need unconditional love and affection?
3 Take each of the Twenty Golden Rules listed above and explain why they are likely to enhance children's self-esteem and contribute to the development of a positive self-image or self-concept.

DO!

1 Plan an activity for a group of children aged 3–5, to encourage and enable the expression of feeling.
2 Undertake a number of observations of children of different ages in different settings. Differentiate between their observable behaviour and your understanding of the feelings underlying or causing the behaviour.

Managing difficult behaviour

Emotional damage may well show itself in anti-social behaviour. Even if you understand the reason for abused children's feelings it may not be easy to cope with their behaviour. The way you respond to difficult behaviour will affect children's self image and self-esteem. Appropriate responses can help to alleviate the effects of abuse.

It is impossible to give detailed advice about how to respond to all the situations that you may encounter. The following points simplify some underlying principles for managing difficult behaviour. They may be difficult to live up to in practice, but it is important to set high standards. Abused children may already have suffered considerable emotional damage at the hands of an adult in a position of trust.

Do!	Don't!
Reward positive or acceptable behaviour	Punish aggressive behaviour with violence
Routinely give praise, time and attention	
Remain calm and in control of your feelings	Presume that a child's behaviour is aimed at you personally
Respect the child	
Reassure the child that you will go on loving them	Pretend that everything is all right if it is not
Recognise how the child's behaviour makes you feel	
Reason with the child	Promise what you cannot do
Restrain the child gently if necessary	Presume that you are always right
Respond consistently to similar events	

Practical points for managing difficult behaviour

We all respond more to praise and encouragement than punishment. If punishment cannot be avoided, keep it as low-key as possible. Seek to make punishment a removal of attention from the child, rather than a drama that they will want to repeat because it brings them attention.

THINK!

1 Why does the way you respond to difficult behaviour affect children's self-image or self-esteem?
2 How can appropriate response help to alleviate the effects of abuse?
3 Why is praise and encouragement more effective than punishment?
4 Why is it important to keep punishment as low-key as possible?
5 In what ways can children of different ages be safely restrained to prevent them hurting themselves or others?

DO!

Before any incidents occur in your workplace, you need to consider how you will control yourself and remain calm under stress.
1 Discuss with staff in your workplace their experiences of handling difficult behaviour; include the negative as well as the positive experiences.
2 Draw up a list of ideas, based on their experience of coping, that may help you.
3 Discuss the difficult behaviour of a particular child with an appropriate member of staff in your workplace. After consultation, design a programme of behaviour modification to reward or reinforce positive behaviour and deter negative behaviour.

Prevention and protection

Parents, professionals and even politicians share responsibility for the prevention of child abuse and the protection of children. Part of this responsibility involves teaching children to protect themselves. This alone will never prevent all abuse, just as teaching children about safety will not prevent all accidents. Nevertheless it would be negligent to fail in this responsibility. Many adults are reluctant to tackle the subject of protection from abuse because they:

- feel embarrassed or ashamed
- do not want to introduce the subject of sex in a negative way
- are unsure how to tackle the subject.

Much insight into the area of protection for children in this country has come from the work of the Kidscape Campaign for Children's Safety. Kidscape's basic concepts of child protection are:

- children learning to trust, recognise and accept their own feelings

Children need to learn to trust, recognise and accept their own feelings

- children understanding they have a right to be safe
- children understanding that their bodies are their own and that no one should touch them inappropriately
- kisses, hugs and touches should never be kept secret, even if they feel good.

These concepts and the skills that children need to put them into practice can be taught through the existing curriculum in schools. They can also be incorporated into themes and topics in pre-school settings. If taught well, they will encourage children's confidence, assertiveness and communication skills, as well as contributing to their protection. They are relevant to all children, including disabled children and children with learning difficulties, who may be especially vulnerable.

1 For the children in your workplace devise an activity or story that seeks to encourage and enable them to do each of the following:

- express and trust their feelings: this may include feelings about anything, but particularly things they don't like
- think and talk about touches that feel good, safe and comfortable and touches that feels bad, unsafe or are secretive
- say no in an assertive way, even to someone they love, and get help when someone tries to take away their rights, for example through bullying
- understand that if it is not possible to say no, because of fear or the threat of violence, caring adults will understand and support them
- get help when they need adult assistance
- learn that there are times when the rules of being polite do not apply
- know the difference between safe secrets and unsafe secrets
- differentiate between telling tales to get someone into trouble and getting help when someone is threatening their safety
- know how to deal with bullies
- understand the difference between presents and bribes and to recognise tricks.

2 What would you need to ensure before putting these activities into practice with regard to parents, colleagues and the children themselves?

3 Devise a list of 'What if...?' questions for the children in your workplace to encourage discussion of potentially dangerous or abusive situations. For example, 'What if you were being bullied by someone who made you promise not to tell?' or 'What if a grown-up told you to run across the road and there was a car coming?'

There is a large number of books and resource materials concerning protection (for example, videos) that are available to use with children. In general they will need to be used in an interactive way if they are to be truly effective. They need to be part of a programme offering children the opportunity to discuss the issues raised. They should not be used by people unprepared for handling children's fears and worries or any disclosure of abuse.

PROTECTING YOURSELF FROM ALLEGATIONS OF ABUSE

There may be times when child-care workers are themselves accused of abuse. Sadly, although rare, there are occasions when these allegations are founded. All those who work directly with children need to consider how to avoid allegations. There may already be guidelines in the establishment in which you work. If so you should ensure that you know what they are and follow them. If not, the following common-sense ideas, from *The Kidscape Training Guide*, may be used to help you to draw up guidelines for your own workplace.

- In the event of any injury to a child, accidental or otherwise, ensure that it is recorded and witnessed by another adult.

- Keep records of any false allegations a child makes against you. Record dates and times.
- Get another adult to witness the allegation, if possible.
- If a child touches you in an inappropriate place, record what happened and ensure that another adult knows (do not make the child feel like a criminal).
- On school trips always have at least two members of staff.
- Do not place yourself in a position where you are spending excessive amounts of time alone with one child, away from other people.
- In residential settings, never take a child into your bedroom.
- Do not take children in your car by yourself.
- If you are involved in a care situation, try to have someone with you when changing nappies, clothing or bathing a child.
- Never do something of a personal nature for children that they can do for themselves, for example wiping bottoms.
- Avoid going on your own to the toilet with children.
- Be mindful of how and where you touch a child. Consider using a lap cushion with young children or disabled children who may need to sit on your knee.
- Be careful of extended hugs and kisses on the mouth from children. This may be particularly relevant to those working with children with learning difficulties.
- Always tell someone if you suspect a colleague of abuse.

THINK!

1 Do you think that all of the above guidelines are necessary or practical in your workplace?
2 Are there some guidelines you would add to this list?
3 Devise incident report forms suitable for recording:
   a) accidental or non accidental injury to a child
   b) allegations made against staff members in your work place.

Key terms
You need to know what these words and phrases mean. Go back through the chapter and find out.

Indicators	Compulsivity
Disclosure	Rituals
Observation	Pseudo-mature behaviour
Monitoring	Ethnicity
Referral	Gender
Liaison	Anti social behaviour.
Self-esteem/-image/-respect	Behaviour modification
Bizarre behaviour	Over compliant
Hypervigilance	Anatomically correct

22 CHILD PROTECTION PROCEDURES

> **This chapter includes:**
> - **Aims and principles of child protection procedures**
> - **Agencies and professionals involved in child protection**
> - **Referrals and procedures for the investigation of suspected abuse.**

Aims and principles of child protection procedures

The child protection procedures for any area include:
- a description of the signs and symptoms of abuse (described in Chapter 20)
- information needed by each agency about who to refer a concern to
- details of the consultation, investigation and protective measures that follow a referral (see page 317).

AIMS

Child protection procedures aim to:
- protect all children from all possible kinds of abuse in any setting
- give clear instructions for action to anyone involved in the care of children if they suspect that a child is at risk
- support all workers by providing an understanding of their different roles and promoting co-ordination between them.

Child abuse is a social and health problem that occurs among people of all races, religious groups, cultures and social backgrounds. It affects both disabled and non-disabled children. It takes place in a variety of settings including families and institutions (for example schools and children's homes). The Children Act (1989) recognises the need and right of children from every background and in every setting to be protected from abuse. The act makes clear recommendations about how this should be done, requiring each local authority to form an Area Child Protection Committee (ACPC).

The Area Child Protection Committee

The ACPC writes, monitors and reviews the child protection procedures for its area. To do this it uses the guidelines provided by the Children Act (1989). The ACPC consists of representatives of all the agencies who aim to protect children. This includes the social services department, police, probation, education, the health service and representatives of voluntary organisations,

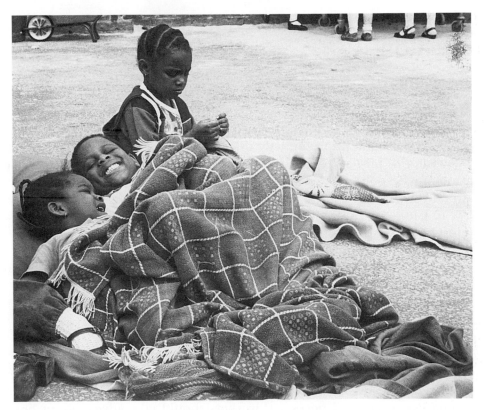

Child protection procedures aim to protect all children from all possible kinds of abuse in any setting

especially the NSPCC. The committee promotes a close working relationship between all professionals.

PRINCIPLES

The Children Act (1989) completely revised the law relating to child protection. The act bases child protection on some key principles:

- the welfare of the child is of the greatest importance
- professionals should work in partnership with parents at every stage
- the child's wishes should be taken into account
- unnecessary delay in procedures should be avoided
- a court order should only be made if it positively contributes to a child's welfare.

CHECK!

1 What is the ACPC?
2 Which organisations have representatives that make up the ACPC?

Agencies and professionals involved in child protection

RESPONSIBILITIES OF AGENCIES

Investigation

There are a number of different agencies and professionals involved in child protection work, some more directly than others. The only agencies with the legal (statutory) power to investigate and intervene are the social services department, the police, the National Society for the Prevention of Cruelty to Children (the NSPCC) and The Royal Scottish Society for the Prevention of Cruelty to Children (RSSPCC). The basis for an effective child protection service must be that all professionals and agencies:

- work co-operatively on a multi-disciplinary basis
- understand and share aims and objectives, and agree about how individual cases should be handled
- are sensitive to issues associated with gender, race, culture and disability.

Equality of opportunity

The Children Act (1989) makes it very clear that although discrimination of all kinds is a reality, every effort must be made to ensure that agencies do not reflect or reinforce this in their practices. All people have a right to good, non-discriminatory services. If necessary, workers should take advice about how to achieve this. We must give equality of opportunity to all involved. Child-care workers must take account of gender, race, culture, linguistic background and special needs throughout their working practices. All workers involved in child protection must have an open mind about whether abuse has or has not taken place and must avoid making any stereotypical assumptions about people.

There are ways to increase equality of opportunity and some of these are listed below:

- anyone who interviews a child or parent needs to use appropriate language and listening skills
- it may help when black families are being investigated, to involve a black worker, or at least someone with appropriate cultural knowledge and experience
- it may be necessary to make arrangements for children and parents to be interviewed in their home language
- if a parent or child has communication difficulties, for example a hearing impairment, assistance must be given during interviews
- remember that children and parents with disabilities have the same rights as others
- the gender of those being interviewed needs be taken into account: it may be better to involve a worker of the same gender. This is especially true in cases where the victim of sexual abuse is female and the alleged perpetrator is male.

1 Can you think of any times when people might be stereotyped and discriminated against because of their social or cultural background?
2 Discuss any difficulties you have had in working together with parents whose child-care practices differ from your own.

ROLES OF AGENCIES

The social services department

Social services departments have a wide range of statutory duties and responsibilities to provide services for individuals and families. The child protection work of social services departments is only a part of its child-care services. Social workers are usually involved in both child protection work and other aspects of work with children, families and other client groups. This gives them a broad awareness of the facilities that are available to help and support all families.

Local authorities, through their social services departments, have a statutory duty under The Children Act (1989) to investigate any situation where they have reasonable cause to suspect that a child is suffering or is likely to suffer significant harm. They take the leading role both in investigation, in child protection conferences, and keeping the child protection register. To meet this need some social services departments have appointed social work specialists to advise and support other social workers.

Social services departments should have a system for the public to refer their concerns about individual children to them. They should provide a telephone number for the public and children to contact them.

Local authorities must now involve parents throughout the child protection process, as long as this is consistent with the welfare and protection of the child. They must:

- give parents full information about what is happening
- enable parents to share concerns openly about their children's welfare
- show respect and consideration for parents' views
- involve parents in planning, decision making and review.

The guardian *ad litem*

The Children Act (1989) recognises that children can find it difficult both to speak for themselves in court and to understand the decision-making process. A guardian *ad litem* will help with both of these.

Guardians *ad litem* are people appointed by the courts to safeguard and promote the interests and welfare of children during court proceedings. The guardian is an independent person, usually with training in social work.

The police

Police officers have a duty to investigate cases of child abuse referred to them. Their focus is to determine and decide whether:

- a criminal offence has taken place

- to follow criminal proceedings if there is sufficient evidence
- prosecution is in the best interests of the child and the public, and what is the best way to protect a child victim.

The police share their information with other agencies at child protection conferences. Co-operation and understanding at this level are essential.

The police also have a unique emergency power to enter and search premises and detain a child in a place of protection, without application to a court.

DO!

1 Describe in your own words the police powers described in the preceding section.
2 When do you think this power might be used?

The probation service

Probation officers have responsibility for the supervision of offenders. Through this they may become involved in cases of child abuse. They will inform social services if they are concerned about the safety of a child who is in the same household as an offender.

The health service

All health service workers are committed to the protection of children. They play an important role in supporting the social services department and provide on-going support for children and their families.

General practitioners and community health workers can play an effective part in the protection of children. They may identify both stresses in a family, and signs that a child is being harmed; they may make an initial referral and attend a child protection conference.

Health visitors and school nurses monitor children's health and development. They are in a good position to identify children who are being harmed or who may be at risk.

A doctor with a specialist knowledge of child abuse is consulted following a referral of suspected abuse. This doctor will produce a written report; this can be used in any legal proceedings.

The education service

Teachers and other staff in schools have daily contact with children. They are therefore in a good position to observe both physical and behavioural signs of abuse. The education service is not an investigative agency, and must refer any suspicions to the social services department.

All school staff need to know referral procedures. Each school should have a trained senior member of staff who is given specific responsibility for referral to and liaison with social services. This person is called the designated teacher.

Schools should be notified of any child whose name is on the child protection register. This alerts them to observe the child's attendance, development and behaviour.

Schools may also be involved in prevention through a personal and social education programme. They can, for example, help children to increase their personal safety by using assertiveness skills.

Educational welfare officers and educational psychologists also have important roles to play. Following abuse they help and support the child in the school and home environment. They may contribute at child protection conferences.

The NSPCC (RSSPCC in Scotland)

The National Society for the Prevention of Cruelty to Children is the only voluntary organisation that has statutory powers to investigate and to apply for court orders to protect children. It has teams of qualified social workers, the child protection officers, to do this. The society works in close liaison with social services departments.

The NSPCC is involved in the prevention of abuse, the support of vulnerable children and their families and in research into the extent and nature of abuse.

Other voluntary organisations

There is a wide range of national and local voluntary organisations that provide services to support children and their families. National voluntary organisations such as Barnados, The Children's Society and The National Children's Home all provide and run family support centres. PARENTLINE and ChildLine provide a telephone counselling and support service for parents and children.

There are many locally based voluntary organisations. Some of these specifically support families and children from ethnic minority groups.

DO!

1 Find out about any national and local voluntary organisations in your area that help to protect children and support their families.

CHECK!

1 What does a guardian *ad litem* do?
2 What is the name of the person in school who has special responsibility for child protection?

Referrals and procedures for the investigation of suspected abuse

REFERRALS

Referral is the process by which suspected abuse is reported by one person to another. Referrals of suspected abuse come from two main sources:

- members of the public, including family members
- professionals who work with children in a range of settings.

Referrals by members of the public

If any person either knows or suspects that a child is being abused or is at risk of harm, that person should inform one of the agencies with a statutory duty to intervene (that is the police, social services department and the NSPCC/RSSPCC). Members of the public are entitled to have their referrals investigated.

Referrals by professionals

Professionals have a duty to refer any case of suspected abuse. In order to be able to respond to and make referrals, professionals need:
- appropriate training to recognise the signs of abuse and neglect
- to be aware of the locally agreed procedures they must follow if they suspect abuse
- to know the procedures for the setting in which they work. They must know their own role, and their responsibility for referral. If they suspect abuse they should know how to respond and whether it is appropriate either to report this to a designated person or to refer it themselves.

MEDICAL EMERGENCIES

Any member of staff who discovers that a child has an injury, whatever its cause, should first decide whether the injury requires immediate medical treatment or not. If it does, the child must be taken to the accident and emergency department of the local hospital. It is better to have parental permission and involvement, although it may be appropriate in child protection cases to consult social services about gaining this.

DO!

1 Try to study a copy of the child protection procedures for your area. (These are public documents. They should be available through your place of work or local authority outlets.)
2 In any organisation there should be clear lines of responsibility for consultation and referral of suspected abuse. Make sure that you are clear about what you should do if you suspect abuse.
3 If you are in a workplace, find out the name of the designated person for child protection.

RECORD KEEPING

Following the making of a referral the person involved must make a clear record. Well kept records are essential for good child protection practice. This can be achieved by:

- the person in charge of an agency (for example a head teacher or an officer in charge) ensuring that staff make accurate records of any observations made or action taken
- making the records immediately, or at least within twenty-four hours. This is especially important, because only then can they be used as evidence in court
- each agency having a policy stating the purpose and format for keeping records
- being clear about how to maintain confidentiality and safeguard the information, as well as knowing with whom they may share it.

DO!

1 Discuss with a friend, colleague or any other person the difference between a fact, hearsay and opinion.
2 Write down some sentences about an imaginary event. Include in this some examples of factual statements, hearsay reports and statements of your opinion. Make a mark beside the sentences which should not be included in a child protection report.
3 If possible find out about the specific record-keeping policy and practice that exists in a workplace that you have contact with.

CONSULTATION

Following a referral, the social services department (and the NSPCC if involved) and the police will consult one another. They will decide whether there are grounds for an investigation and will agree their respective roles in this investigation.

INVESTIGATION

Following a consultation, a local authority has a duty to investigate a referral if they have reasonable grounds to suspect that a child is suffering or is likely to suffer significant harm. Two aims of the investigation are to establish the facts and to decide if there are grounds for concern.

To establish the facts, social workers interview the child, the parent(s), carers, anyone who has a personal interest in the child and any appropriate agencies and professionals. This may include a medical examination with an appropriate doctor. Accurate recordings of any interviews should be made. As with any records, it is important to record only the facts and to understand the difference between fact, hearsay and opinion. New provisions under the Criminal Justice Act (1991) will allow a video recording of an interview with a child to be used as a child's main evidence in criminal proceedings

If cause for concern is established during an investigation, there will be an initial child protection conference. This will normally take place within eight days of the initial referral.

A third aim of the investigation is to find out the source of the risk, how great it is, and to decide what action, if any, to take to protect the child/ children).

The investigation must also establish in particular whether the police or the authority needs to exercise any of its powers under the Children Act to protect the child from any person or situation as an emergency.

POLICE PROTECTION

If it is considered that there is an emergency, the police can take a child into police protection. They can remove a child to suitable accommodation (for example foster care), or ensure that the child remains in a safe place (for example a hospital).

Police protection cannot last for longer than 72 hours. During this time an officer who has special training (a designated officer) will inquire into the case. The officer must inform the child, those with parental responsibility and the local authority of the steps taken. An appropriate court order (for example an emergency protection order) must be obtained if the child continues to need protection.

EMERGENCY PROTECTION ORDERS

If it is decided that a child needs further protection during an investigation, the police or the local authority can apply for an emergency protection order. To make this order, a court must be satisfied that:
- the order is in the child's best interests
- the child is likely to suffer significant harm if they are not removed from their present accommodation.

This order enables a child to be removed to safe accommodation or kept in a safe place. The court can also say who is allowed to have contact with the child while the order is in force.

An emergency protection order lasts for a maximum of eight days. An authority can ask a court to extend the order for a further seven days if it needs more time to investigate. If the parents of a child were not in court when the order was made, they can, after 72 hours, put their own point of view to the court and apply for the emergency protection order to be removed. The court may appoint a guardian *ad litem* to protect a child's interests during this period.

DO!

1 Try to find out any situations when an emergency protection order might be applied for.

CHILD ASSESSMENT ORDERS

If during the investigation a child is not considered to be in immediate danger, but the authority wish to make an assessment of the child's health, development or the way the child has been treated, the authority can apply to the court for a child assessment order, providing that:

- the parents or carers of a child are unco-operative during the investigation
- there is sufficient concern about the child
- the authority believes that the child may suffer significant harm if an assessment is not made.

The authority has to convince the court that they have made reasonable efforts to persuade parents or carers to co-operate with an assessment.

An order has to say on which date the assessment will begin. It will then last for a maximum of seven days. The court may appoint a guardian *ad litem* to protect the child's interests during the period of the order. Children can refuse to undergo any assessment or examination (providing they have sufficient understanding to make an informed decision about this).

THE INITIAL CHILD PROTECTION CONFERENCE

Following an investigation, if there is enough cause for concern, an initial child protection conference is called. It is usually held within eight working days. (It must be held within fifteen days.)

The initial child protection conference brings together the family, professionals concerned with child protection (social services, health, the police, schools, probation), and other specialists who can give advice (psychiatrists, psychologists, lawyers). It enables them to:

- exchange information
- make decisions about the level of risk
- decide whether the child needs to be registered
- plan for the future.

One of the ways that you may contribute to the protection of children is by providing information to other professionals at a child protection conference. This may take the form of a general report about a child's development, or a more specific report of something you have observed or witnessed.

The principle of working in partnership with parents must form the basis of the child protection conference. Parents and carers will as a matter of principle be included in conferences. There may, however, be occasions when parental involvement may not promote the welfare of the child and they will then be excluded from all or part of the proceedings. Children are encouraged to attend conferences if they have sufficient understanding. They can take a friend to support them.

If a child is considered to be suffering or likely to suffer significant harm, the conference may decide to register the child. It will appoint and name a key worker and also recommend a core group of professionals to be involved in a child protection plan. The key worker will be from the social services department or the NSPCC. However, it may agree that other workers from the core group will have more day-to-day contact with the child and family.

The child protection register

Following a decision to register, a child's name will be put on a central child protection register. This must be kept in each social services area office. It will list all the children in the area who are considered to be at risk. A child's name is only registered following agreement at a child protection conference. The registration of a child means:

- the protection plan for the child will be formally reviewed at least every six months.
- if a concerned professional believes that the child is not adequately protected, or that the plan needs to be changed, they can ask the social services department (or the NSPCC) to call a child protection review
- any professional who is worried about a child can quickly refer to the register to see if the child is considered to be at risk, or if there is a protection plan in force.

Initial child protection plan

The initial child protection plan that is made by the core group of professionals after the conference will:

- include a comprehensive assessment of the child and the family situation
- form the basis for future plans of work with the child and family.

A care order

If a conference concludes that a child is at risk, the social services department may apply to a court for a care order. If made, this places the child in the care of the local authority. It also gives the authority parental responsibility in addition to the parents. A care order gives the local authority the power both to care for the child and to determine the extent of parental involvement. A child may either be placed in the care of foster parents or in a children's home.

An interim care order

If assessments are not complete enough to decide on making a full care order, the court may make an interim care order. This may not last initially for more than eight weeks; a subsequent order may only last for four weeks.

A supervision order

If it is considered that a care order is not necessary, the court may make a supervision order. This gives the local authority the right to supervise, advise, befriend and direct the care of a child who remains at home. It is effective for a year.

A child protection review

To ensure that a registered child continues to be protected from abuse, and that his or her needs are being met, a review of the child protection plan by those involved must be held regularly, at least every six months.

De-registration

De-registration (the removal of a child's name from the child protection register) should be considered at every child protection review. Alternatively, a conference can be called by any agency to consider de-registration. The grounds for de-registration are:

- the original factors which led to registration no longer apply: the home situation may have improved or the abuser has no further contact with the child
- the child and family have moved to another area (when this happens the other area will have to accept the responsibility for the case)
- the child is no longer a child in the eyes of the law: this follows an 18th birthday or marriage before this age
- the child dies.

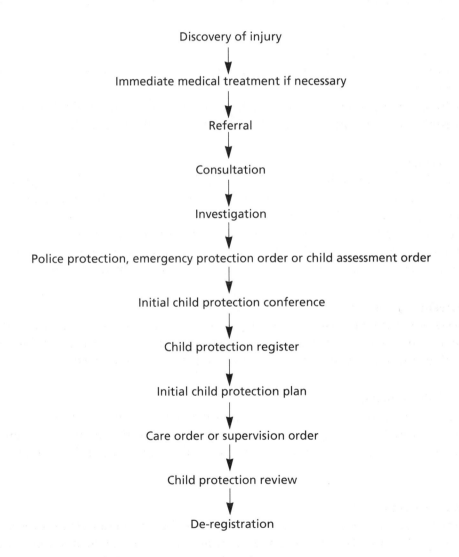

Discovery of injury

↓

Immediate medical treatment if necessary

↓

Referral

↓

Consultation

↓

Investigation

↓

Police protection, emergency protection order or child assessment order

↓

Initial child protection conference

↓

Child protection register

↓

Initial child protection plan

↓

Care order or supervision order

↓

Child protection review

↓

De-registration

The possible path of child protection procedures

1 Produce a report based on the following imaginary situation.

You are a nursery officer in a day nursery. Imagine that you have been asked to present a written factual report at an initial child protection case conference. The officer in charge will be giving an overview report of a child in your group. Your factual report will be primarily about the child's development. The report should cover the following:

- how long the child has been with you
- how often the child is with you during the week
- a description of the child when she arrives and leaves the nursery, including her physical and emotional state
- how the child responds when leaving and greeting their carer
- the stage of the child's physical, intellectual, language, emotional and social development
- the nature of your contact with the child's parents or carers
- whether you work alongside the parents in the nursery.
- any special cultural, gender, physical or educational needs of the child.

2 Produce a second report based on the following imaginary situation:

As a nursery officer you have observed a parent speaking rather aggressively to their child when leaving the child at the nursery. This concerns you and you speak to the parent about it. You later notice some finger tip bruising on the child's upper arms. You know that they were not there the day before. You report the matter to your officer in charge. She tells you that she will follow the child protection procedures. She instructs you to write a factual report about everything you have heard and seen, and to draw a diagram of where the bruises are.

Key terms

You need to know what these words and phrases mean. Go back through the chapter and find out.

ACPC	Investigation
Equality of opportunity	Emergency protection orders
Guardian ad litem	Child assessment orders
Designated teacher	Initial child protection conference
Referral	Child protection register
Consultation	Care order

Bibliography and further reading

J Bastiani, *Working with Parents (A Whole School Approach)*, Windsor/NFER/Nelson, 1989

Michele Elliott, *Dealing with Child Abuse*: The Kidscape Training Guide, Kidscape, 82 Brook Street, London W1Y 1YS, 1989

David N Jones, John Pickett, Margaret R Dates and Peter Barbor, *Understanding Child Abuse*, 2nd edition, Macmillan Education Ltd., Houndsville, Basingstoke, Hampshire RG21 2XS, 1987

J Laishley, *Working with Young Children*, Hodder and Stoughton, 1987

J and L Lindon, *Caring for the Under 8s*, Macmillan, 1993

Stephen Moore, *Sociology Alive!*, Stanley Thornes (Publishers) Ltd, 1987

Wendy Stainton Rogers and Jeremy Roche, *Children's Welfare and Children's Rights: A Practical Guide to the Law*, Hodder and Stoughton, 1994

Working Together under the Children Act 1989, HMSO, London, 1991

An Introduction to the Children Act 1989, HMSO, London, 1989

Child Abuse and Neglect: An Introduction, The Open University, Milton Keynes MK7 6AN, 1989

Index